Pay Determination
and
Industrial Prosperity

To Karin, Anna, and Mark
and
Coral, Claire, and Felicity

Pay Determination
and
Industrial Prosperity

Alan A. Carruth
and
Andrew J. Oswald

CLARENDON PRESS. OXFORD
1989

Oxford University Press, Walton Street, Oxford OX2 6DP
Oxford New York Toronto
Delhi Bombay Calcutta Madras Karachi
Petaling Jaya Singapore Hong Kong Tokyo
Nairobi Dar es Salaam Cape Town
Melbourne Auckland
and associated companies in
Berlin Ibadan

Oxford is a trade mark of Oxford University Press

Published in the United States
by Oxford University Press, New York

British Library Cataloguing in Publication Data
Carruth, A. A. (Alan A)
Pay determination and industrial prosperity.
1. Great Britain. Personnel. Remuneration.
Determination. Econometric models
I. Title II. Oswald, A. J. (Andrew J)
331.2'15'0941
ISBN 0–19–828692–9
ISBN 0-19-877296-3 (pbk.)

Library of Congress Cataloging-in-Publication Data
Carruth, Alan A.
Pay determination and industrial prosperity/Alan A. Carruth and
Andrew J. Oswald.
Bibliography: p.
Includes index.
1. Wages. 2. Industrial relations. 3. Profit. 4. Wages—Great
Britain—Econometric models. I. Oswald, Andrew J. II. Title.
HD4909.C23   1989   331.2'15—dc20   89-8735
ISBN 0–19–828692–9
ISBN 0-19-877296-3 (pbk.)

Set by Gecko Ltd, Bicester, Oxon
Printed in Great Britain by
Courier International Ltd., Tiptree, Essex

Preface

This book began on the M6, southbound, close to Carlisle. The year was 1986 and we were driving home after a conference at St Andrews University. Unfortunately the M6 was disposed of more quickly (Carruth was driving) than was our monograph.

The book has benefited from discussion with many colleagues at Kent, the London School of Economics, and elsewhere. We should like to thank, in particular, Steve Bazen, Charlie Bean, Wilfred Beckerman, Danny Blanchflower, Simon Burgess, Louis Christofides, Andrew Clark, Rod Cross, Richard Disney, Saul Estrin, Richard Freeman, Mary Gregory, Jonathan Haskel, Andy Henley, Richard Jackman, Tim Jenkinson, Richard Layard, David Marsden, Sheena McConnell, David Metcalf, Steve Nickell, Chris Pissarides, Penelope Rowlatt, Tony Thirlwall, Alistair Ulph, and Sushil Wadhwani. David Card, Bertil Holmlund, John Pencavel, and Robert Solow often provided food for thought *par avion*. Some of these people may even agree with us.

Early versions of the book's results were presented in University seminars at Essex, Glasgow, INSEAD (Paris), Kent, the London Business School, the London School of Economics, Oxford, Southampton, Stirling, and Surrey. The suggestions we received there are gratefully acknowledged.

The book is intended primarily as a research monograph, but much of it should be accessible to undergraduates in economics, business, and industrial-relations courses. We have made efforts to write most of the book in straightforward English. There are sections, nevertheless, which are written for specialists, and we apologize to the general reader for what may look like needless jargon, mathematics and statistics. Even the more difficult chapters have concluding sections which write down our message, and why we think it worth taking seriously, so it is our hope that the main ideas are intelligible.

Some sections of the book draw upon our published articles. Chapter 2 includes material from the 1985 *Scandinavian Journal of Economics* and the 1986 *American Economic Review*. The last part of Chapter 3 uses versions of tables which appeared in the 1987 *Oxford Bulletin of Economics and Statistics*. The same journal published preliminary annual results, and theoretical equations, related to those in Chapters 6 and 7. We are grateful to the editors of these journals for permission to include this material.

Part of the book provides new econometric evidence on the role of lagged profits in shaping pay. The estimation uses David Hendry's software package PC-GIVE. To assist other researchers to evaluate our work the book includes a Statistical Appendix which provides the data on which the regressions are based. We have also included there the estimates from standard TSP software.

A conscious effort is made here to combine forms of evidence which conventionally appear apart. We hope readers will not eschew the parts which look unfamiliar. To do so would be to miss much of this book's point.

Andrew Schuller of Oxford University Press, and the anonymous readers, made many useful suggestions. Special thanks are due to the anonymous referees: their perceptive criticisms forced us to improve the book. We are particularly grateful to Joanne Putterford, who typed the manuscript, for her patience in the face of numerous revisions. Liz Blakeway kindly helped with some of the work.

The Economic and Social Research Council, through its funding of the Centre for Labour Economics at LSE, contributed materially to the work reported in this study. The essential role of such grants will be known to those interested in relevant economic research.

Contents

1

Introduction

Of the many prices in an economy, the price of labour is one of the most influential. It moulds the levels of employment and unemployment; it helps to determine the distribution of income; it shapes people's decisions about how hard to work and whether to set up their own businesses. Despite this, the wage-rate and the forces which fashion it are not well understood. Whatever their teachers' private doubts, most students continue to be taught that, like the price of strawberries, labour's price emerges from the meeting-point of a demand curve and a supply curve.

The purpose of this study is to contribute to the construction of an empirically valid model of wage determination. Although some of the findings may apply elsewhere, Britain is the country upon which most attention is focussed. Secondary evidence, principally for the United States, is also discussed.

The inquiry began as an econometric investigation of real-wage movements in the British economy. It was stimulated by a now famous puzzle. Why, throughout the 1980s, did the wage-rate in Britain rise so quickly? Unemployment over the period averaged more than three million, so that roughly one in eight Britons were without work. Yet this remarkable degree of excess supply seemed, on the face of it, to have little impact on the level of pay settlements. Real earnings grew between 1981 and 1987 by a quarter, and nominal earnings almost doubled (tables 40 and 41 of HMSO *Economic Trends*, 1988). The labour market did not look as if it could justify its title.

Our preliminary work, begun in 1986, suggested that the answer might lie in the behaviour of profitability — or some more general measure of industrial prosperity — over the time period of interest. Lagged profits appeared to be statistically significant in a real-wage equation for Britain (early results were given in Carruth and Oswald (1987a)), and the growth in profits, illustrated in Table 1.1, had become well documented.

2 *Introduction*

Table 1.1 *British profits (1980 prices, £bn.)*

Year	1979	1981	1983	1985	1987
Real profits[a]	22.2	16.0	19.7	27.9	38.5

a Gross trading profits net of stock appreciation for all industrial and commercial companies (income arising in UK) excluding North Sea oil companies. Further details are contained in Chapter 7.

It soon transpired that there were many other kinds of evidence which pointed in the same direction. There was too much material for even a long article: a monograph looked a more appropriate vehicle. This study is the result.

Three themes run throughout the book. First, for at least fifty years there have been economists who have claimed that pay levels depend upon variables such as product prices and profits. Moreover, empirical evidence in various forms has existed for most of that time. Second, it is possible to argue, using quarterly and annual British data, that lagged profit per employee helps to determine the real wage. The resulting model encompasses alternatives and has higher explanatory power. Third, even those who distrust time — series empirical research may be able to assuage some doubts about the hypothesis that profit (or an equivalent measure of product market prosperity) affects pay. This is because other kinds of evidence are available. In part the study contains the methodological message that, in a largely non-experimental subject like economics, one way to assess a proposition is to discover whether it is supported by numerous and dissimilar types of empirical proof. A valid argument ought to be visible from many angles, and the view should be independent of angle.

In the competitive model of the labour market an employer pays a wage-rate dictated by the balance of supply and demand in the whole market, not one governed by the firm's internal profitability or productivity. The classic statement is Hicks's *Theory of Wages* (1932, reprinted in 1963). Writers on labour markets have often objected, however, that the price of labour is better thought of as fixed by non-competitive pressures. Hicks himself grew disenchanted with his 1932 monograph — as his preface to Hicks (1963) makes clear. One reason for the inadequacy of competitive theory is the fact that in reality wages are often determined by collective bargaining. On page 155 he writes 'the power of trade unions to raise or retain wages above the competitive level is much greater in times of good trade . . . Once an employer is making large profits, and expects those profits to continue in the near future, he is an easy mark for union demands.' A few years later came John Dunlop's work, carried out on the other side of the Atlantic, and written up in part in Dunlop's (1944) *Wage Determination Under Trade Unions.* There followed *Trade Union Wage Policy* (1948) by Arthur Ross. Whilst at odds with Dunlop over many issues, Ross agreed that product market pressures — factors such as financial prosperity — play an important role. Thus we find both 'a union's bargaining power may vary considerably between one group of employers and another, because of . . . differences in . . . the profit rates of employers. . .' (Ross (1948, p.15)) and 'changes in . . . profits . . . tend to affect wage rates' (Dunlop (1944, p.vi)). These three writers offered little or no systematic empirical evidence for their view. That was provided first by Slichter (1950).

Sumner Slichter, of Harvard University, was one of the most distinguished US economists of the post-war era. Some of his work is described in detail in Chapter 4. A central theme in Slichter's writings was the idea that the competitive model is 'too simple and needs to be supplemented' (Slichter (1950, p.91)). He argued that employers pay high wages when they can afford to do so, and used statistical methods to defend this ability-to-pay hypothesis. Despite a prolific amount of writing, Slichter was gradually forgotten as a new generation of labour economists emerged. That group concentrated on the effects of human capital on wage levels and neglected earlier economists' worries about the competitive paradigm. An illustration of this is the fact that there is no reference to Sumner Slichter (not even to the definitive Slichter, Healy, and Livernash (1960)) in the recently available 1,300 page *Handbook of Labor Economics* edited by Ashenfelter and Layard (1986). At much the same time as Slichter wrote, Lester (1952) independently proposed a similar set of ideas, and also rejected the competitive paradigm.

British research of a conceptually similar kind was done by a team of economists led by Donald MacKay (reported especially in MacKay *et al.* (1971)). This work drew upon information from personnel records in sixty-six engineering plants between 1959 and 1966. Its central conclusion was that competitive theory is inadequate as a framework for understanding modern labour markets. Thus on page 391: 'even where managements are unwilling to concede higher wages readily, they may find it difficult to resist wage claims which are likely to be pushed strongly when profits are high . . . the conditions at plant level may have an effect on wages in a manner which is rigorously excluded from the traditional model.' MacKay *et al.* argued that competitive forces set only the outer limits of a wage band (or 'range' in Lester's terminology (Lester (1952) and Lester and Shishter (1948))) within which employers must pay.

These writers believed that industrial prosperity influences non-union wages as well as union rates of pay. When workers are difficult to replace quickly and costlessly, and have scarce skills, it is possible (as Lindbeck and Snower (1988) and others have argued) for them to have negotiating power even without formal union representation. Bilateral monopoly, in other words, may be pervasive; it is not necessarily the preserve of the trade union. A union bargaining model then has wide application.

Our study's second theme is more modern in origin and execution. Chapters 6 and 7 develop and estimate a model of real-wage determination using British data from 1954 to 1983. A principal concern is to test for profit effects upon pay. As a bench-mark, and to provide a foundation for the statistical model, the framework of Layard and Nickell (1986) is used. A more general version of the wage equation in that work, in which profitability is entered as an explanatory variable, is found to explain the data most effectively. Thus Chapter 7 attempts to encompass previous empirical inquiries.

It is usual, before estimating a time-series model, to begin by examining the raw data themselves. Fig. 1.1 plots real average earnings and real company profits for thirty-four years from 1953. Two points stand out. The first is that earnings is a much smoother series than profitability. The second is that there is fairly clear evidence of a positive correlation. For example, both series have six peaks and six troughs, although in the case of the real-earnings variable these are around a steady trend, and in both cases the most dramatic of the peaks and troughs coincide at the end of the period. It also appears that, especially from the 1970s onwards, profits lead wages by a year or so.

The figure reveals that in the 1970s and early 1980s the British

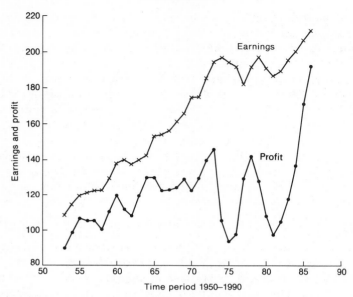

Fig 1.1. *Real earnings and profit (excluding North Sea companies) 1953–1986*

Key: Real earnings is average weekly earnings for full-time male manual workers (all industries) deflated by the Retail Price Index. Real profit is gross trading profits net of stock appreciation (income arising in UK) excluding North Sea oil companies deflated by an Output Price Index.

economy generated a 'natural experiment'. Profits fell sharply, increased, dropped again, and then rose even more markedly. Any theory which predicts that pay follows profitability would have to predict the same strong changes in the real wage. This is what occurred.

Fig. 1.1 cannot begin to be conclusive, because some underlying variable may have been at work. However, it constitutes prima-facie evidence that real earnings move with lagged real company profits. Any positive relationship (ignoring trend, which will be a function of real growth) between the two should be considered noteworthy, because, as profitability in a company is a declining function of its wage-rate, it might be expected that once de-trended the series of Fig. 1.1 would fluctuate in opposite directions.

It is natural to ask why, as Fig. 1.1 suggests, profits earned by firms and the wage paid to employees should move together. Later chapters explore this in detail, but one answer emerges from the simplest kind of economic model.

Consider a firm which bargains with a trade union. Assume that the firm wishes to maximize its profit, whilst the trade union wants to drive its wage as high as possible. The two sides' interests conflict. Assume for simplicity that in the event of a delay or breakdown in negotiations (such as a strike) the firm earns zero profit and the union's members receive some low level of outside income. Bargaining theory then suggests — see the proof at the end of the chapter — that the equilibrium level of pay may be written as the sum of two components:

$$\text{wage} = \text{outside (delay) income} + \text{profit per employee} \qquad (1)$$

Thus, in a bilateral bargaining model, workers benefit as their employer becomes more profitable. Gains are shared.

It is not necessary to rely on bargaining theory. A relationship between pay and profit can be justified on grounds of 'fairness'. Psychologists such as Adams (1965) have suggested that agents will divide gains according to the formula of Equity Theory:

$$\frac{\text{Income of agent } A}{\text{Effort of agent } A} = \frac{\text{Income of agent } B}{\text{Effort of agent } B}$$

The manager of a profitable firm may thus think it natural, and only just, that some of any surplus be passed on to employees. Alternatively, and more formally, equation (1) also emerges from Nash's (1953) mathematical model of fair division. Much of the remainder of our study shows how notions of fairness may matter in real-life collective bargaining.

The third theme of this investigation has a more strongly methodological flavour. Economists are used to evaluating theories by narrow methods — by time-series econometric tests, or cross-section econometric tests, or the examination of institutional evidence, or the study of economic survey data, or experimental methods in a laboratory. It is rare in the economics literature for authors to appeal, in an eclectic way, to more than one of these criteria (so-called 'pluralist' methodology). Whilst understand-able, this inevitably discourages later researchers from drawing upon a wide range of evidence, and arguably helps to produce a perception — one common among theorists — that the conclusions of applied economics are fragile. The use of a single method of empirical assessment is also inefficient. Later chapters of the study consider in turn a number of forms of empirical evidence. These include evidence from the following:

(1) collective-bargaining documents,
(2) industrial-relations surveys of establishments,
(3) cross-section regression estimates,
(4) time-series regression estimates,
(5) experiments documented in the economics and psychology literature.

Different economists are likely to give different weights to the approaches. It is their *combined* value which this study attempts to stress: all of (1)–(5) are shown to point in the same direction.

The text has the following structure. Chapter 2 surveys old and new theories of wage determination. It reveals that economists have been preoccupied with the search for a model in which pay is insensitive to product market pressure. Later chapters suggest that this is misguided. Chapter 3 is concerned with industrial-relations evidence and reveals that wage-bargainers place much emphasis on product market conditions. Early econometric work is assessed in Chapter 4, which concludes that, although almost all the early time-series research is unreliable, there is credible cross-section evidence of an effect of profitability upon wages. Social psychology enters in Chapter 5: relevant experimental results are examined. The study's suggested model is set out in Chapter 6 and estimated in Chapter 7. Chapter 8 contains conclusions. The Statistical Appendix at the end of the book gives the data used in our study, in order to assist other researchers to verify some aspects of the work, and, for a similar reason and as a check, reports the results of estimating our preferred equations with different software.

Appendix: Proof of Equation 1

Denote profit by π, the wage by w, and outside income during a delay by $\hat{w}$. Under non-cooperative bargaining (Binmore, Rubinstein, and Wolinsky (1986), for example), or Nash's (1953) axioms, the bargained wage can be written as a solution to the problem

$$\text{Maximize } (w - \hat{w})\, \pi(w) \qquad (A1)$$
$$w$$

which is easily generalized to the asymmetric case. This assumes a zero profit level in the fall-back or disagreement state, which is restrictive, and that $\pi(w)$ is a maximum profit function. Under appropriate assumptions about differentiability and concavity, the solution to the maximization is

$$\pi(w) + (w-\hat{w})\, \pi'(w) = 0. \qquad (A2)$$

By a standard duality result, employment, n, is equal to $-\pi'(w)$. Hence the above equation can be written as

$$w = \hat{w} + \frac{\pi(w)}{n} \qquad (A3)$$

The bargained wage is equal to the sum of outside income (during a delay) and profit per employee.

Generalizations of equation $(A3)$ are straightforward. Chapter 6 examines variations on this analysis. A valuable introduction to non-cooperative bargaining theory is provided by Sutton (1986).

2

Wage Determination:
Theories of Inflexibility

2.1 Introduction

Economists have been interested in wage inflexibility for many years. Chapter 3 of John Hicks's 1932 *The Theory of Wages*, for example, contains a discussion of the 'element of rigidity due to the desire of employers to maintain good relations and safeguard the future' (p. 57).

The purpose of this chapter is to summarize a number of modern theoretical contributions to the theory of wages. As will become clear, theorists in this field have concentrated almost wholly upon one particular kind of wage rigidity, namely, the inflexibility of pay in response to changes in the employer's product demand. These models study wages which are inflexible in the face of what might be called 'internal' pressure. They do not, in general, explain why pay might be insensitive to 'external' pressure from, for example, the aggregate level of unemployment in the economy. Whether or not this is a serious difficulty depends on the appropriate definition of wage rigidity. Our view is that modern theories of pay inflexibility have misled economists by encouraging them to ignore the effects of product market prosperity upon wage rates.

There are four main ways to derive models in which the firm's wage-rate is inflexible:

(1) competitive theory
(2) efficiency wage models
(3) trade-union models
(4) labour contract theory.

As with any taxonomy of this kind, there are occasional examples of theoretical work which does not fit neatly into a single part of the classification, but this fourfold grouping has advantages.

2.2 Competitive Theory

It is possible to devise a competitive theory of wage inflexibility. Consider a single small labour market or sector. Assume that the demand curve for labour has normal properties, so that it is smooth and downward sloping over the relevant range. Assume also, and crucially, that workers can swiftly move into and out of this industrial sector, which is therefore best thought of as an industry in which little training is required.

The sector's wage-rate, under these assumptions, will be inflexible in the face of product demand shocks. If the firms in the sector cut their wage-rates, workers will leave. If firms want more labour, there is no need to raise pay. This sector must simply offer the same wage (or, more correctly, because conditions of work may be different in this sector, the same level of *utility*) as is being paid elsewhere in the labour market. The supply curve of labour, to the industry, is (as in Fig. 2.1) horizontal. Hence a change in the demand curve will not affect the equilibrium wage-rate. A rise in the demand for shop assistants, for example, would on this view produce no noticeable change in their wage-rates, because cleaners and clerks could and would switch jobs immediately if shop assistants' pay began to increase.

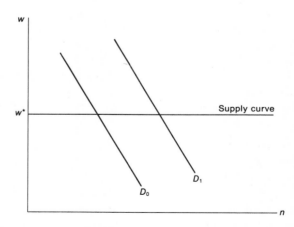

Fig 2.1.   *Wage rigidity in a competitive industry with mobile workers*

Is this theoretical model so simple that it is not worth taking seriously? The answer depends on what the model is expected to explain. Later sections of the book will summarize evidence that, even in unskilled labour markets, wages do seem to respond somewhat to product market conditions. Moreover, the real world contains trade unions and cartels. As a literal explanation of the world, therefore, the framework represented in Fig. 2.1 appears to be inadequate — in part because labour is in practice probably less mobile than required. The model is also unsatisfactory as a theory of aggregate wage rigidity. No economists argue that the labour supply curve in the whole economy is perfectly elastic. What the competitive argument does point to, however, is a possible explanation for the observed rigidity of the relative wage structure of an economy. Evidence of such stability is documented in Phelps-Brown (1977), Dickens and Katz (1987), and Krueger and Summers (1987).

2.3 Efficiency Wage Theory

If, as is widely argued, wages do not fall in a recession, this may be because firms do not wish them to fall. As a general point, a reduction in pay may alter the attitudes and behaviour of the work-force, and perhaps even of some of the other agents with whom the firm deals. Yet that in itself need not worry a firm which is considering whether to reduce wages, because in principle the firm can *require* its workers and other agents to behave in certain ways. It can insist, for example, that a worker will fill 120 boxes a day, and sack any individual who falls below that standard. Then it is difficult to see why a firm could not cut pay, whilst monitoring workers' output, without having to concern itself with how employees will react. The difficulty for firms, however, is that it is not always possible to measure how individuals are behaving.

Efficiency wage models assume that the wage-rate affects the quality of work, broadly defined, that the firm can extract from its work-force. The idea was proposed originally by Leibenstein (1957) for underdeveloped countries. He argued that employers would not cut the wage of their workers because to do so would make their employees so underfed that they would be of no use. This is a nutritional theory of pay stickiness. It sounds far-fetched even for underdeveloped countries; but the approach has been modified, for the industralized economies, and applied in the work of Stiglitz (1974, 1984), Salop (1979), Solow (1979), Weiss (1980), Yellen (1984), Shapiro and Stiglitz (1984), Malcomson (1981), and Akerlof (1982), among others.

Assume that the firm's output depends on two variables. Call them employment and quality of work. In principle the firm should then set two price variables — a payment for employment and a payment for quality. This would then be analogous to its two payments, in conventional models, for labour and capital, and the result would be efficient. However, consider the case where, for some reason, the employer must fix only a single price to control both employment and work quality. Then inefficiencies may result. In particular, an employer may be reluctant to cut wages in a slump, because of fears that the quality of work might fall excessively.

A famous, if loosely documented, example of this is given in Weiss (1980). The author begins his paper with the following claim:

In 1975, the administration of the Stanford Linear Accelerator Center (SLAC) declared its intention to lay off 10 per cent of its workforce. The workers then voted to take a 10 per cent wage cut voluntarily to stop the layoffs. The offer was refused by the management of SLAC. The reason offered by SLAC was: if the wages were cut 'the best workers would quit'. (p. 526).

Weiss then presents a model in which the firm does not know the identity of its best workers, and where by raising the wage the employer increases the quality and productivity of its work-force. Although this is one way in which to justify the efficiency wage hypothesis, it is not the most common one. The conventional explanation relies upon the idea that workers vary their effort at work.

Assume that the firm sells its product at price p. Its production function is taken to be $f(n, e)$, where n is employment and e is the effort put in by its typical employee. Each worker receives the wage w. Workers elsewhere receive wage $\bar{w}$.

A worker's effort is assumed to depend positively on the wage. Hence $e = e(w)$ is an increasing function. There might be many explanations for the assumption of an $e(w)$ function, but a common one is that higher pay leads to higher morale and hence higher productivity. Psychologists have laboratory evidence for this, and tests of so-called 'equity theory' can be found in Adams (1963) and Adams and Rosenbaum (1962), among many others. Chapter 5 studies this issue. The $e(w)$ function may also be derived as rational behaviour in a model where workers can shirk (see Shapiro and Stiglitz (1984), among others).

The firm's maximization problem is then as follows:

$$\text{Maximize } \pi = pf(n, e) - wn \qquad (1)$$
$$w, n$$

subject to

$$e = e(w) \qquad (2)$$
$$w \geq \bar{w}. \qquad (3)$$

Consider the case where the second constraint does not bind (otherwise the solution is trivial). Then the first order conditions for a maximum are

$$n : pf_n(n, e) - w = 0 \qquad (4)$$
$$w : pf_e(n, e) e'(w) - n = 0, \qquad (5)$$

whereupon they can be combined to give

$$\frac{we'(w)}{e(w)} = \frac{nf_n(n, e)}{e(w)f_e(n, e)}. \qquad (6)$$

The left-hand side is the elasticity of the effort function.

It is now possible to derive the most famous result in efficiency wage theory. Almost all writings in this literature assume that output depends on the *product* of employment and effort. Hence the production function takes the multiplicative form $f(ne)$. Under this assumption

$$\frac{f_n(n, e)}{f_e(n, e)} = \frac{e}{n}. \qquad (7)$$

Inserting this into the right-hand side of (6), and simplifying, gives

$$\frac{we'(w)}{e} = 1. \qquad (8)$$

This is the key efficiency wage theorem and implies that the wage, which is set so as to make the elasticity of the effort function equal to unity, is independent of product and labour market conditions. A change in the firm's product price p, or (unless they enter the effort function) wages elsewhere $\bar{w}$, will not induce the firm to change its own wage-rate. Moreover, as long as the wage which satisfies (8) is above $\bar{w}$, there is involuntary unemployment. Outside workers would like to join this firm and would be willing to do so for a reduced wage. But the firm will not cut its rate of pay, because it knows that employees would respond by lowering their effort at work.

The principal objection to this, as a theory of sticky wages, is that it requires that the production function be of the form $f(ne)$. Why effort and total employment should enter multiplicatively is unclear. Yet in the general case, $f(n, e)$, the wage-rate is not fixed. In general equation (6) implies that the wage will vary as employment does, and hence as the product price does.

What happens if the firm can observe and enforce some level of effort? The formal problem is then

$$\text{Maximize } \pi = pf(n, e) - wn \qquad (9)$$

subject to

$$n, w, e$$

$$u(w, e) \geqslant \bar{u}, \qquad (10)$$

where $u(w, e)$ is a worker's utility function, increasing in pay and decreasing in effort, and $\bar{u}$ is the utility level available elsewhere. The first-order conditions, which now include one for effort e, are

$$n : pf_n - w = 0 \qquad (11)$$

$$e : pf_e + \lambda u_e = 0 \qquad (12)$$

$$w : -n + \lambda u_w = 0 , \qquad (13)$$

where $\lambda \geqslant 0$ is a Lagrange multiplier on constraint (10).

In this model there is no simple restriction which will generate wage inflexibility. Furthermore, involuntary unemployment will not exist. The mathematical reason is that, for the second of the first order conditions to hold, it is necessary that λ be strictly positive. For a maximum, however, the complementary slackness condition is

$$\lambda[u(w, e) - \bar{u}] = 0 . \qquad (14)$$

Thus the term in square brackets must be zero, which requires that the firm offer the same utility level as elsewhere. There is then no involuntary unemployment in equilibrium.

The propositions of these models are clearly disturbingly sensitive to the exact assumptions made. Another criticism of efficiency wage theory is that it has been little tested. Although both Krueger and Summers (1988) and Wadhwani and Wall (1988) address this issue, their evidence is consistent with many theoretical approaches. Those who propound the merits of efficiency wage theory have to show that it explains the data of the world more effectively than its rivals. Whether that can be done remains an open question. Moreover, the wage rigidity proposition of efficiency wage theory is of questionable robustness.

2.4 The Economics of Union Wage Determination

To construct a model of trade-union behaviour it is necessary to specify the aims of, and constraints on, union actions. Recent work has followed John Dunlop's (1944) lead in the assumption that the primary concerns of labour are (real) pay and jobs.

The literature relies extensively on an indifference map, drawn on a diagram with the wage on one axis and employment on the other, like that in Fig. 2.2. Higher combinations of the wage and the number of jobs give greater utility to the union (I_1 is preferred to I_0, and so on). The convexity of the curves is the result of the assumption — typical in other branches of economic theory — that, at the margin, scarce things are valued most highly. Farber (1978), McDonald and Solow (1981), Oswald (1982*a*), and others have used a special mathematical form for such a trade-union utility function. Farber (1978) and McDonald and Solow (1981) assume

   (1) that the utility of the labour group can be thought of as being measured by the utility of a 'representative' individual,

   (2) that the individual faces some probability of being employed and one minus that probability of being unemployed,

   (3) that unemployed union workers receive income from some outside source,

   (4) that all individuals have declining marginal utility of income.

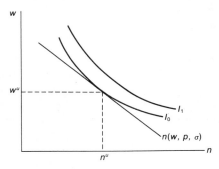

Fig 2.2.   *The monopoly union model*

Formally, then, the union's utility is to be thought of as the expected utility of its typical worker. Oswald (1982*a*) makes the closely related assumption that the union has 'utilitarian' preferences: its welfare is the sum of its members' utilities. This replaces (1) with the assumption that

(1') the utility of the labour group is measured by the sum of its members' utility levels,

omits (2) altogether, and keeps (3) and (4).

The 'expected utility' and 'utilitarian' representations of a union's preferences are probably now used more than any others. They include as special cases Dunlop's (1944), Heiser's (1970), and Johnston's (1972) assumption that the union's maximand is the wage-bill (possibly including outside unemployment benefits), and Rosen's (1970), Calvo's (1978), and De Menil's (1971) assumption that it is the 'rent', namely that total surplus over the wage-bill under perfect competition. For empirical purposes, however, John Pencavel has proposed and used extensively a 'Stone–Geary' utility function, which also generates convex union indifference curves. The details are pursued in a later subsection.

Where the current competing models differ from one another is in their assumptions about the constraints on union behaviour. Dunlop (1944) was one of the first to develop the *monoply union model*, which is represented in Fig. 2.2. The union is assumed to recognize the fact that there is a demand for its members' services. This is the crucial assumption — one still often criticized today — which completes the model and makes it capable of being used to make predictions about behaviour. The trade union would like both very high wages for its members and plenty of jobs for them. It knows, however, that when workers become more expensive their employer will want to hire fewer. Hence there is assumed to be an optimal wage target (w^u), which the union feels to be its best compromise between a high wage and a large level of employment. This is the idea behind Fig. 2.2's formal representation.

Although the paper by McDonald and Solow (1981) begins by discussing the monopoly union model, it rejects it on the grounds that there is a flaw in the model's internal logic. Their criticism, which goes back to Leontief (1946), is that both the union and the employer could do better by jointly negotiating a point to the right of the labour demand curve. We would not expect negotiating agents to pass up the opportunity for joint gains, they argue, and hence we should not expect the monopoly union model to be a good picture of the world. The authors' alternative, the *efficient bargain model*, postulates that the union is constrained by the employer's profit-level and not (directly) by the labour demand curve. The stronger the union the more it will achieve both greater employment and larger rates of pay.

Fig. 2.3 shows the possible outcomes, drawn in as a contract curve or 'Pareto efficiency locus', in a wage-employment diagram. Curves π_1 and π_0 are iso-profit contours, each showing combinations of pay and jobs that produce particular levels of profits. They are the firm's indifference curves. The dotted line, CC', marks out the tangency points between the labour group's indifference curves and those of the employer. The labour demand curve, drawn as pf' to represent marginal product, is the set of turning-points of the iso-profit contours. In effect the diagram represents

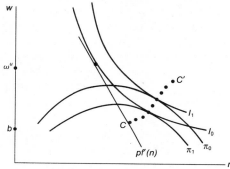

Fig 2.3.   *The efficient bargain model*

the old idea that pay is determined in a bilateral monopoly. A number of solution concepts in co-operative game theory can be used to suggest how a particular point on CC' is chosen (McDonald and Solow (1981) contains a discussion of these).

Both models suggest that unions will raise pay, and empirical evidence supports this hypothesis (Ashenfelter (1978), Blanchflower (1984), Freeman and Medoff (1984), Lewis (1963), Metcalf (1977), Parsley (1980), Pencavel (1977), Minford (1983), and Stewart (1983)).

However, there is one especially important difference between the monopoly union model and the efficient bargain model. In the former the firm has the power to set employment unilaterally. That cannot be true, however, of the second: 'More complicated institutional arrangements are necessary for the achievement of efficient bargains. In particular the union has to exercise some sort of influence over the level of employment . . .' (McDonald and Solow (1981, p. 900)). McDonald and Solow go on to claim that this might be achieved by direct negotiation over employment or by the fixing of manning restrictions like man–machine ratios. The latter is not proved in the paper, and economic theory has not yet shown whether it can be proved (papers by Johnson (1985) and Clark (1988) raise doubts).

A third model of union behaviour is what might be called the *right-to-manage model*. Due to Nickell (1982) and Nickell and Andrews (1983), but implicit in many other studies (see Freeman and Medoff's (1984) discussion of the economic effects of unionism, for example, and Jackman and Layard (1987), Pissarides (1986, 1988), and Newell and Symons (1987)) this sets out to construct a model around two stylized facts about labour markets. The first is that wages are something over which there is bargaining; the second is that, in general, that is not true of employment. Hence the right-to-manage model takes the labour demand curve itself, not the contract curve of Figure 2.3, to be the locus along which wage bargains are struck. Fall-back utility levels are assumed for each side and a co-operative solution concept from game theory is used to pick one point. More intuitively, the employer chooses employment as he sees fit, and the union tries to drive the wage as high as possible. The negotiated wage-rate then depends on the parties' bargaining strengths.

An interesting generalization is developed in Manning (1987).

Moene (1988) is the first analytical paper to examine how different union actions affect fall-back utilities.

2.4.1. *Details and Results*

In this section we discuss more formally the ideas outlined in the previous subsection. Assume that the union cares mainly about its members' real wages and the level of employment in its industry. Assume for the moment that each worker is paid w and that the number of jobs in the industry is n. Define an increasing, quasi-concave utility function for the union, $U(w, n)$. Why should a union have such a utility function? Some early writers, like Fellner (1949), Cartter (1959), Akerlof (1969), and Atherton (1973), argued for this general form on intuitive grounds; but most of the first writings in the field offered a more specific rationale. The notion, for example, that the trade union is to be thought of as maximizing the wage-bill (possibly including government payments to unemployed members) has often been made. A very closely related assumption is that the union's preferences can be represented as $U = n(w - w^c)$, where w^c is the competitive wage-rate. More recently, however, writers have normally followed one of two assumptions, those of:

(1) a general quasi-concave union utility function, usually of a specific structural form (Stone–Geary, for example)
(2) an expected-utility, or utilitarian, function.

These are worth studying in detail, although it must be borne in mind that some writers reject this kind of neoclassical methodology: see, for example, Ross (1948), Marsden (1986), and Martin (1980). The results in Pemberton (1988), however, suggest that an analytical compromise between Ross (1948) and this approach is feasible.

The first approach can be found in the writings of Calmfors (1982), Carruth and Oswald (1981), Corden (1981), Dixon (1987), Hersoug (1983), Kotowitz and Mathewson (1982), Mulvey (1978), Oswald (1979 and 1982c), Rees (1977), and Warren-Boulton (1977). However, it has become particularly influential in the empirical work of Dertouzos and Pencavel (1981), Pencavel (1984a and 1984b), and Macurdy and Pencavel (1986). They adopt the Stone–Geary functional form

20   *Theories of Wage Inflexibility*

$$U = (w - \gamma)^\theta (n - \delta)^{1-\theta}, \qquad (15)$$

where γ and δ may be thought of as 'minimum' or 'reference' levels of wages and employment. The parameter θ captures the relative importance of 'supernumerary' wages and employment to the trade union. This assumption has a number of advantages. First, it is simple and familiar (from consumer theory). Second, it nests as special cases some other assumptions about union preferences. The wage-bill utility function occurs when $\theta = \frac{1}{2}$ and $\gamma = \delta = 0$. The rent utility function is produced when $\theta = \frac{1}{2}$, $\delta = 0$ and $\gamma = w^c$. Dertouzos and Pencavel (1981) also argue that the assumption captures the notion of a comparison wage-rate — that the union might care about 'relativities' — if γ is thought of as the standard of comparison. Third, the Stone–Geary function is reasonably easy to handle in econometric work.

Nevertheless, there is a difficulty with the Stone–Geary union utility function (one which applies to all similar functional specifications). It is not derived explicitly from conventional axioms about workers' preferences. There is apparently no way to show why, for example, risk-averse employees would, as a group, behave as if maximizing a Stone–Geary function.

The second approach to union utility functions, (2), is a little different. In its simplest form this function can be written either as

$$U = \frac{n}{m} u(w) + \frac{(m-n)}{m} u(b) \qquad \text{Expected utility} \qquad (16)$$

or

$$U = nu(w) + (m-n) u(b) \qquad \text{Utilitarian} \qquad (17)$$

where $u(.)$ is the concave utility function of an individual worker, m is the membership of the trade union and b is the level of unemployment benefit (or an alternative wage). If m is fixed, these obviously have exactly the same properties; but if membership is variable, and influenced by the union, the two forms will not be equivalent. The rationale for the utilitarian form is straightforward; the union is assumed to treat people identically and to care about the sum of their utilities. This is not a moral justification, it should be stressed, but merely an economic interpretation. In its expected utility form the union's preferences reflect the fact that there are two states of nature for each member of the union. If the individual is lucky, he is employed at wage w; if he is unlucky, he takes home unemployment pay (or an alternative wage, earned in a competitive sector) b. Because n people are employed, membership is m, and everyone is treated equally, each worker is assumed here to face a random draw — a point we discuss later — in which the probability of getting a job at utility $u(w)$ is n/m, and the probability of having utility $u(b)$ from unemployment is $(m-n)/m$. If workers care about leisure time then their utility from being unemployed can be written $v(b)$, say, without upsetting the form of these utility functions.

The approach to union preferences captured in equations (16) and (17) was apparently developed independently by at least half a dozen authors. By chance, although characteristically in the history of economic thought, the idea was conceived in a number of countries at around the same time. It seems to have appeared first in a journal article by Dreze and Modigliani (1981), although in a slightly different form Farber's (1978) article actually predated this, and was then followed by McDonald and Solow (1981), Calmfors (1982), Oswald (1982a), and Sampson (1983). But it can also be found in unpublished work by De Bruyne and Van Rompuy (1981), Moore (1981), and Sampson and Shephard (1978), and was probably previously known to American labour economists. The advantage of this approach is that the union's utility function has a clear microeconomic foundation; individuals' preferences, and the size of the membership, appear explicitly. Hence it is possible to see how the group's preferences change as, say, members become more risk-averse or the size of the union declines. Equations (16) and (17) are also simple enough to generate convenient estimating equations: see, for example, Brown and Ashenfelter (1986) and Carruth and Oswald (1985). Furthermore, the rent and wage-bill forms of union preferences again emerge under special conditions. The form $U = n(w - w^c)$ requires risk-neutrality of individuals; the form $U = nw$ follows from risk-neutrality plus the assumption that membership equals employment.

There are generalizations of the expected utility or utilitarian analysis of union preferences (surveys are available in Farber (1986), Oswald (1985), and Pencavel (1985)). The approach sketched above makes the implicit assumption that union members are homogeneous. But there have been attempts in the literature to allow for individuals' heterogeneity. Farber's (1978) well-known paper assumes that the union aims to satisfy the desires of the median-aged member, because that minimizes the risk that the union leaders will lose their own jobs. In a framework similar to that in equation (2), Farber treats the union as maximizing the median member's expected utility. Blair and Crawford (1984), however, show that in fact a voting equilibrium need not exist in his model. Frank (1985) and Kuhn (1988) analyse a union's seniority wage structure. Atherton (1973), Booth (1984), Prachowny (1987), and Strand (1983) also recognize the heterogeneity of the union's workers. Dynamic models of union behaviour are examined in Blanchard and Summers (1987), Burda (1987), and Kidd and Oswald (1987).

The important question of seniority is pursued by Grossman (1983). He assumes that workers are indexed by $i \in [0, n_t]$, where n_t is the size of the union at the start of period t. Grossman lets seniority decrease with the index i and assumes that all firing depends on the criterion of seniority within the union (Oswald (1987) provides US evidence in favour of this). Uncertainty enters the analysis, because the price of output is unknown *ex ante*, and is also discussed by Atherton (1973), Black and Bulkley (1984), Blair and Crawford (1984), Hall and Lilien (1979), Oswald (1982b), and in the large and influential literature on labour contract theory — where unions are treated as groups of atomistic workers — such as Azariadis (1975), Baily (1974), Hart (1983), and Moore (1985). This branch of the literature is discussed later in the chapter.

The literature now seems to be dominated by two of these models of the trade union — a dichotomy which many articles stress including Brown and Ashenfelter (1986), Macurdy and Pencavel (1986), Card (1986), Eberts and Stone (1986), McDonald and Solow (1981), Bean and Turnbull (1986), Svejnar (1986), and Ben-Ner and Estrin (1985). Empirical tests between them have so far produced no clear winner.

2.4.2. *The Monopoly Union*

Imagine a union which runs a closed shop and can control either entry into the profession or the wage-rate. Say that the union faces many small firms and that it would be prohibitively costly to negotiate with all of them. To keep the model simple, let the trade union fix the wage, and assume that firms set employment unilaterally. Take the union utility function to be that in equation (17) and take membership, m, to be fixed. For simplicity write the firm's decision as

$$\text{Maximize}_{n} \; pf(n) + (\sigma - w)n, \qquad (18)$$

where p is the exogenously given price of output, $f(n)$ is a concave production function, n is employment (the only input), w is the wage and σ is an employment subsidy by the government. Let workers face a linear income tax schedule, such that their take-home pay each is $\omega = w(1-t) + s$; hence the marginal tax-rate is t, and s is a flat income benefit. If we write the demand curve for labour as $n(w, p, \sigma)$, the union utility function after the labour demand and tax schedules have been substituted in becomes a function $U = R(w, p, m, b, s, \sigma, t)$. The union's desired wage-rate, which can be represented as a tangency in Fig. 2.2, is the solution to

$$\text{Maximize}_{w} \; R = u(w(1 - t) + s)\, n(w, p, \sigma)$$
$$+ [m - n(w, p, \sigma)]\, u(b). \qquad (19)$$

At an interior maximum, then,

$$R_w = u'(\omega)(1-t)\, n(w, p, \sigma) + [u(\omega) - u(b)]n_w(w, p, \sigma) = 0 \quad (20)$$

This says simply that at the optimum the union's marginal benefit from raising the wage must equal its marginal cost from doing so. The marginal benefit is the increase in utility gained by each worker multiplied by the total number of employed members. The marginal cost is the number of members who lose their jobs multiplied by the utility a member loses when he or she is transferred into the pool of unemployed workers.

The comparative static predictions (following the method of Oswald (1982a)) each emerge from one further differentiation (dw/db takes the sign of R_{wb}, and so on). The key results — ignoring corners, such as $m = n$ — are as follows.

(1) An increase in unemployment benefit raises the union's desired wage-rate.

Proof. $R_{wb} = -u'(b) n_w > 0.$ (21)

Of special interest here, however, is the effect of product market prosperity.

(2) A rise in the price of the product has no effect on the union's desired wage-rate whenever the elasticity of labour demand is constant.

$$\text{Proof.} \quad \frac{u'(\omega)(1-t)w}{u(\omega) - u(b)} = \frac{-wn_w}{n} \equiv \epsilon, \tag{22}$$

by the first-order condition. The left hand term, and hence w, is fixed if ϵ is constant. There are a number of other standard results.

(3) A change in membership does not affect the union's desired wage-rate.

$$\text{Proof.} \quad R_{wm} = 0. \tag{23}$$

(4) A rise in the worker's income subsidy lowers the union's desired wage-rate.

$$\text{Proof.} \quad R_{ws} = u''(\omega)(1-t) n + u'(\omega) n_w < 0. \tag{24}$$

(5) An increase in the employment subsidy to firms has an ambiguous effect on the union's desired wage-rate.

$$\text{Proof.} \quad R_{w\sigma} = u'(\omega)(1-t) n_\sigma + [u(\omega) - u(b)] n_{w\sigma} \gtrless 0. \tag{25}$$

(6) A change in the marginal rate of income tax has an ambiguous effect on the union's desired wage-rate.

$$\text{Proof.} \quad R_{wt} = -u''(\omega) w(1-t) n - u'(\omega) n - u'(\omega) wn_w \gtrless 0. \tag{26}$$

(7) The wage is higher, and employment lower, than at a competitive equilibrium.

Proof. Competition would imply $pf'(n) + \sigma = w^c = b$. By the first-order condition, and concavity of $f(n)$, $w > w^c$ and $n < n^c$.

Results 1 and 6 capture effects which pivot the union's indifference curves towards either its wage goal or its employment goal. Results 4 and 5 are ambiguous because incentives at the margin can outweigh or be outweighed by income effects. Result 3, that membership does not matter, stems from the fact that neither the marginal benefit nor the marginal cost to the union depends here on the size of the membership pool. This is probably seen as the most unattractive of the seven predictions, because economists tend to think that membership is an important influence on union behaviour. One way around the result is to assume that equilibrium is at a corner where employment equals membership (see Carruth and Oswald (1987*b*)), another is somehow to let membership affect bargaining power, a third is to think of membership as a choice variable for the union. None has been much explored. Result 7 says that the union rations jobs and raises the value of marginal product and therefore the wage-rate.

Result 2, which is of particular interest, states the condition under which a demand shift will maintain exactly the same equilibrium wage rate (so that, geometrically, the 'expansion path' is horizontal). Wage rigidity in the monopoly union model, therefore, takes the form illustrated in Fig. 2.4. Crucially, pay inflexibility rests upon the constancy of the elasticity of labour demand.

The only obvious way to get around such a restriction is to impose an alternative: kinked preferences (as in Oswald (1986*b*)) would be one possibility. But this also is unhappily restrictive.

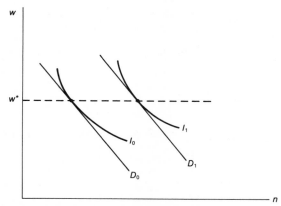

Fig 2.4.   *Wage rigidity in the monopoly union model*

2.4.3. *Efficient Bargains*

The equilibrium in the monopoly model is inefficient: the outcome does not lie on the bargaining-contract curve. This idea can be represented as in Fig. 2.3. Efficient bargains — there are an infinite number — lie on the CC' locus of tangency points between indifference curves and iso-profit contours. Hence, by moving from the monopoly equilibrium, ω^u, both parties can gain. The competitive equilibrium is given by the intersection of the labour demand curve and the horizontal labour supply curve (fixed by the height of the reservation wage).

Perhaps the simplest case is that where profit is $pf(n) - wn$ and the union's utility is $u(w) n + (m - n) u(b)$. Efficiency requires that one be maximized subject to an arbitrary level of the other. The equation of the contract curve, therefore, is

$$\frac{u(w) - u(b)}{u'(w)} = w - pf'(n), \qquad (27)$$

which is essentially equation (17) in McDonald and Solow (1981). The same equation appears repeatedly in work on labour contract theory, which is discussed in the next section.

Various results can be proved.

(1) The contract curve slopes upwards in wage-employment space.

$$\text{Proof.} \quad \frac{\mathrm{d}w}{\mathrm{d}n} = \frac{pf''(n)u'(w)}{[w - pf'(n)]u''(w)} > 0. \qquad (28)$$

(2) A rise in unemployment benefit (or the reservation wage) shifts the contract curve up to the left.

$$\text{Proof.} \quad \frac{\partial w}{\partial b} = \frac{-u'(b)}{[w - pf'(n)]u''(w)} > 0. \qquad (29)$$

(3) An increase in the price of output shifts the contract curve down and to the right.

$$\text{Proof.} \quad \frac{\partial w}{\partial p} = \frac{u'(w)f'(n)}{[w - pf'(n)]u''(w)} < 0. \qquad (30)$$

(4) Equilibrium employment is higher than in the equivalent competitive labour market.

Proof. Add $u'(w)b$ to both sides of the first-order condition for efficiency, (27), and write as $u(w) - u(b) + u'(w)(b - w) = u'(w) [b - pf'(n)]$. The left hand side is positive by concavity of $u(.)$. Hence $b \geqslant pf'(n)$, so the value of the marginal product of labour is lower than the competitive reservation wage b. This imples that employment has been pushed beyond the level which would be generated without a union in the labour market.

(5) If the labour demand curve's elasticity is constant, and the bargaining outcome is fixed by the 'fair shares' rule $wn = kpf(n)$, where k is the share parameter, the wage will be unaffected by changes in the price of output.

Proof. Differentiate the two equations, the contract curve and the sharing rule, to give

$$\begin{bmatrix} -u''(w)\,[w - pf'\,(n)] & -u'(w)\,pf''\,(n) \\ n & -kpf'\,(n) \end{bmatrix} \begin{bmatrix} \mathrm{d}w \\ \mathrm{d}n \end{bmatrix} =$$

$$\begin{bmatrix} -u'(w)f'\,(n) \\ kf(n) \end{bmatrix} \mathrm{d}p \qquad (31)$$

It follows that when $\epsilon = -(\partial n/\partial w)\,(w/n)$ is constant, namely when $f'(n)/f''(n)n$ is a constant, $\mathrm{d}w/\mathrm{d}p = 0$.

Result 5 is an especially simple form of the 'wage stickness' which McDonald and Solow (1981) wish to highlight. Again the constancy of the labour demand elasticity is required. More generally, they assume that in a slump the efficiency locus, given by the contract curve, shifts up; but the equity locus, of which the 'fair' division rule is one, shifts down. When these two are off-setting, as in Fig. 2.5, the wage is rigid.

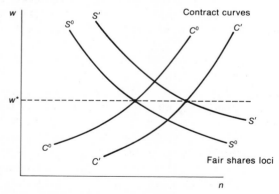

Fig 2.5.   *Wage rigidity in the McDonald–Solow model*

In Carruth and Oswald (1987*b*) we derive a wage rigidity theorem of a related kind. It is shown there that the wage of an expanding firm is inflexible in the face of product price changes when (i) the union assigns no utility weight to employment, (ii) there is a Nash bargain with a zero profit fall-back for the firm, and (iii) the production function has constant elasticity. The paper justifies (i) by the assumption that 'insiders' in an expanding firm want higher pay for themselves rather than jobs for 'outsiders'. Solow (1985), Black and Bulkley (1984) and McDonald (1985) analyse variants of this approach. Chapter 6 of the book treats senior employees as those with insider power, and develops an alternative framework.

In summary, there are a number of ways to derive wage rigidity results in trade-union models. All of them, however, rely on special assumptions about functional form.

2.5 Wage Determination and the Theory of Implicit Contracts

In the middle of the last decade a number of American economists developed a model of wage inflexibility which was to become known as 'implicit contract' theory. Its aim was to improve upon, and get away from, the traditional idea that wages and employment are determined in competitive markets and so by the interaction between demand and supply curves. Baily (1974), Azariadis (1975), and Gordon (1974) wrote down mathematical models in which the wage was predicted to be rigid across booms and slumps. The explanation for this result lies in the authors' assumptions about the different attitudes to risk of the firm and its work-force.

Imagine that a group of workers is employed by a single firm and that a new labour contract, or collective bargain, is to be negotiated. Product market conditions in the future are uncertain, but both sides have some clear idea about the chances of boom and slump. Assume, moreover, that both the workers and the employer will be able to observe correctly the firm's performance (the selling price of the product, profitability, and so on) once the future arrives. This is known in the jargon as the assumption of *symmetric information*. How, then, will the firm and its workers design the labour contract? The answer depends on their feelings about risk. The implicit contract theory of the mid 1970s drew upon the assumption that workers are averse to risk but that firms are not. The mathematics then showed what intuition would suggest: the parties' desired form of labour agreement is one in which the wage stays constant regardless of whether the firm's sales go well or badly. Firms take the risk; employed workers do not. This is jointly efficient in that workers are happy to accept a lower average wage if it is a fixed wage (and so can be relied upon). The firm earns higher average profits and bears the risk.

This theory caused a stir in the economics profession. It appeared to provide a rationale for the apparent stickiness of real wages in the real world, and hence was seen as opening doors to a new and better kind of macroeconomic theory.

Although an influential model, it has been criticized on a number of grounds. One weakness is that the model predicts that employment will be larger than that in the equivalent kind of competitive, atomistic market, and that fluctuations will be smaller than in such a setting (for example, (Akerlof and Miyazaki (1980), Pissarides (1981)). Yet the theory's aim was to explain why unemployment equilibria could exist. A second weakness is that once lay-off pay is introduced into the model it can be shown that the number of jobs will be exactly the same as in a competitive labour market (for a recent proof, see Grossman and Hart (1981)). Oswald (1986*a*) and Oswald and Turnbull (1985) discuss the evidence of lay-off pay. A third is that the famous wage rigidity result disappears once the firm is assumed to dislike risk (Grossman and Hart (1981)).

In 'implicit contract' models, the wage is rigid because that is the optimal way in which firms can provide income insurance for their workers. The theory assumes that workers are risk-averse and that firms are risk-neutral. A common justification for the latter assumption (that each firm aims to maximize its expected profit) is that an employer can spread his risks more easily than the typical employee. Firms may also have better access to the capital market. In this framework the efficient form of labour contract, or collective agreement, is one in which firms pay a guaranteed wage-rate. In a more general setting this prediction goes back at least to Borch (1962), who wrote on the theory of insurance markets.

Although this idea may be an important reason for wage

stickiness, it is not often remembered that implicit contract theory rests upon a number of rather unpalatable axioms. It is relatively easy to eliminate the famous wage rigidity prediction, by altering the assumptions very slightly.

Consider a firm which aims to maximize expected utility,

$$EV = \int v(pf(n) - wn) g(p)\mathrm{d}p, \qquad (32)$$

where $v(.)$ is a concave and increasing function, p is the exogenous product price, $f(n)$ is a production function with conventional properties, w is the wage rate, n is employment, and $g(p)$ is (the firm's view of) the density function for the uncertain product price. Define profit as $\pi = pf(n) - wn$. When $v(.)$ is linear the firm is riskneutral. Assume that the firm has a pool of workers who are committed to it once they have agreed a 'contract'. Let the pool be of size unity. Assume that workers do not know in advance which of them will be employed, and that, if employment is below unity, jobs will be allocated randomly. The expected utility of the typical worker can then be written

$$EU = \int \{nu(w) + (1 - n)u(b)\} h(p)\mathrm{d}p \qquad (33)$$

where $u(.)$ is a worker's (concave) utility function, b is the income of an unemployed worker, and $h(p)$ is the workers' view of the density function of prices.

An optimal wage contract consists of a wage schedule $w(p)$ and an employment schedule $n(p)$ which maximize the firm's expected utility subject to some minimum level of expected utility for workers. Less formally, to obtain any employees at all, the firm has to offer as good a job package as being offered elsewhere. To do that in the most efficient way it must choose a contingent wagerate and a contingent employment level which provide a suitable compromise between the interests of both sides to the agreement. Workers here are 'told' how wages and employment will depend on the product price. They agree to $w(p)$ and $n(p)$ in advance; eventually the price, p, becomes known; then some of the workers in the labour pool are hired.

The formal problem is as follows:

$$\begin{array}{l} \text{Maximize} \\ w(p), n(p) \end{array} \quad \int v(pf(n) - wn) g(p) \, \mathrm{d}p \qquad (34)$$

s.t.

$$\int \{nu(w) + (1-n)\,u(b)\}\,h(p)\,\mathrm{d}p \geqslant \bar{\mu} \qquad (35)$$

in which the variable $\bar{\mu}$ represents the 'going' or market level of expected utility of a worker. Let $\lambda \geqslant 0$ be the multiplier corresponding to the constraint. Then the Lagrangean for this constrained maximization is

$$L = \int v(pf(n) - wn)\,g(p)\,\mathrm{d}p$$
$$+ \lambda \int \{nu(w) + (1-n)u(b)\}\,h(p)\,\mathrm{d}p. \qquad (36)$$

At an interior optimum, therefore, the following first-order conditions are satisfied:

$$w(p): -v'(\pi)\,g(p) + \lambda u'(w)\,h(p) = 0 \qquad (37)$$
$$n(p): v'(\pi)\,[pf'(n) - w]\,g(p) + \lambda[u(w) - u(b)]\,h(p) = 0 \qquad (38)$$

These are the wage and employment solutions to the model. The first is a wage function (or schedule) defined on price p. The second is an equivalent employment function.

The famous Baily–Azariadis–Gordon wage rigidity theorem stems from a special case of this model. It assumes that the firm is risk-neutral, so that $v'(\pi)$, which is the firm's marginal utility of profit income, is constant. It also assumes, although this is rarely mentioned, that $g(p) \equiv h(p)$, namely that both sides have identical perceptions of the likely probability distribution of the firm's eventual selling price. Under these assumptions equation (37) reduces to

$$-1 + \lambda u'(w) = 0, \qquad (39)$$

because $v'(\pi)$ becomes unity by the assumption of risk-neutrality, and $g(p) \equiv h(p)$ can be cancelled throughout. Equation (39) establishes the theorem. It can be rearranged as

$$u'(w) = \frac{1}{\lambda}$$

$$= \text{a constant.} \qquad (40)$$

Hence the optimal labour contract is that which makes the marginal utility of wages a constant (the same constant for every different output price p). There is only one (real) wagerate which fixes the marginal utility at just the right amount. Thus the wage is perfectly inflexible.

It is apparent from the mathematics — though not from the superficially attractive intuition that wage rigidity is a way in which firms provide 'insurance' — that each of the following three conditions must be satisfied.

(1) The firm must be exactly risk-neutral.

(2) Both the firm and the employees must have the same views about the probability distribution of the firm's product price.

(3) Employees must be chosen by random draw.

Whenever at least one of these is violated, the theory of labour contracts will not predict wage rigidity. To the best of our knowledge there is no compelling empirical evidence for these conditions.

2.6 Contract Models with Asymmetric Information

There are a number of variants on the same contractual theme. One due to Hall and Lilien (1979), Calvo and Phelps (1977), and Grossman and Hart (1981) is the theory of labour contracts under asymmetric information. Although this is similar in spirit to early implicit contract theory, it introduces the assumption that firms may be much better informed than their workers. Many models make the extreme assumption that only the firm is able to observe the selling price and profitability of its product. In this case it is not possible to have an employment contract — either implicit or explicit — which makes pay and employment levels contingent upon the product price. Interestingly, these models do not predict that the wage will be rigid, however, but rather that the optimal contract will tie pay to the amount of employment (assumed to be observable to both sides). Consider the following assumptions.

1. Each worker has a utility function $u(.)$. The function is concave, increasing, bounded, and twice differentiable. It is to be thought of as the utility from real income. Leisure is taken to have no value. The wage income when working is w, and is b when not

working. Only a single unit of labour is supplied by each worker.

2. There is a fixed labour pool, normalized at size unity. Employment is n, defined on the closed interval $[0, 1]$.

3. The preferences of the labour group (or trade union) are described *ex post* by the utility function $U = nu(w) + (1 - n) u(b)$, which is a quasi-concave function defined on wages and employment. Labour's preferences *ex ante* are described by the group's expected utility function, EU.

4. The firm or employer has a utility function, $v(.)$. It is concave, increasing, bounded and twice differentiable, and is to be thought of as measuring the utility from profit income, π. The firm maximizes expected utility, Ev.

These assumptions give the nature of the agents' preferences. They are similar to assumptions made in the early contract literature. Another especially important assumption is the following:

5. The utility of an unemployed worker, $u(b)$, is independent of the firm's actions.

This follows Baily (1974), Azariadis (1975), and Holstrom (1984) and plays a crucial role in labour contract models under symmetric information.

It is also necessary to specify the form and nature of uncertainty, the structure of technology, and the minimum profit (utility) necessary to keep the firms (workers) from withdrawing from the market.

6. The firm's output price, θ, is uncertain. It is distributed according to the density function $g(\theta) > 0$ on the closed interval $[\underline{\theta}, \bar{\theta}]$. Only the firm observes θ.

7. Output is given by a production function $f(.)$. The function is concave, increasing, bounded, and twice differentiable.

8. A firm elsewhere in the economy earns expected utility v^*.

9. No one will work for the firm in state θ if $u(w) < u(b)$.

These assumptions describe a world of the following kind. A firm aims to employ some workers to produce a good which it will eventually sell in a competitive market. No one can be sure what the price will be, but the employer must recruit today. It would like to offer its workers a deal in which their pay depends on the selling price of the product. This cannot be done, however, because the employees will not be able to observe the price. By way of example, auto workers, say, can observe for certain only the sticker prices on the automobiles they help to manufacture, and cannot know what dealer and customer discounts are being offered across the country. To get any workers at all, it is assumed that the company must pay a wage that is greater than government unemployment benefit or the alternative reservation wage. This is because employees can quit. It is assumed, though, that the firm cannot leave costlessly if a bad state of nature occurs, and hence requires only the average utility it would expect to get by switching into another sector.

One possible form of the employment contract would be for the firm to pay a fixed wage across all states of nature, but a risk-averse firm is not going to be happy with such an agreement. It would prefer to share some of its risk. There is a way to achieve this, namely, by having a labour contract in which pay, w, is linked to the number of jobs, n. Employment can be observed by both sides, so a contract of form $w(n)$ is feasible.

If the wage is a function of employment, profits can be written

$$\pi = \theta f(n) - w(n)n. \tag{41}$$

The firm's utility is $v(\pi)$, and it will be useful to define a function

$$r(n, \theta) = v(\theta f(n) - w(n)n) \tag{42}$$

which the firm is to maximize, by its choice of employment, once the product price θ is known. For well-behaved optima, therefore, the number of jobs is chosen so that

$$r_n - v'(\pi)[\theta f'(n) - w'(n)n - w(n)] = 0 \tag{43}$$

and $r_{nn} < 0$. Let $n(\theta)$ be the function which solves this. Then it turns out that employment is an increasing function of the price of output, namely,

$$n'(\theta) = - v'(\pi)f'(n)/r_{nn} > 0, \tag{44}$$

which will be used later on. Finally, because the optimization problem to come can be set up most concisely using a maximum value function, let

$$v(\theta) = \max_{n} r(n, \theta). \tag{45}$$

By an envelope result, therefore,

$$v'(\theta) = v'(\pi)f(n) > 0, \tag{46}$$

which measures the rise in the firm's *ex post* utility that is caused by an increase in the product price. The employer does better as states of nature improve.

The optimal form of employment contract is to be thought of, as usual, as the solution to a maximization problem. The group of workers — they might be taken to be a trade union but that is not essential — must pick a wage function $w(n)$ which maximizes their expected utility subject to various constraints. This contract will not be first-best Pareto optimal, because of the existence of asymmetric information about conditions in the product market, but will in the obvious sense be a second-best optimum. There are various ways to characterize it mathematically. The simplest is to work not with a wage function defined on employment, but rather with two functions defined on the state of nature θ. Hence one could derive a function for pay, $w(\theta)$, and a function for jobs, $n(\theta)$, and let these together define implicitly the wage as a function of the employment level. We use a variant of this in which the choice variables are $v(\theta)$ and $n(\theta)$, but this is only a matter of convenience.

The full problem can be written as

$$\underset{v(\theta), n(\theta)}{\text{maximize}} \int_{\underline{\theta}}^{\bar{\theta}} \{nu(w) + (1 - n)u(b)\}\, g(\theta)\, d\theta \tag{47}$$

subject to

$$\int_{\underline{\theta}}^{\bar{\theta}} v(\theta)\, g(\theta)\, d\theta \geq v^* \tag{48}$$

$$v'(\theta) = v'(\pi)f(n) \tag{49}$$

$$u(w) \geq u(b), \tag{50}$$

where for brevity the wage employment, and profit variables have not been written explicitly as functions of θ. The maximand is the expected utility of the labour group, and the choice variables here are the utility of the firm and the number of jobs. Equation (48), the first of the three constraints, states that the employer's expected utility (when setting employment optimally) must be at least what it can achieve in another sector of the economy. The second constraint, equation (49), captures the fact that the firm will move on to its labour demand curve once the price of output is known. It implies and is implied by the condition that the value of the marginal product of labour be equal to its marginal cost.

Equation (50), the third of the constraints, stipulates that an individual worker be no worse off, *ex post*, than he or she would be by drawing government unemployment benefit. This is a feasibility condition.

The firms' utility from profits, $v(\pi)$, is monotonic, so can be inverted. At the optimum the employer's utility is $v(\theta)$. Thus it is possible to define profits by the function $\pi(v(\theta))$, which is the inverse of $v(\pi)$. The product of the derivatives of these two functions is unity. The relationship $\pi(v)$ provides a way to write the wage as a function of the realized product price. It is, by rearrangement of the definition of profits,

$$
\begin{aligned}
w &= (\theta f(n) - \pi)/n \\
&= (\theta f(n(\theta)) - \pi(v)\theta)))/n(\theta).
\end{aligned}
\tag{51}
$$

These points mean that both the wage and the profit level can be substituted out of the optimization problem described by equations (47) to (50).

The problem will be solved here by integrating equation (49) by parts and using the result to form a Lagrangean. Let the multiplier on the first constraint be λ, that on the second be $\psi(\theta)$, and that on the third be $\phi(\theta)$. The Lagrangean is then

$$
L = \int_{\underline{\theta}}^{\bar{\theta}} \{ [nu(w) + (1 - n)u(b) + \lambda v(\theta)] \} g(\theta) - v(\theta)\psi'(\theta) -
$$
$$
\psi(\theta)v'(\pi)f(n) + \phi(\theta)[u(w) - u(b)] \} \, d\theta.
\tag{52}
$$

There are, strictly speaking, some endpoint terms from the integration by parts, but for simplicity they have been omitted. The first-order conditions for an interior optimum include

$v(\theta)$: $[\lambda - (u'(w)/v'(\pi))]g(\theta) -$
$\quad \psi'(\theta) - (v''(\pi)/v'(\pi))\psi(\theta)f(n) - \phi(\theta)u'(w)/(v'(\pi)n) = 0$ (53)

$n(\theta)$: $\{u(w) - u(b) + [\theta f'(n) - w]u'(w)\}g(\theta) -$
$\quad \psi(\theta)v'(\pi)f'(n) + (\phi(\theta)u'(w)/n)[\theta f'(n) - w] = 0$ (54)

$\psi(\underline{\theta}) = \psi(\bar{\theta}) = 0$ (55)

$u(w) - u(b) \geq 0 \qquad \phi(\theta) \geq 0.$ (56)

Equation (55) gives the transversality conditions: the multiplier $\psi(\theta)$ must start and end at zero. Equation (56) is the complementary slackness condition (50): the multiplier $\phi(\theta)$ is zero when the inequality $u(w) \geq u(b)$ fails to bind. The analysis will concentrate on the case in which constraint (56) is not strictly binding (it is straightforward to incorporate).

The first points that need to be established are about the sign and behaviour of the multiplier $\psi(\theta)$ which corresponds to the differential equation (49). It turns out to be possible to show that $\psi(\theta)$ cannot be negative. It must begin at zero, become positive for some states of nature, and then return to zero for the best state of nature. The proof (given in the Appendix to this chapter) shows that once $\psi(\theta)$ becomes negative it remains negative. This would violate the transversality condition $\psi(\bar{\theta}) = 0$, which is what makes it possible to rule out negative values for the multiplier.

The model can generate equilibria in which there is both involuntary unemployment and underemployment. Involuntary unemployment will be defined here as an outcome in which the utility from work, $u(w)$, is strictly greater than the utility from being unemployed, $u(b)$. This seems to be the most natural definition. It captures the idea that there can be an individual without a job who would like to change places with a similar individual who is employed. A definition of underemployment and overemployment is also needed, and the normal one will be used. The value of the marginal product of labour is $\theta f'(n)$: the value of the reservation wage is b. Overemployment will be said to exist when $\theta f'(n) < b$ and underemployment will be said to exist when the inequality is reversed. The intermediate case is, as we should expect, the efficient competitive outcome $\theta f'(n) = b$. As noted earlier, conventional implicit contract theory solves the problem

$$\max_{w(\theta),\, n(\theta)} \int_{\underline{\theta}}^{\bar{\theta}} [nu(w) + (1 - n)u(b)]g(\theta)\, d\theta \qquad (57)$$

subject to

$$\int_{\underline{\theta}}^{\bar{\theta}} [\theta f(n) - wn]\, g(\theta)\, d\theta \geq \pi^* \qquad (58)$$

with first-order condition

$$u(w) - u(b) - u'(w)w = -u'(w)\theta f'(n). \qquad (59)$$

By adding $bu'(w)$ to both sides we have

$$[u(w) - u(b)] + u'(w)(b - w) = u'(w)[b - \theta f'(n)] \geq 0. \qquad (60)$$

which is positive by concavity of the $u(.)$ function. The production function $f(n)$ is also concave so that $b \geq \theta f'(n)$ implies that employment exceeds that at the point at which $b = \theta f'(n)$. This again is the overemployment result of early contract theory. Notice, however, that involuntary unemployment ($u(w) > u(b)$) can certainly exist. The second generation of work on labour contracts (see Grossman and Hart (1981), for example) uses an amended version of the framework developed earlier. In this case private unemployment insurance b is set to the point at which there is full insurance. Underemployment, $\theta f'(n) - b > 0$, does occur, but it is all voluntary.

It is not surprising that, by taking an element from each of the two generations of contract theory, we can produce a model in which there are insufficient jobs and dissatisfied unemployed workers. The proof adds $g(\theta)bu'(w)$ to both sides of equation (54), and imposes the assumption $\phi = 0$, so that

$$g(\theta)[u(w) - u(b) + u'(w)(b - w)] = u'(w)g(\theta)[b - \theta f'(n)] + \psi(\theta)v'(\pi)f'(n). \qquad (61)$$

Concavity of the worker's utility function again ensures that the left-hand side is positive. In this model, however, it is not the case that overemployment follows immediately. The reason is that $\psi(\theta)$ is necessarily positive, so that underemployment can exist at the same time as equation (61) is satisfied. It is the mixture of the assumptions of asymmetric information and imperfect unemployment insurance which generates the possibility that underemployment and involuntary unemployment can occur simultaneously.

Some other results can be established. First, there exist at least two intervals, $[\underline{\theta}, \theta^1]$ and $[\theta^2, \bar{\theta}]$, on which there is overemployment. Equation (61) makes it clear that when $\psi(\theta)$ is zero, the usual overemployment conclusion (as in equation (60)) goes through. That must occur, by the transversality condition, in the best and worst states of nature. By continuity, therefore, there exist intervals at either end of the support of $g(\theta)$ on which the value of the marginal product of labour drops below the reservation wage. Second, the same argument can be used to prove that, for the lowest price ($\underline{\theta}$) and the highest price ($\bar{\theta}$), the model simply replicates the equilibrium of a Baily–Azariadis–Gordon model. This is formally equivalent to the result in optimal non-linear tax theory (Mirrlees (1976), for example) that the marginal tax-rate should be zero at the top and bottom ends of the skill distribution. Third, equation (59) reveals that, as noted earlier, in first-generation contract theory the wage exceeds the value of the marginal product of labour. Yet this is no longer true once asymmetric information is introduced. Inspection of equation (61) shows that $w > b$ and $w \leqslant \theta f'(n)$ can hold simultaneously.

It is useful to provide a more intuitive account of the forces which lead to overemployment or underemployment. The first is a response to a missing insurance market. By assumption, in this and early contract models, there is no private unemployment insurance scheme to allow workers to avoid the risk of a drop in utility if fired. Workers must therefore find some other way, if they can, to guard against the vagaries of the market. The optimal one is to ensure that the firm takes on more employees than would be justified on the grounds of technical efficiency. That reduces the risk of unemployment. The greater is workers' risk-aversion, the larger will be the extent of the overemployment. Underemployment has quite a different cause. When there is asymmetric information about prices, the optimal labour contract ties pay to the number of jobs, which is observable and carries some information about the employer's success in the product market. Thus, crucially, pay is not rigid. The wage is an increasing function of employment whenever, at the optimum, the value of the marginal product of labour exceeds the wage rate. Equation (43) states this formally. In this case, however, there is a reason to employ fewer individuals than would be optimal in the equivalent market with a competitively fixed wage: the marginal cost of labour is higher than in the equivalent market with wage taking by firms. This apparent inefficiency (it is second-best efficient) is the indirect result of the fact that workers do not have access to the same information as their employer. Whether the model is a satisfactory one is an empirical question. What matters for our purposes is that it does not generate wage rigidity.

2.7 Conclusions

This chapter has described and criticized four theories of wage inflexibility. Each provides a way to show why a rational firm may not change its rate of pay when its product demand changes, but each generates pay rigidity only in special and arguably implausible circumstances.

The first argues that, with a competitive aggregate labour

market and perfect labour mobility, a sector which experiences a decline in demand must continue to offer the going market rate of remuneration. If firms in the depressed sector do otherwise, they will lose all their workers. The drawback of this approach is that the necessary 'frictionless' competitive conditions seem unlikely to hold in Western economies.

The second, the efficiency wage hypothesis, has recently attracted much professional attention in the American literature. According to this model, firms do not wish to cut wages in a recession, because their employees would reduce effort so much that the wage-cut would be self-defeating. One objection to this idea is that, in practice, employers may immediately be able to see and penalize those workers who 'shirk'. Efficiency wage theory assumes, perhaps implausibly, that this is impossible. A more crucial objection, for our purposes, is that wage rigidity occurs only under restrictive assumptions (that the production function is multiplicative in effort and output, for example).

The third explanation focuses upon the role of trade unions. Both the monopoly union and efficient bargain models can generate wage rigidity. However, special assumptions are required, such as that the elasticity of labour demand be a constant, and this must count as a weakness. Union models can just as easily produce wage flexibility as they can wage inflexibility.

The fourth approach, labour contract theory, is one of the most famous ways to provide a rationale for wage inflexibility. Once again, however, restrictive assumptions are required. The Baily–Azariadis–Gordon theorem, for example, only holds if the firm is strictly risk-neutral, lay-offs are by random draw, and both employer and employees have identical beliefs about the probability distribution of product prices. Recent more general versions of contract theory (Grossman and Hart (1981) for example), based on the assumption of asymmetric information, do not predict that wage-rates will be inflexible.

In conclusion, there have been many attempts by economists to prove wage rigidity theorems. All derive the result that the employer's equilibrium rate of pay is independent of its level of product demand or price. Yet none appears to be robust: wage flexibility is the general case and wage inflexibility the special case. It is conceivable that this modern literature has had too narrow a focus and has misled.

APPENDIX
A Proof of the Non-negativity of $\psi(\theta)$

The analysis of the main section of the paper relies on the fact that the multiplier $\psi(\theta)$ is weakly positive. The proof is as follows. Equation (53) is a linear differential equation of first order. It can be rewritten — setting ϕ to zero on the assumption that (50) does not bind — as

$$\psi'(\theta) = \left[\lambda - \frac{u'(w)}{v'(\pi)} \right] g(\theta) + \psi(\theta)\rho f(n). \qquad (A1)$$

where $\rho \equiv - v''(\pi)/v'(\pi)$. The solution to the equation can be found by integrating it using the condition $\psi(\underline{\theta}) = 0$. That solution is

$$\psi(\theta) = \int_{\underline{\theta}}^{\theta} \left[\lambda - \frac{u'(w)}{v'(\pi)} \right] g(x)H(x)\mathrm{d}x \qquad (A2)$$

where

$$H = \exp \int_{\underline{\theta}}^{x} - \rho f(n)\mathrm{d}z, \qquad (A3)$$

and x and z are used to denote the variable of integration.

The endpoint conditions, equation (55), also ensure that $\psi(\bar{\theta}) = 0$, which is the key to the proof of the multiplier's non-negativity. Define a new variable

$$A(\theta) \equiv \lambda - u'(w)/v'(\pi). \qquad (A4)$$

If $\psi(\theta)$ is to satisfy the transversality requirement, $A(\theta)$ must change sign over the interval $[\underline{\theta}, \bar{\theta}]$. The derivative of that function is

$$A'(\theta) = \frac{u''(w)}{v'(\pi)} \frac{\mathrm{d}w}{\mathrm{d}\theta} + \frac{u'(w)v''(\pi)}{[v'(\pi)]^2} \frac{\mathrm{d}\pi}{\mathrm{d}\theta} \qquad (A5)$$

By earlier definitions, $w = (\theta f - \pi)/n$, $\pi = \pi(v)$ and $v'(\theta) = v'(\pi)f(n)$. Hence

$$A'(\theta) = -\frac{u''(w)}{nv'(\pi)} [\theta f'(n) - w]n'(\theta) - \rho(u'(w)/v'(\pi)f(n) \qquad (A6)$$

The derivative $n'(\theta)$ is known to be positive. Hence negativity of $A'(\theta)$ would be guaranteed by the condition $w > \theta f'(n)$. We wish to prove $\psi(\theta) \geq 0$. Assume not, in order to obtain a contradiction. Equation (54) in the text then implies that $[\theta f'(n) - w]$ is negative. This ensures $A'(\theta) < 0$. Thus, once $\psi(\theta)$ takes a negative value, it remains negative. For an optimum, however, $\psi(\theta)$ must return to zero at $\theta = \bar{\theta}$. Hence $\psi(\theta) < 0$ implies a contradiction.

3

Wage Determination:
Industrial–Relations Evidence

3.1 Introduction

Chapter 2 stressed that microeconomic models of wage determination show why there may be wage inflexibility in the face of changes in product demand, but also questioned the robustness of such rigidity theorems. It is now appropriate to examine whether their predictions hold good for labour markets in a country like Britain.

One natural way to try to understand how wages are determined is to study real-world examples. It should thereby be possible to pick out recurring elements and so identify some pattern behind the myriad of influences. This can be characterized as the inductive or industrial relations approach. It does not start with theory, or the construction of models, but rather with the observation of detail.

This chapter collects together various kinds of industrial relations evidence. It assumes that such evidence is complementary to that provided by the statistical and econometric methods upon which later chapters focus. Chapters 4 and 7 are concerned with such analyses, and they dominate applied economics in the 1980s. Ever since Adam Smith (1st edn. 1776), however, a knowledge of labour market institutions and facts has been seen by most as essential. A notable modern statement of 'neo-institutionalism' is contained in Kerr (1983).

One particular idea runs throughout the chapter. It is that *wages are determined in part by the past profitability of the employer*. This has a long history in the labour economics literature, but has been omitted from most of the work of the last two decades. The idea (sometimes known as the ability-to-pay argument) is central to this book's thesis.

Many factors affect pay. In 1947 the Chicago Association of Commerce and Industry became convinced that wages were 'the most important single problem facing American business'. In response, they commissioned Professor Sumner Slichter, of Harvard University, to write *Basic Criteria Used in Wage Negotiations*. Slichter (1947) contains one of the earliest comprehensive analyses of the determinants of pay within a system of collective bargaining. The author identified seven principal criteria used in wage negotiations (p. 8):

1. The minimum necessities of workers.
2. Changes in the cost of living.
3. The maintenance of take-home pay in the face of reductions in hours.
4. Changes in the productivity of labour.
5. The ability (or inability) of the employer to pay.
6. The alleged effect of higher or lower wages upon consumer purchasing power and employment.
7. The wages paid in other industries or places.

The first of these criteria is particularly important in administering minimum wage legislation, but it is also frequently used by unions in wage negotiations. The third criterion is used only by unions. The remaining five criteria are used by both employers and unions.

Forty years later this taxonomy remains an accurate one. In particular, as the evidence of the chapter will reveal, wage-rates within a firm appear to be influenced by the financial health of that firm.

3.2 What are Wage Negotiations Like?

A book on wage determination would be incomplete without a description of real-world wage-bargaining. The best way to provide that is to reproduce what firms and unions actually say when they negotiate. It is impossible, because of the lack of reliable source material, to do this in a statistically representative way, so examples must suffice.

This section summarizes the first two rounds of the 1986 pay negotiations between the Engineering Employers and the collected body of their trade unions (the CSEU). A principal reason for this choice is that both sides prepared written documents, stating their arguments and counter-arguments, and recording the precise discussions — available from transcripts — which took place. Normally such debates are confidential.

There are two objections. First, it is never possible to be sure that a single wage negotiation is representative. Second, this is an example of national wage-bargaining, in which the parties represent large numbers of disparate employees and firms. Some advantages, however, are also apparent. The sector is unusually helpful to the investigator in that it provides exact statements from both sides. It is also an important and interesting part of the British economy. Section 3.3, moreover, will show that systematic survey evidence confirms the significance of the factors identified by the engineering unions and employers. Thus, although the following is but one special case, it may convey the flavour of broader matters.

3.2.1. *The Unions' Case*

On 17 October 1986 the Engineering Employers' Federation and the Confederation of Shipbuilding and Engineering Unions met to discuss a pay claim. The employers' side was led by R. G. Hooker, and the unions' side by G. H. Laird. The unions' claim was outlined by W. Jordan; the employers' reply was read by J. S. McFarlane.

The union proposed five items.

(1) A substantial increase in minimum time rates of pay.
(2) A reduction in the basic working week to thirty-five hours without loss of pay.
(3) Six weeks annual holiday.
(4) The adult rate to be paid at 18 years.
(5) That an equal opportunities (that is, anti-racist) policy
 • clause be inserted in the national agreement.

We shall concentrate on the discussion about the first and most commonly debated issue — the claim for a higher wage-rate.

After an initial statement of the five objectives, the union side began in the following way.

MR JORDAN. First let me say that we of the CSEU are committed unreservedly to the strength and profitability of the engineering industry, and our members' efforts are testimony to that. We are also strongly committed to the prosperity of all who are in the industry. However, the evidence is that the profits in the industry are being unevenly distributed. Our claim is about righting this injustice.

We know that optimism expressed about economic growth this year has been clouded by such uncertainties as the drop in oil prices and effect of the United States' huge budget deficit on world trade. However, longer-term forecasters say that the outlook for late 1986 and 1987 is brighter.

Now pundits, with unnerving regularity, alter their optimistic or pessimistic insight on economic recovery, but we must deal with the facts of our industry as they are. There is no more solid fact than that since 1979 more than 1.8 million workers have lost their jobs in manufacturing. This has meant that a third of engineering's workforce has gone and, along with them, valuable skills.

But throughout this period of radical retrenchment, reorganisation and change, your member firms, in their annual statements and through the Federation, have acknowledged the tremendous contributions made by our members to revitalise their companies and industry.

In progressing our claim, we not only look at the current situation and future prospects but also at the sustained rise in profits, output and productivity in recent years, achieved with the co-operation and effort of our members.

These were the opening paragraphs of the written wage-claim document, and it seems likely that they contain the most powerful of the unions' arguments. The role of past and expected profits is obviously here given central importance. It is also of interest that Jordan's focus was upon factors internal to the industry, rather than upon external pressures from the UK labour market itself.

The CSEU then went on to provide precise figures.

MR JORDAN. In 1985 profits of industrial and commercial companies were up 29 per cent. Even excluding North Sea oil companies and British Telecom, profits still reached 21 per cent, and as significant in the context of this claim, dividends rose by 27 per cent.

Over the longer period since 1980, profits have increased by 60 per cent in real terms and it is confidently predicted by stockbrokers Phillips and Drew that profits in industrial companies will go up by 17 per cent this year.

Further, the rate of return on capital in manufacturing rose by 8 per cent last year. This is higher than in any year since 1973 and equal to the boom years of 1972 and 1973.

We know that this represents a mixed bag, as results vary considerably in engineering, as elsewhere, but the fact is that many companies in engineering have seen their profitability rise significantly in recent years and others expect to show impressive financial improvements by next year. Later in our claim we will provide a number of examples, using pre-tax profit as a yardstick. Growth in output and increased productivity are important economic indicators. Taking into account allowances made for distortions caused by the fall in employment, the following points are worth making.

Output rose in manufacturing by 3.9 per cent in 1984 and 2.9 per cent in 1985, according to *British Business*. The increase in engineering output was 4.5 per cent in both years.

Between 1982 and 1986 manufacturing productivity increased by 21 per cent. Similarly, productivity — that is output per head — rose by 28 per cent in engineering during this same period.

The improvements in strength, profitability and competitiveness that these statistics represent have been bought dearly by job loss, increased effort and acceptance of change by our members. It is they who have borne the brunt of managements' effort to reduce production costs.

Although the theme remains the same, the later parts of the document broaden the arguments by introducing matters of productivity and effort. The next stage of the argument was to decry the low rate of investment in the industry, and to urge management to adopt new technology and to involve union members in such planning. Inadequate training and skill shortages were also criticized. At this point, union negotiators returned to the issue of financial health, and brought in also notions of wage comparability.

MR JORDAN. Mr Chairman and gentlemen, our contention is that our industry has passed through one of the worst periods in the history of engineering, but has maintained a strength, as reflected in levels of profitability, that is due primarily to the sacrifice and efforts of our members. If that strength is to be maintained and built on, the minimum pay and conditions levels have to be improved substantially. You can afford to do it.

I therefore ask you to give serious considerations to each facet of the claim and will now deal with the first item: a substantial increase in the national minimum time rates.

We are seeking a substantial increase in NMTRs that will reflect the going rate of settlements.

In manufacturing, the average settlement rate is 7.75 per cent and in engineering the majority of increases range from 5 per cent to 8 per cent, while the underlying increase in average earnings in manufacturing is 7.5 per cent.

We believe that the consequences of the Chancellor's mis-management seem to be catching up with him, even as the North Sea bubble bursts. So the use of the currently predicted level of inflation to quantify 'substantial' would be highly speculative, and events of this week add weight to our judgement.

However, it has to be said, the level of NMTRs is a measure of how highly an industry values its workforce. Not so many years ago our industry was near the top of the manual workers' wage league. A recent Industrial Relations Review survey covering the lowest grade basic rate shows that out of 103 national negotiating groups engineering was only 94, tenth from the bottom. Those on a basic working week of 39 hours or less involved 87 groups, with engineering being seventh from the bottom. Appendix 1 will demonstrate this.

As for skilled workers, many industries and firms, in both the private and public sectors where our skilled members are doing similar work, receive considerably higher basic minimum rates than in engineering, and Appendix 2 will demonstrate that fact.

The unions then suggested that a pay rise would ease skill shortages in the industry, pointed out that by international standards British engineering labour costs were low, and provided data on eighteen countries' wages and national insurance charges.

Next on the agenda was a comparison with executive remuneration.

MR JORDAN. Whatever arguments you muster in replying to our claim, I hope you will avoid linking our justified submissions for an adequate NMTR with the offensive call from the Government and the CBI for low wage settlements. To do so would be a study in hypocrisy at a time when so many managers and directors are now receiving large salary increases, often topped by bonuses, shares and other perks.

A number of top salary surveys have been published recently. Inbucon, management consultants, the Engineering Council and the salary survey organisation, Remuneration Economics, all paint a consistent picture of those that run industry rewarding themselves well. Do our members deserve a lesser treatment?

He went on:

Earlier I mentioned the sharp increase in profitability for industrial and commercial companies, with particular reference to manufacturing industry. Now I would like briefly to consider engineering and individual sectors.

The mechanical engineering sector has been in the doldrums, but last year brought the best annual growth for 10 years, with a rise in output of 7 per cent over 1984. The trend is continuing but at a slower rate. A number of companies in this sector have either recorded substantially increased profits or anticipate doing so later this year or in 1987.

The union document gave the table shown as Table 3.1.

Table 3.1 *Examples of pre-tax profits in engineering*

Company	% Percentage increase of pre-tax profits over previous year or interim
Adwest[a]	16
Aerospace Engineering	16.5
APV[a]	66 (interim figure)
Brown Boveri Kent[a]	18
Deritend[a]	33
GKN[a]	16
Jones and Shipman[a]	98
Johnson Matthey[a]	50
Parkfield Group[a]	75
Ramsomes Sims and Jeffries[a]	33 (interim figure)
RHP Group[a]	52 (interim figure)
Siebe[a]	91
Sterling Industries	31
F H Tomkins	109
Triplex[a]	97
Tube investment[a]	61
Valor[a]	42
Vickers[a]	50
Weir[a]	32
Woodhouse and Rixson[a]	18

[a] Federated Firms or Parent Company/Subsidiaries are members.
Sources: Investors Chronicle or Newspaper cuttings.

Its Appendix 5 (not reproduced here) contained detailed statements on the profitability of ten well-known firms. This included quotes from company reports and financial newspapers.

The remainder of the wage-claim document, and the 17 October meeting, was concerned with the proposed reduction in working time, and the other items listed as (3)-(5) above. The employers' team gave their preliminary reactions to the claim document, and the sides agreed to meet again.

3.2.2. *The Employers' Response*

Exactly one month later, on 17 November 1986, the parties met to consider the employers' response. This began with an attack upon the unions' view that engineering profitability was high. In other words, the employers' group were not arguing that it was inappropriate for the unions' wage demand to reflect profitability, but rather that union perceptions were faulty.

DR MCFARLANE. As an introduction to our reply to the detailed items of your claim, I would like to report our general view of the situation in the engineering industry. In doing so I am responding to those of your statements in which you referred to engineering output, profits and productivity.

The general problem which we face is a shortage of orders. You suggested that there was a steadily growing output in engineering but we do not find this to be confirmed by our members' recent experience nor by the Government's official index of engineering production. That index shows output in the first eight months of 1986 to have been 2 per cent lower than in the same months of 1985.

The employers' team stated that certain sectors were paying only small wage increases.

DR McFARLANE. . . . false pride should not lead us to propose an increase that is inconsistent with settlements at domestic level which, in hard-hit areas like the West Midlands, are generally below 5 per cent, and increasingly below 4 per cent as I shall mention again in a moment. You will have noticed the recent acceptance, following a vote, of a 3 per cent settlement at Leyland Trucks. I understand that in the shipping industry the unions are recommending acceptance of an increase of £3 per week on their basic rates, which equates to an approximately 3.4 per cent increase in weekly earnings. I am sure also that you will have noticed recent announcements of further redundancies at Automotive Products, at British Timken and at other companies. This bears out what I said earlier about the present state of trade in some sectors of our industry.

Perhaps you will let me quote from the Federation's latest economic trends report, which was published a month ago:

'After several years of growth, UK engineering output turned down in the summer of 1985. A gradual recovery is now indicated, starting in the second half of 1986. It is expected to continue throughout 1987.

However, little or no growth is forecast in the mechanical engineering and metal goods sectors.'

This forecast recovery is slow by comparison with the growth rate for 1983 and 1985 and takes the forecast levels of output at the end of 1987 approximately up to, but not significantly beyond, the peak levels in 1985.

I would like to emphasise that last point. Our forecast does indeed indicate a somewhat brighter outlook for next year, but even at the end of 1987 our forecast output levels are not significantly higher than those achieved in 1985.

The question of how far there has been a recovery was taken up by the *Financial Weekly* recently which said that recent half-year results of companies have 'confirmed current doubts about a real recovery in British engineering'. As one of they analysts said 'The figures confirm that it's pretty difficult out there. No matter how good you are, there's nothing you can do if the demand isn't there'.

The next step in the argument was to predict further declines in employment in the industry, and to examine the reasons for low investment.

The discussion then turned again to profitability.

DR McFARLANE. You have made several statements to us about the supposedly high level of profits. The latest national accounts analysis by the Department of Trade and Industry shows that the estimated average rate of return before interest and tax, at current replacement cost, in manufacturing in 1985 was just 7.2 per cent. In other words real profits, before deducting interest and tax, were 7.2 per cent of the total capital employed. That is certainly not an excessive real return on investment when money put into a building society has earned a higher return, risk-free, in the last 12 months.

You have said that the rate of return on capital in manufacturing last year was higher than in any year since 1973 and equal to the boom years of 1972 and 1973. The DTI's latest figures show a different picture — with real rates of return of 8.1 per cent in 1972 and 1973 but only 7.2 per cent in 1985. These years, 1972–73 and 1985, were, as you have described them, relative boom years. In the intervening years rates of return have been much lower — falling to 2.8 per cent in 1975 and 2.7 per cent in 1981. We show in our Appendix 1 the DTI's estimates of manufacturing profitability for each year from 1960 to 1985. You will see from the chart that despite the recent improvement the rate of return remains far below the levels achieved in the 1960s. I must emphasise that the very low levels of profitability in the 1970s and 1980s are the prime reason for investors not having supported manufacturing industry. We urgently need to raise profitability in order to attract the funds required for fixed investment, for research and development and for training.

In presenting your claim you listed in your Appendix 4 some 20 companies whose profitability has risen substantially in the latest available accounting years and you have identified some large percentage increases. If I may refer again to the DTI figures for average profitability in the whole manufacturing sector, shown in our Appendix 1, you will see that manufacturing profitability rose from 2.7 per cent in 1981 to 7.2 per cent in 1985. The average profitability of 7.2 per cent is therefore an increase of some 170 per cent over 1981. But in calculating such percentage increases we must not lose sight of the fact that the actual real return on capital in 1985 was still only 7.2 per cent and the average in the last ten years was only 4.8 per cent. When you start from a low base, even a slight improvement gives rise to an increase that in percentage terms looks impressive.

The employers continued on this theme, stressing how far British productivity was below that in other economies. They also pointed out that the national minimum time rates had to cover both financially weak and strong parts of the industry: 'Arguments based on the profitability of particular companies may have their place in domestic bargaining but not in trying to arrive at agreed minimum rates for the whole of the industry.' This was the nearest that the employers came to disagreeing with the principle that high profits can justify high pay. Again comparability came up.

DR McFARLANE. You asked that we should increase NMTRs in line with the level of domestic settlements. I would like to examine this point quite carefully as we can find no evidence to support your statement that the average settlement rate in manufacturing is 7.75 per cent.

The trend in settlements is now clearly downwards. Our most recent figures indicate that, for the three-month period July–September 1986, 65 per cent of domestic settlements in member companies have been at or below 5 per cent and of these nearly half were at or below 4 per cent. The figures are even more revealing if we take an area of particular importance to engineering, the West Midlands. For the same three-month period over 75 per cent of settlements were at or below 5 per cent and no less than 40 per cent were at or below 4 per cent.

The other factor the employers were keen to emphasize was the low rate of price inflation. Dr McFarlane continued:

I would like now to come to a factor which was rather overlooked by you which I did refer to at our last meeting. It is the rate of inflation as measured by the Retail Price Index. Our NMTRs are not, of course, linked to the RPI but the rate of inflation is certainly one of the factors, among others, that we need to take into account on assessing what offer we make to you.

The October figure, declared last Friday, showed an annual increase over the figure for October 1985 of 3 per cent. This is a welcome reduction on the rate of inflation which was declared this time last year which was for a year on year increase of 5.4 per cent. We welcome this drop in inflation as I am sure you and your members do. We must all be interested in the real level of earnings and not simply in pushing up the rate of inflation by agreeing increases in wages which contribute to an inflationary spiral.

At this point the employers' side turned on to the other elements in the union claim document (much time, for example, was given to the question of racial discrimination). The employers then made their offer (£105.28 for skilled workers, £75.80 for unskilled). In response, Mr Jordan wished 'to register extreme disappointment' and, after discussion, the CSEU retired. When the unions returned, they had calculated the offer to be worth 3.7 per cent, and described it as 'paltry' and 'dangerous'. After further discussion, the parties agreed to adjourn and to agree a date for future negotiations.

It would be a mistake to draw sweeping conclusions on the basis of this single example of wage negotiations. The engineering industry has special features, and interpretation is complicated by the fact that bargaining here is about national minimum rates of pay. Moreover, internal pressure may work more effectively at company level.

Nevertheless, the kinds of factors to which the bargainers pointed are likely to be influential in many different settings. One of these is the idea of wage comparability. There is nothing new in this view: 'comparisons play a large and often dominant role as a standard of equity in the determination of wages under collective bargaining' (Ross (1948, p. 50)). Brown and Sisson (1975), among others, provide recent case-study evidence. A second factor, and one more crucial for later points of our argument, is that of employers' financial performance.

There is a striking difference between the spirit of these wage negotiations and the nature of the wage inflexibility theories summarized in Chapter 2. The employer's performance in the product market, and the state of demand generally, was the first issue discussed by the wage-bargainers in the real-life engineering case. By contrast, as Chapter 2 makes clear, a significant part of the microeconomic theory of labour markets has aimed to prove the reverse.

Although we shall not examine it in detail, another useful source of information is the TGWU pamphlet *The Ford Wage Claim* (1971). Published by the Transport and General Workers' Union, this is a written statement of the workers' pay-claim for 1971 against the Ford Motor Company Limited. It was presented by Mr Moss Evans on 27 November 1970 in a London meeting of the two sides.

The parallels with the recent engineering industry claim described above are so strong as to make unnecessary a full description. The 1971 document, for example, contains the following passage.

It is a simple statement of fact that on all key economic and financial indicators Ford's is well out in front of the rest of the British car industry. It takes the lead in terms of efficiency and output per worker. It has secured remarkably high rates of profit . . . Ford's should see it as shameful that the one area in which its standards do not lead the industry, in which it is a laggard, is the pay of its manual workers. Indeed, the disproportion between the reward going to profit from Ford's operations and that going to the workers is so great that we reckon, after a perusal of your accounts, that the trading profit per vehicle produced last year was almost certainly greater than manual workers' wages per vehicle produced. We think there is some room for redistribution of the rewards.

As in the engineering pay-claim document, detailed union calculations of employers' profits are included in the pamphlet.

The purpose of this section is not to make a scientifically rigorous case for the idea that an employer's prosperity shapes its wage-rates. It is instead to raise that hypothesis and to convey its real-life flavour. Anecdotal and individual case-study evidence rarely proves anything, but is commonly the mainspring of the search for proof, and is in that sense valuable. Whether the material described above is misleading rests upon whether the central discussions about financial prosperity are peculiar to these examples. Five British surveys suggest that they are not.

3.3 Survey Evidence

There have been a number of recent questionnaire studies of the determinants of British wage-rates. The Confederation of British Industry, for example, began in 1979 a regular Databank Survey of pressures upon pay settlements; it studies the settlement group rather than the firm or union. Gregory, Lobban, and Thomson, (1985, 1986) have analysed the answers returned to the CBI. The Databank consists of a structured sample of establishments, stratified by industry and region. Although coverage began with manufacturing industry alone, it was gradually extended to private sector services. The manufacturing survey, on which Gregory, Lobban, and Thomson concentrate, contains approximately 1,200 establishments and covers approximately 2,000 settlement groups. This sample covers nearly 600,000 workers. The typical response rate to a CBI survey is two-thirds.

For each establishment in the sample, management nominates up to three groups, whose settlement levels are recorded. When there are more than three relevant groups within the establishment, management is asked to select the three most important, with the suggestion that these might be 'the two largest manual groups and the largest staff group'. Where both staff and manual workers are covered by collective agreements, it is requested that management include a group from each category. The average response is 1.7 group reports per establishment.

The principal question in the survey is about the pay increase resulting from each settlement (the 'settlement level'). This is asked as follows: 'Please give us your best estimate of how you think gross average earnings (including the value of any productivity deal) will rise over the year as the result of the settlement.'

In responding to the Databank Survey, managers report the relative importance of factors influencing pay negotiations. Table 3.2 lists the possible answers, plus some recent figures. Respondents must choose to reply using one or more of the answers 'very important', 'fairly important', or 'not important'. The ratings are therefore qualitative. They are for manufacturing industry only.

Table 3.2 *CBI Databank responses*

		Proportion of respondents citing the factor as 'very important' (%)		
		1979/80	1981/2	1983/4
Factors exerting upwards pressure on pay				
a.	Level of establishment/ company profits	11	16	21
b.	Management able to pass on pay increase in prices	6	3	4
c.	A need to improve recruitment	22	6	9
d.	Cost of living	60	45	40
e.	Threat of industrial action	2	2	3
f.	Industrial action	3	1	2
Factors exerting downwards pressure				
g.	Level of establishment/ company profits	45	60	45
h.	Management unable to pass on pay increase in prices	38	52	51
i.	Risk of redundancy	20	35	21
j.	Miscellaneous			
Other factors				
k.	Comparisons with employees in same company	24	23	21
l.	Comparisons with employees in same industry	21	13	17
m.	Comparisons with employees in same locality	27	15	18
n.	Comparisons with national pay levels	26	16	19
o.	Employer organisation agreement	16	19	9
p.	Non-official employer organisation agreement	6	4	3

Source: Gregory, Lobban, and Thomson (1985, p. 350).

Gregory, Lobban, and Thomson (1985) report that there is a tendency for managers to cite several pressures simultaneously. Their article records the answers from 1979-84. Within Table 3.2, five factors are especially strongly and reliably cited. They are:

d. Cost of living
g. Level of establishment/company profits
h. Management unable to pass on pay increases in prices
i. Risk of redundancy
k. Comparisons with other employees in same company

The single most commonly mentioned category (Gregory, Lobban, and Thomson (1985), table 4 p. 350), averaged over five years, was 'level of establishment/company profits' as a *downward* pressure on pay settlements. It was cited by more than half of the respondents in the survey.

In 1983/4, the most recent year reported in Gregory, Lobban, and Thomson (1985), 21 per cent of firms cited profits as an upwards pressure, 40 per cent cited cost of living, 45 per cent cited profits as a downwards pressure, 51 per cent cited 'management unable to pass on pay rises', 21 per cent cited risk of redundancy, and 21 per cent cited comparisons with other employees in the same company.

A new survey of British establishments has recently produced fairly similar results. This is encouraging, because its sample is quite different. Blanchflower and Oswald (1988a) examine the 1984 Workplace Industrial Relations Survey, which was sponsored by the Department of Employment, the Policy Studies Institute, the Economic and Social Research Council, and the Advisory, Conciliation, and Arbitration Service, and provides a unique source of data on the factors which personnel managers claimed affected the most recent pay settlement. The Survey is a nationally representative sample of approximately 2,000 British establishments (defined as 'places of employment at a single address or site') in both the public and private sectors. The sample was drawn from the 1981 Census of Employment. To be included in the sample an establishment had to have at least 25 employees (full or part-time) both in 1981 and in 1984, so that new and small establishments were omitted. The response to the survey questionnaire was 77 per cent. Agriculture and coal-mining were the only important industries to be excluded from the survey. Blanchflower and Oswald use the data obtained from personnel managers — more precisely, the 'senior person at the establishment dealing with industrial relations, employee relations or personnel matters'

— in 1,267 private sector establishments.

The design of the sample involved the selection of workplaces with different sampling fractions, with larger establishments having higher probabilities of selection than smaller workplaces. Weights were applied to restore the number of cases in each establishment size band to their proper proportions. Approximate sampling errors attached to a single estimate, assuming a 95% confidence level, are given below.

	10% or 90%	20% or 80%	30% or 70%	50%
Approximate sampling error	1.6	2.3	2.5	2.8

Hence, where the survey shows that, for example, 30 per cent of all establishments had a particular feature, there is a 95 per cent probability that the true proportion is in the range of 27.5 per cent to 32.5 per cent.

All those managers interviewed for the survey were asked the question: 'What factors influenced the level of pay decided upon in the most recent settlement?' This was asked twice — once for a pay settlement for manual workers and again for a pay settlement for non-manual workers. One of the advantages of the questionnaire is that, in the case of the question above, respondents were allowed to answer entirely in their own words. Managers were not prompted, nor were they required (as in the CBI survey) to tick specific boxes on the interview form. They were permitted to cite as many influences as they wished (though typically they only gave one or two).

Table 3.3 contains the results. The many different answers given by managers were grouped into thirteen classes. This classification was done *ex post* by the survey team. The table reports the percentages of managers citing each of those different factors in wage settlements. For example, the top left-hand figure of 11 in Table 3.3 indicates that, for those establishments employing unionized manual workers, 11 per cent cited the reason 'All establishment could afford'.

The most common answers were:

(1) Profitability/productivity

(2) Increasing cost of living
(3) Going rate in industry
(4) External pay structure
(5) All establishment could afford.

It is unfortunate (if not surprising) that the single most cited

Table 3.3 *Factors cited by managers as influencing the level of pay in the most recent settlement* (%)

Cited influences	Union sector[a] manuals	Non-union sector manuals	Union sector[b] (non-manuals)	Non-union sector[b] (non-manuals)
All establishment could afford	11	5	9	7
Increasing cost of living	34	29	37	32
Going rate in industry	15	23	13	19
Merit/individual performance	4	20	5	33
Published norms	3	2	3	4
Internal pay structure	2	3	6	15
External pay structure	15	15	9	11
Government regulation	6	3	10	2
Strikes	1	0	0	0
Profitability/productivity	34	35	37	38
Economic climate	9	2	13	3
Other	13	7	15	6
Not answered	8	3	11	1
Number of establishments	488	613	356	904

Notes: 1. Because managers could cite more than one influence, the columns sum to more than 100 per cent.

2. Union status of establishment is determined by whether or not unions were recognized at the workplace for purposes of bargaining.

3. The 'other' category includes answers such as 'union pressure, change in payment systems, retention/recruitment, change in working practices', *inter alia*. This information was kindly supplied by Neil Millward.

[a] establishments with manual workers.
[b] establishments with non-manual workers.

Source: Blanchflower and Oswald (1988[a]).

reply, (1), should be an amalgam of two slightly different concepts, but that is how the computer coding was done, and confidentiality restricts further analysis.

The results are similar to those of Gregory, Lobban, and Thomson (1985, 1986). The powerful role which managers assign to profitability is particularly noteworthy.

A similar study, though smaller and for an earlier period, is reported in Daniel (1976). This was in a sense a forerunner of the Workplace Industrial Relations Surveys. It consisted of, in 1975,

(i) interviews with managers in a sample of 254 British establishments representative of manufacturing industry;
(ii) second-stage interviews with leaders of management negotiating teams in 148 of the sampled establishments;
(iii) interviews with leaders of union negotiating teams in a sample of 98 of the stage (ii) establishments.

Among many other things, Daniel tabulates the items 'spontaneously mentioned by management negotiators as being among the chief considerations' in the wage offer to unions. The answers are shown in Table 3.4.

Table 3.4

Answer	Proportion of managers (%)
Items relating to the establishment's/ firm's ability to pay	61
Items relating to comparability/pay of other groups	51
Rise in the cost of living/rate of inflation	36
Items relating to pay structure/wage-work bargain	30
Company/national agreement	11
Social contract/government guidelines	11
Easing recruitment/turnover problems	6

The base for these calculations was 148. On average members cited 2 out of 7 variables.

Equivalent questions were asked of the sample of 98 union
negotiators. For them the spontaneously mentioned items are
shown in Table 3.5.

Table 3.5

Answer	Proportion of Union Officials (%)
Rise in the cost of living/price increases	75
Comparability/earnings increases of other groups	51
Changes in payment system	41
The establishment/firm's ability to pay	15

As for managers, respondents typically mentioned two of these
factors.

One of the interesting features of the two sets of results is that,
although similar influences are mentioned by both sides, the
ordering of priorities is quite different (and in large part is
reversed). Inflation is third on the managers' list; ability to pay
comes first in the minds of management but fourth in the mind of
workers' representatives.

The comparative uniformity in answers from these three different surveys is not something which can easily be ignored. There is
much evidence that profitability (or more generally 'ability to pay')
is uppermost, or close to uppermost, in the minds of those
managers who set, or negotiate about, wage-levels. This is the
engineering case, of Section 3.2, writ large.

Another small but interesting survey was done by Kaufman
(1984). In the summer of 1982 the author interviewed twenty-six
firms in Wales, the West Midlands, and Greater London. The
sample was chosen to achieve a cross-section of firms within each
area, sampling some large unionized firms, but concentrating on
small non-union ones. The median employment level was seven.
The regional distribution of the employers is shown in Table 3.6.
Although the sample was not a correct random draw, Kaufman's
findings are suggestive.

Table 3.6

Regions	No. of firms	Region's 1979 unemployment rate (%)	Region's 1982 unemployment rate (%)
Greater London	11	3.8	9.5
West Midlands	10	6.1	16.2
Wales	5	8.3	16.5

First, Kaufman discovered that the patterns of wage increase, over the previous five years, were fairly uniform. Two-thirds of firms reported that between 1977 and 1980 they had raised pay at or above the rate of price inflation, but that from 1980 to 1982 real pay had declined. In six firms nominal earnings had stayed static in one of the previous two years; none had cut nominal pay. The author's questions included:

What has happened to your wage levels during the past 5 years? During this or last year? How were these wage changes determined? Were inflation, comparability or profits important? Could you presently find qualified personnel at less than current wages?

Kaufman was interested especially in the issue of how wage-fixing was affected by the record level of unemployment at the time of interview. A list of his other questions is contained in Kaufman (1984 p. 105).

Second, the author concluded that neither union nor non-union wages responded quickly or strongly to the existence of excess labour supply. All but one of the unionized firms believed that they could find qualified workers at lower wages. Half of the non-union employers thought the same.

Third, the main reason given for not reducing pay was the possible effect on effort and morale. The firms 'felt that wage reductions, especially those unaccompanied by credible information concerning a financial crisis, would . . . be treated as an affront' (p. 107). Kaufman did conclude, however, that those newly started firms could and did pay lower wages.

Fourth, the author found that, among those firms which had implemented real-wage reductions, 'profits were the most commonly cited factor' (p. 107). He drew the judgement that a prerequisite for such reductions is the belief that severe cutbacks or closure will be necessary unless pay cuts are enacted. Firms attempted to 'hold real wages constant during the initial stages of financial difficulties and resorted to real wage cuts only if a financial crisis developed' (p. 107).

One other empirical study contains relevant results. In the early 1970s a research team at Glasgow University set out to analyse the wage and employment behaviour of sixty-six engineering plants. The study, reported in MacKay *et al.* (1971), examined personnel records on 75,000 manual workers over the period 1959-66. It had two main aims. The first was to describe and present information on a range of labour market issues 'obscured by a blanket of ignorance' (p. 10). The second was to use the observations as a test of the predictions of the competitive theory of labour markets.

The MacKay project is interesting both because it draws a distinction between 'ins' (those already employed by a plant) and 'outs' (non-employees), and because it attempts to distinguish between internal and external pressures upon pay. Although it is not possible to do justice to the research in a few paragraphs, the book's principal conclusions included the following:

1. Certain plants paid high wages over an extended period, and their identity was widely known throughout the market. However, these plants did not appear to be seeking to recruit a larger number of employees.

2. The inter-plant wage structure was stable over time.

3. There were substantial and persistent wage differentials for the same kinds of labour across different plants. (The authors recognized that this finding is not inconsistent with the competitive model if pay advantages are offset by non-pecuniary factors, yet:

Unfortunately for the theory these explanations . . . do not seem to be adequate to explain away the wage differentials observed. There is simply no indication that the low wage units in our study offered especially favourable conditions in other respects so that net advantages were equalised (p. 390).

4. The authors believed it improbable that high-wage plants enforced hiring standards high enough to equalize efficiency wages.

5. Low-wage plants had more quits.

6. Where a plant was a high-wage payer for one group of

workers it tended to be a high-wage payer for all employees, and whenever one group fell out of line that tended to be made good subsequently.

MacKay *et al.* were therefore drawn to the judgement that competitive theory can not satisfactorily explain observed wage behaviour, because the conditions at plant level affect wages in ways that can not be well understood within the classical framework.

First, 'market forces appear to set only the outside limits within which the wage bargain will be struck' (p. 391). Second, 'what we are suggesting is that the labour force will benefit in the form of higher wages if the plant enjoys high profitability, economies of scale, efficient management or methods of production, monopoly elements in the product market, and so forth' (p. 391). Third,

'an employee's increases in earnings over any substantial period of time will depend more on the plant in which he is employed than on the external conditions for the particular skill he possesses. This is in direct contrast to the prediction of the competitive model, which is that the economic circumstances of the employing unit will be irrelevant in explaining an individual's increase in earnings, for this will be determined by the demand and supply conditions for his particular type of skill. It is extremely difficult to find support for this prediction in our evidence' (p. 391).

3.4 Concession Bargaining

The most extreme form of linkage from profits to pay levels is so-called 'concession bargaining'. Also sometimes called 'reverse collective bargaining' (Henle, 1973), this is the phenomenon of wage-cuts in firms close to bankruptcy. It has been documented by industrial relations specialists for many years.

One of the earliest studies is Shultz and Myers (1950), based on two field projects. The first was of the men's shoe industry in south-eastern Massachusetts; the second examined a New England community in which the partial shutdown of a large textile mill had produced 13 per cent unemployment. In the case of the shoe industry there had been a shift over two decades in the market for shoes. Customers had switched away from high-quality, high-price products towards cheaper shoes of lower quality. The Massachusetts producers made high quality shoes and gradually lost business. Shultz and Myers document the declines in pay which this generated, and conclude that 'they represent the dominant theme of wage activity in this section of the industry: the adjustment of wages to the realities of business and employment conditions' (p. 370). The authors draw similar judgements about the textile mill community. Here textile factories had been closing down in nearby areas, and some employees were on short time. The authors cite a union leader who said of the employer (in explanation of his own failure to press for wage demands): 'You can't push that guy anywhere except out of business' (p. 370). Another union representative said:

When I am called in by local people to help prepare contract demands, I ask them 'How many days are you working a week? How much back-log of orders is there? How does business seem? What is happening in the other plants in the area? Is there much unemployment?' If they say, 'yes' as they are saying now, I tell them, 'Well, there's your answer.' (p. 371)

Textile workers, according to Schultz and Myers, accepted lower pay and greater workloads because of the financial difficulties of their employers.

Further American evidence on concession bargaining is plentiful. Juris (1969) is another example, and reports the results of research on ten plants in the meat-packing industry in 1962/3. In that period, the two dominant trade unions in meat-packing had to decide whether to accept pay reductions. Jobs and profitability were threatened by shifts in purchasing and sales patterns, and by changes in technology. Most of the ten plants accepted wage-cuts. Hernstadt (1954) provides further empirical evidence (for the textile industry) and discusses attitudes to concessions.

Similar work was done by Henle (1973). He examined twelve examples of concession bargaining covering about 20,000 employers. The trade unions concerned were industrial, including the electrical, rubber, aluminium, and bakery workers, and machinists and print workers. Most of the establishments were more than 25 years old; many were less efficient than their competitors. They employed an older work-force than average, and were in the older industrial regions in the USA.

Henle argues that 'each of these cases originated in a management decision that a particular operation or plant was no longer profitable and must be cut back, moved, abandoned, or sold' (p. 957). The author attributes some of this to the 1970–1 recession, some to alteration in tastes or technology, and some to import competition. Table 2 of Henle (1973) documents the wage and benefit decreases which were precipitated by employers' financial problems. Most were substantial. The author argues that:

'The critical factor in gaining employee approval for a renegotiated settlement did not depend on management's ability to support its arguments with wage and fringe benefit comparisons, financial information, and data on orders, operating rates, and bids on government contracts. While this general information was useful, employees seemed to have been persuaded more effectively by the information they obtained on the job: the flow of work, the number of employees on lay-off . . .' (p. 960)

Henle concludes that wage settlements reflect the perceived financial performance of the employer.

The most recent case of US concession bargaining occurred in the early 1980s. Many cases are studied in Mitchell (1982) and Cappelli (1985), *inter alia*. Cappelli, for example, examines the 1981 negotiations in the tyre and meat-packing industries, and argues, in line with earlier work, that 'the force driving unions to bargain over concessions is the possibility of job loss through layoffs and plant shutdown' (p. 95). The author's evidence includes regression results explaining the incidence of concessionary behaviour. Mitchell (1982) lists forty-six cases of wage concessions between 1979 and 1982, and estimates the number of workers affected at a little under 2 million. More instances are detailed in Flanagan (1985).

A new study by Addison (1986) identifies further examples of concession bargaining. An important class of cases comes from the automobile industry around 1980. Pay reductions at Chrysler pushed levels almost one-quarter lower than at Ford and General Motors, and those employers then went on to negotiate concessions. Competition from Japanese imports was considered partly to blame. Addison argues that the secular forces which produced concession bargaining in the first half of the 1980s may be expected to continue to keep down union workers' remuneration.

Is there concession bargaining in Britain? Research is limited, but our article Carruth and Oswald (1987*a*) collects evidence of a kind similar to that for the United States. The Appendix to this Chapter summarizes the cases of which we know: the time period studied was the exceptional recession at the beginning of the 1980s. As in the USA, it appears that severe financial problems can and do produce sizeable wage reductions in Great Britain.

3.5 Conclusions

The principal message from the evidence studied in this chapter, which draws on institutional industrial relations material, is that wage levels appear to depend upon employers' profitability. Confirmation of this is suggested by the fact that different kinds of sources all point to the same conclusions.

1. Many of the early American writers argued that the employer's ability to pay was of importance in collective bargaining. Among this group were distinguished labour specialists (such as Sumner Slichter) who knew a great deal about industrial relations practices.

2. As a practical example, the chapter has described a recent British wage negotiation (for the engineering industry) in which the wage claim documents repeatedly stress the role of past and prospective profits. The employers' side did not question this in principle. Instead they attempted to convince the union side that profitability was poor.

3. Five kinds of surveys on wage determination have been summarized. One is that conducted annually by the CBI, another the 1984 Workplace Industrial Relations Survey, a third the 1976 study by William Daniel. The other two are Kaufman (1984) and MacKay *et al.* (1971). All show the important weight given to employers' financial performance.

4. When plants are close to shutting down, wage reductions are sometimes negotiated. Evidence, for Britain and the United States, has been summarized in the chapter. Instances of this kind of concession bargaining have been known to labour economists since at least the 1940s.

Different economists are likely to assign different weights to empirical findings of the form examined in this chapter. Most of the studies, for example, rely on statements about what managers and workers' representatives *believe* influence pay settlements; much of it is qualitative. Our own judgement is that the material described here is one kind of evidence for a prosperity (or ability-to-pay) effect upon wage determination.

APPENDIX
Recent Cases of Significant Real Wage Cuts in Britain

Company/ number of employees affected	Settlement	Details
Acrow	12-month pay freeze, 1983	The unions agreed in order to help the company restore profitability and re-establish a five-day working week.
Blackett Hutton	Pay cut of around 9 per cent to last for 3 months, 1982	The pay cut was achieved by making a 5 per cent reduction on basic pay and the suspension of a plant-wide bonus scheme worth about 4 per cent. The company, a steel castings manufacturer, also made 200 employees redundant.
British Caledonian (5,250)	Pay freeze for 7 months initially, 1981, but extended into 1982.	Individual employees were asked to forgo their index-linked pay increases for 1981. The employees were due for a pay increase in January 1982 when the 2-year index-linked agreement expired, but salaries were again frozen for most of 1982.
British Leyland	3.8 per cent pay increase, 1981	The workers rejected the company's initial offer but after securing concessions on bonus payments they accepted the deal. Change in RPI for October 1981 was 11.7 per cent, and for TPI 14.9 per cent.
British Midland Airways	12 month freeze, 1981	The freeze was agreed with the unions in view of the financial position of the company.

continued

British Steel (115,000)	6-month pay freeze, 1981	The 'McGregor Plan' provided for a 6-month pay freeze and then a 7 per cent pay increase (the actual increase negotiated later was 8 per cent). The package, which also included 20,000 redundancies, was opposed by the main union, the ISTC. In response to the proposed package, and as an alternative to the redundancies, workers and union officials in the tinplate section of BSC's business offered a voluntary pay freeze for the next year, in effect foregoing the 7 per cent pay increase. The offer was not taken up by management.
Bronx (400)	6-month pay freeze, 1981	Management offered to review the situation after the six month freeze but no guarantees were made that any rise would be forthcoming.
Christie-Tyler (2,300)	Wage-cuts of up to 10 per cent, 1982	Each employee at the South Wales furniture manufacturer agreed to take a direct cut in gross earnings to prevent future job losses. Some workers took cuts of up to 10 per cent to save an estimated 1,000 jobs. However, the company was one of the highest paying firms in the region, with current average earnings around £200 per week (up to £400 for some manual workers) and a guaranteed minimum wage of £87.60).
Ductile Group	4-month pay	Due to the financial position of

continued

(700)	Freeze, 1981	the company a freeze was imposed by management. Subsequently an 8-month deal was negotiated involving a 5 per cent pay increase.
Dunlop	Pay increases ranging from zero to 6 per cent offered, 1981	Under the company's decentralized plant bargaining structure some plant managements were offering zero increases to their workforces. Despite union opposition several low settlements (below 5 per cent) followed.
GEC Machines (2,000)	6-month pay freeze, 1981	Management imposed a 6-month freeze with no guarantee of any wage increase after the 6 months.
Hoover (1,470)	6-month pay freeze, 1982	In 1981 the company proposed a 10 per cent wage reduction and an indefinite freeze until the company returned to probability, but this was rejected by the unions. Instead a national level agreement on productivity and other changes were introduced to achieve a similar reduction in costs. The company subsequently decided to close Perivale factory and the workers in Cambuslang (Scotland) agreed to a six-month pay freeze in 1982 with a 7 per cent increase to follow in January 1983.
Hyster Corporation (500)	Wage cut, 1983	The employees reluctantly accepted the principle of a wage cut with a promise by the company of new investment and around 1,000 extra new jobs. The plant is, however, non-union and pays above-

continued

ICL (4,000 manuals, (18,000 staff)	12-month pay freeze, for manual workers, and a 7-month freeze for staff, 1981	average rates as part of its non-union policy The company announced in January that manual workers' wages would not be increased during 1981. For staff employees this effectively meant a 7-month freeze given their settlement date of June. The unions did not oppose it.
John Branch	Pay cut, 1981	Bonus earners at this building firm agreed to take a 10 per cent cut in their bonus earnings, amounting to a reduction in take home pay of around £1–4 per week.
London Works Steel Co. (480)	6-month pay freeze for staff employees, 1981	Both deferrals were negotiated with the unions, but no guarantees were made about future increases.
May and Baker	Indefinite pay freeze, 1981	Due to the severe financial position of the company the unions agreed that settlements be deferred until the company's position improved. After about 7 months sales had picked up and pay negotiations were reopened. At some plants the subsequent increase was backdated to the original settlement date.
Norvic Shoe Co.	12-month pay freeze, 1981	Because of the company's financial predicament the workers volunteered to have their pay frozen for a year in the effort to keep the factory in business. The workers were due for a 3 per cent cost of living increase in February 1981.
Pan American World Airways	10 per cent reduction in	In August 1981 the company proposped a 10 per cent wage-

continued

(UK) (1,055)	the wage bill, 1981–2, then a 10-month pay freeze in 1982.	cut but the unions preferred to eliminate the bonus-equivalent to an 8.3 per cent reduction. By September 1981 a formula was reached for 1982 involving the non-payment of the annual holiday bonus entitlement (normally paid in advance and due in January 1982), which saved 8.3 per cent, with a further 1.7 per cent saved through productivity improvements. The pay increase negotiated in March 1982 was also to be frozen until January 1983. Ninety per cent of the workforce voted in favour of the agreement, which guaranteed no redundancies.
Talbot	2.5 per cent pay increase, 1981	The company's deal was originally rejected by the work-force, but the company refused to change its offer and after the union secured some concession on bonus payments the deal was accepted.
Thorn Brimar	12-month pay freeze, 1982–3	No pay increase was awarded in October 1982, the annual settlement date, and there was no pay review until October 1983.
Tilgham Wheelabrator	12 month pay freeze, 1981–2	In August 1981, because of financial difficulties, the company decided to freeze wages until August 1982.

Source: Industrial Relations Review and Reports (in various issues, but especially No. 256, September 1981). *Financial Times* (various issues). *Incomes Data Services* (various issues).

4

Previous Econometric Evidence on the Link From Profits to Wages

> If instead of relating wage increases to unemployment and the
> rate of change of unemployment, Professor Phillips had
> related them to the increase in production, or to the increase
> in profits of the previous year, I am confident that he would
> have found an even better correlation . . .
> (Nicholas Kaldor (1959), p. 293.

4.1 Introduction

For many economists there is only one kind of admissible evidence
— that from econometric studies. In this chapter, therefore, we
provide a survey of econometric work on the link from product
market pressures (especially profits) to pay determination. The
purpose is to argue that a coherent theme emerges from the
juxtaposition of scattered individual inquiries.

The first thing which is noticeable when reading the literature is
that, apparently unknown to most writers at the time, there were
simultaneously two rather different currents of research. The first,
based upon cross-section regressions, stems originally from the
work of Sumner Slichter. It continues today — the use of more
sophisticated tests has done relatively little to alter Slichter's
insights — in research such as Dickens and Katz (1987) and
Krueger and Summers (1987). The second current, stimulated by
quite different pressures, is that of aggregate time-series analysis.
This began as an attempt to investigate whether Phillips's wage
inflation model could be improved by the addition of variables
such as current or past profits. Kaldor (1959), in a lecture at the
London School of Economics, appears to have been the first
publicly to propose the idea. By the middle of the 1980s, however,
this current of research (one stressing product market influences)

had almost completely disappeared. One contributory factor may have been its peremptory dismissal in Laidler and Parkin (1975).

These two traditions, the cross-section approach and the aggregate time-series work, ran in separate but parallel channels for approximately three decades. Rather than split them into two, we discuss them in rough chronological order. This is partly because there are, inevitably, or or two works which span the divide. Hamermesh (1970) is an early example, Nickell and Wadhwani (1987) a more recent one.

4.2 Early Work

It is appropriate to begin with the seminal cross-section evidence in Slichter (1950). The author begins by pointing out that the same quality of labour receives quite different remuneration in different plants (something noted also by Lester (1952), MacKay *et al.* (1971), and more recently Nolan and Brown (1983), Dickens and Katz (1987) and Krueger and Summers (1987)). As an example, Slichter cites the distribution of wage rates across 85 plants in Cleveland (USA) in February 1947 (see Table 4.1).

Table 4.1 *Hiring rates for common labour in Cleveland, February 1947*

Cents per hour	Number of plants.
50–60	4
70–74	2
75–79	1
80–84	12
85–89	13
90–94	22
95–99	17
100–104	6
105–109	8

His thesis is that the 'chaos which seems to prevail in the labour market conceals a pattern of order which can be explained and which sheds light on the influences that determine the inter-industry wage structure of the community' (p. 81).

Slichter collects earnings data on male unskilled labour. The figures are for 1939, after the war-time regulated scales (and before the USA joined the Second World War), and for twenty different industries. The author notes that larger plants are probably over-represented in the data set, which was from a National Industry Conference Board Survey. Because of this there may be some bias in the statistics.

The study's principal conclusions are that unskilled male earnings tend to be high where:

(1) skilled rates are high
(2) the proportion of women is low
(3) value-added per worker is high
(4) the value product of labour is high
(5) payroll costs are a small proportion of sales revenue
(6) firms' post-tax income is a large proportion of sales.

Another, and more general, finding is that the wage structure changes little over time.

The results are based on rank correlation coefficients between earnings and each of the other variables. The highest such correlation, 0.93, was that between value-added per worker and earnings. Chemicals had the highest value-added ($3.48) and paid the second-largest earnings level ($0.69). Cotton had the smallest value-added ($0.75) and the third-lowest earnings ($0.49). The sample of industries in the calculation was thirteen. Similar conclusions emerge from the relationship between earnings and the value product per wage-earner hour. Here, over a sample of nineteen industries, the coefficient of rank correlation was 0.83. In this, chemicals ranked second in both, whilst cotton ranked bottom in value product and second bottom in earnings.

Another measure of financial performance is the size of sales margins (number (6) above). Again Slichter found a significant correlation (0.70), and concluded, in a passage now well-known, that the results suggest: 'the view that wages, within a considerable range, reflect managerial discretion, that where management can easily pay high wages they tend to do so, and that where management are barely breaking even, they tend to keep wages down' (p. 88). Slichter's table (from p. 88) is reproduced here as Table 4.2. It is clear, even from informal inspection, that unskilled male earnings are related to profit margins across this sample of

Table 4.2 *Slichter (1950)*

Industry	Profit/sales	Rank	Average earnings[a]	Rank
Chemicals	12.6	1	0.69	2
Automobiles	8.6	2	0.80	1
Electrical Manufacturing	8.1	3	0.67	4
Printing (papers)	6.1	4	0.62	9
Paint	5.1	5	0.63	7
Rubber	4.9	6	0.67	3
Paper products	4.6	7	0.53	14
Paper and pulp	4.5	8	0.54	12
Agricultural implements	4.2	9	0.65	5
Wool	3.4	10	0.52	15
Printing (books)	3.3	11	0.54	11
Leather	2.9	12	0.56	10
Iron and steel	2.8	13	0.64	6
Cotton	2.6	14	0.49	16
Furniture	2.4	15.5	0.54	13
Boot and shoe	2.4	15.5	0.43	19
Hoisery	1.8	16	0.46	18
Lumber	1.3	17	0.48	7
Meat packing	0.9	18	0.62	8

[a] Hourly earnings, unskilled males.
All figures for 1939.

Source: Slichter (1950, table 6).

nineteen industries. Considering that high pay tends to depress profits, the size of the *net* positive correlation is striking.

Sumner Slichter's main object was to provide evidence against the competitive theory of the labour market. His view was that employers did not 'take' wage-rates, as that model suggests, but had the power to set them within a range determined by product market performance. Other economists were soon to turn to the study of the macroeconomics of wage inflation, but they either did not know of, or failed to see the links with, Slichter's 1950 *Review of Economics and Statistics* paper.

The earliest relevant time-series study appears to be by Klein and Ball (1959). They use quarterly British data and estimate a nominal wage-change equation. The size of pay rises is assumed to depend upon an index of unemployment, the change in the consumer price level, seasonal and political dummies, and, in some of their equations, a profit variable and a productivity variable. Unfortunately Klein and Ball do not report the exact results including either profits or productivity. Profits were taken as an average over the previous four quarters. The authors state that a positive coefficient larger than its sampling error was obtained on the profit variable. Because the other variables were reduced in size, and strong autocorrelation was introduced into the residuals, however, Klein and Ball gave up on profits and provide no estimates. This was somewhat premature. The introduction of profits would almost certainly reduce the size of their few other variables, and in any case it is unclear why this should be known by the authors to be incorrect. Second, if there are omitted variables, or if the correct way to specify profits is as (say) lagged two years, or as a change in profitability, either lagged or not, then the authors' finding of autocorrelation is what would be expected.

The next step in the debate was prompted by Nicholas Kaldor's (1959) attack on Phillips's work. Kaldor argued that wage-rates are determined by the bargaining strength of labour and that this depends upon the prosperity of the industry concerned. According to this view, unemployment itself does not matter, and the Phillips curve worked statistically simply because profits and unemployment were correlated over Phillips's time period.

Lipsey and Steuer (1961) took up the challenge and estimated an encompassing model of wage inflation. Both real profits and unemployment were entered in their framework into an equation explaining the rate of change of money wages. This was estimated on aggregate British data from 1949-58, from 1926-38, and from 1870-1913. The results were mixed, and the authors concluded broadly against the profits theory. Lipsey and Steuer also estimated ten industry wage-change equations, from 1949-58, in which, by studying R^2 values, they claim to have 'conclusively refuted' the view that profits are a more important explanatory variable than unemployment, or even that profit has a minor role.

Although Lipsey and Steuer proceeded in what must have seemed a sensible manner, their results, by modern standards, must be treated with caution. First, it is apparent that even the units of measurement should have given the authors cause for concern. The dependent variable in their regressions is nominal, whereas the independent variables are real. Any change in the nominal price level, therefore, would almost certainly alter the dependent variable in a proportionate way, but might have no effect on the right-hand side of the equation. In fact, the period 1926–38 had relatively low price inflation, and this was the only time-span for which Lipsey and Steuer found any support for the profits theory. Second, many of the authors' equations were estimated with between six and eight degrees of freedom. Third, no tests were done for autocorrelation of the residuals. Fourth, no account was taken of the fact that, from 1870 to 1958, real wages almost doubled. Nominal wages therefore moved systematically in relation to prices, in a way linked presumably to real productivity growth, and this ought to have been incorporated into the model. Bearing these points in mind, the Lipsey–Steuer model appears to be misspecified, and the empirical results are probably of little value.

In 1962 Bhatia correctly pointed out that there was no a priori reason to assume, as Lipsey and Steuer (1961) had done, that the time-lag from profits to pay was of one year or less. He tested both for different lags and for a possible rate of change effect, and used quarterly data for the USA from 1948-59. The most striking part of the article is a graph on page 258 (chart 2) showing a strong correlation between the annual percentage change in earnings and the annual percentage return on equity capital. Bhatia reports many regressions and ends by accepting the profit argument and not the unemployment one. The author suggests that the lag from profits to pay is only two months.

On the face of it Bhatia's paper provides excellent ammunition for the thesis which is propounded in this book. Yet it is likely that his econometric inferences are just as fragile as those of Lipsey and Steuer (1961). Indeed the amazingly close fit, and almost instantaneous link, between profits and earnings might well have alarmed the author.

The true interpretation of Bhatia's chart 2, and accompanying regressions, is probably that the annual percentage rate of return on equity capital moves dominantly with the nominal price index, just as nominal earnings does. Although the article is not clear about the construction of the profit variable, it may well be the nominal profit divided by the capital stock (at historic prices) at the end of the previous period. Such a variable would change, *ceteris paribus*, with the rate of price inflation. On this view the chart in Bhatia (1962) simply depicts two series which move closely with retail prices and hence, on the face of it, closely with each other. This would also explain the puzzlingly short lag — bearing in mind that wage settlements in the USA in this period ranged from one to three years — of two months. On balance, Bhatia's claims that profits enter a wage equation can be given little credence.

Similar problems arise in the Eckstein and Wilson (1962) study of US money wages. The authors estimate wage-change equations in which profits and unemployment are independent variables. Figure 1 of their article shows that wage inflation is almost perfectly correlated with the 'profit rate'. As no price index is entered on the right-hand side of the equation, it is tempting to speculate that, as with Bhatia (1962), the profit variable is picking up changes in nominal variables such as the price level. Further evidence comes from a statement on page 392: 'If profits and prices are used as the explanatory variables, profits cease to be a significant variable because of their high collinearity with consumer prices.' This appears to establish that the Eckstein-Wilson profits variables cannot be a *real profitability* measure (which can hardly move closely with a nominal price index). In addition, many of the industry wage-change equations find no significant profit effect. This is consistent with the view that, as constructed, the aggregate profits variable is dominantly affected by the price level. Industry profitability would fluctuate much more in real terms, and so would be a less perfect proxy for nominal effects.

To check their time-series results, Eckstein and Wilson also investigate cross-section data. Table 5 of their paper appears to offer some chance of valid inference, because the variable omitted from the time-series equations, namely the price index, goes into the constant term of the cross-section ones. Profits always enter positively, but are often not significant. However, there is mild support for the idea that wage changes are correlated with industry profit levels.

Around this time US labour economists were building upon the foundations laid by Slichter (1950). Brown (1962) examines the correlation between wages and industries' ability-to-pay using data from the 1950s. He takes cross-section statistics on eighty-one US manufacturing industries, and calculates nine variables relevant to wage determination. Annual average wage earnings is used as a dependent variable and both simple and partial correlation coefficients are estimated. Brown's findings are set out in Table 4.3.

Table 4.3 *Correlation coefficients for wages and ability-to-pay measures*

	Simple	Partial
Value-added per man hour	0.471[a]	0.093
Degree of concentration	0.406[a]	0.326[a]
Profits per sales dollar	0.411[a]	0.298[a]
Production worker employment/ other employment	−0.560[a]	−0.378[a]
Payroll/value added	−0.168	n.a.[b]
Male employment/total employment	0.608[a]	0.392[a]
Seasonality of employment	−0.227[a]	−0.029
Employment per firm	0.352[a]	n.a.[b]
Change in employment	0.013	−0.124

   [a] significant at 5 per cent level.
   [b] n.a. means not applicable.

Brown draws the conclusion that 'interindustry differences in expected ability to pay are the primary determinants of interindustry differences in . . . earnings' (p. 58).

Brown's profit measure is net of taxes and relative to sales revenue. The correlation coefficient of 0.411 is taken over 59 industries (because of missing profits data). Brown ranks the top ten and bottom ten industries on pay and profitability, and shows that the correlation is stronger at the bottom end. Thus, he argues, 'inability to pay (as reflected by low levels of profitability) is a stronger determinant of wage levels than ability to pay, though both are important' (p. 55).

These results provide interesting evidence — of a kind supportive of Slichter's earlier work — of a link from industrial prosperity to pay. Brown is well aware of their limitations; the correlations cannot prove that there is a causal relation. Nevertheless, six indexes of expected ability-to-pay together explain nearly 75 per cent of the variation in wages.

Perry (1966) is a systematic study of United States wage determination. Although it contains much of interest, the book suffers from the same difficulty as Bhatia (1962) and Eckstein and Wilson (1962): 'profit rates' are highly correlated with nominal price changes. Fig. 3.5 and Fig. 3.7 of Perry's book are strikingly close. It is clear, once again, that inferences drawn from thinking of this profit rate as a real variable are likely to be incorrect.

However, much of Perry's analysis gets around this, somewhat inadvertently, by estimating equations such as that on the author's page 50:

$$\dot{w}_t = -4.3 + 0.37\,\dot{p}_{t-1} + 14.71U_{t-1} + 0.42R_{t-1} +$$
$$(0.05) \qquad (2.19) \qquad (0.07)$$
$$0.80\dot{R}_t + e_t$$
$$(0.18)$$
$$R^2 = 0.87 \qquad DW = 1.2$$

where $\dot{w}$ is nominal wage inflation, $\dot{p}$ is the rate of change of the consumer price level, U is unemployment, R is the profit variable (company earnings divided by stockholders' equity), and $\dot{R}$ is the rate of change of the profit variable. Standard errors are in parentheses.

Although this equation is flawed by autocorrelation, it has a structure which can be sensibly interpreted, and it is possible that the equation's results offer some (necessarily unreliable) information. If, as seems reasonable, R's level is an imperfect proxy for price inflation, it makes sense to add together the coefficients on inflation and the profit levels:

$$R + \dot{p} : 0.42 + 0.37 = 0.79$$

This is not far short of the unit coefficient which neoclassical economics would suggest. If *changes* in R correctly measure the variation in real productivity, the $\dot{R}$ variable's positive sign and significance may identify a link from financial health to the level of pay.

Why is the estimated equation so affected by serial correlation? One likely reason is that the $\dot{R}$ variable is a poor proxy for the change in real profits. Another is that the equation contains no productivity or growth trend term, despite the fact that real wages tend to grow over time. Finally, there is no reason to suppose that the true lag structure is as simple as that in the estimated form.

Equivalent problems occur in an innovative study by Kuh (1967). The author attempts to test the view that productivity rather than profits should enter an equation for wage inflation. The study openly agrees that such attempts are *ad hoc* and presents eclectic quarterly and annual results for US data (mostly for the 1950s). Kuh argues that the best specification includes the (nominal) value of productivity per employee. This is claimed to be slightly superior to one which includes real profit, defined as the ratio of sales to labour income. First, however, the regressions in which the productivity variable is significant have Durbin–Watson statistics which average well below unity. Second, the regressions reveal a coefficient on the rate of price inflation of approximately 0.1, which indicates that the dependent variable is effectively almost wholly nominal. It is then unsurprising that the addition of another nominal variable (plus, in fact, a new term for the wage level) meets with apparent success. Third, Kuh acknowledges in a footnote that the profit specification can work as well as, or better than, the productivity specification if, following a suggestion made to him by Eckstein, he estimates with profit deflated by capital.

In 1968 Eckstein published another paper on pay determination. Again he used American data, quarterly from 1950 to 1963, and finds in favour of a profit effect upon wage-rates. One attractive feature of the result is the fact that the change in prices now enters as an independent variable. For example, the author's table IV finds the level of wage inflation to depend upon price change (with a coefficient of 0.8), unemployment, and the change in profitability. Unemployment enters with a t-statistic of -1.7. Eckstein concludes that 'with one exception, all successful explanations of money wages have employed variables reflecting both the state of the labour market and the state of the product market . . . But in my judgement it is impossible to discover the relative weights to be attached to the specific short-term factors of the precise mechanism through which they operate . . .' (p. 141).

De Menil (1971) contains both an influential theoretical analysis and some empirical results using US data. The author estimates hourly earnings change equations. Data quarterly from 1954 to 1969 are used; eight industries are examined separately. A reasonably representative result (the first equation of the author's table 7.2) for 'Stone, Clay and Glass Products' is shown in Table 4.4. De Menil concludes that the empirical success of the productivity and wage variables is evidence in favour of a bargaining approach to the analysis of pay determination. The significance of value

Table 4.4 *Rate of change of union hourly earnings equation*

Log value of output per employee $(t-1)$	0.15
	(3.2)
Log of non-union wage $(t-1)$	0.09
	(2.4)
Log of previous earnings $(t-1)$	−0.3
	(3.4)
Average of past lay-off rates	−0.17
	(2.9)
A past price inflation measure	0.46
	(1.9)
An incomes policy dummy (1962/3)	0.0005
	(0.27)
+ constant	

$R_2 = 0.46$
$DW = 1.86$
t−statistics in parentheses

productivity per worker might be seen as an indication of an industrial prosperity effect.

The study raises interesting possibilities. Although De Menil's basic theory suggests a wage *level* equation, the estimation uses wage change as the dependent variable. However, the inclusion of the lagged level of pay as an independent variable redresses this. In long-run equilibrium, with zero inflation, the model reduces to a wage level equation with pay depending positively on value productivity and non-union earnings, and negatively on the scale of lay-offs. In general, however, the presence of the inflation term (marginally significant) is then unconventional.

Eliasson (1975) is in a similar mould. He examines data on various Swedish industries between 1948 and 1956. Although mainly concerned with the estimation of profit functions, the author reports some wage equations, including the following annual wage-change equation (see his p. 58) for mining, metal and engineering industries.

The numbers in parentheses are standard errors.

It is hard to know what to make of such results. Unemployment has a surprising sign and is insignificant. Profit margin, defined as a rate of gross profit to value-added, is statistically significant. Inflation enters with a coefficient suitably close to unity. However, it is conceivable that many relevant independent variables are omitted here, and it is not obvious that this is an appropriate specification. At best the results are suggestive.

Howard (1969) adopts what he calls an 'error-learning approach to collective bargaining'. The author argues that, contrary to previous thinking, bargained wage-rates are to be explained by past profit performance. According to his model, parties agree on the wage given their best estimates of future profits, and then later correct for their errors in forecasting. Although the author reports some conclusions based upon regression analysis, the equations themselves are not given, and this makes the research impossible to evaluate. From his description of the work, however, Howard appears — like most others at that time — to have omitted consumer prices as an independent variable. Later research by the same author, Howard and Tolles (1973), estimates wage-change equations on US data from 1950–70. The only variables are lagged profitability up to three years earlier and lagged unemployment up to three years earlier. Not surprisingly, as the profit rate is partly nominal and there are no other nominal variables, it is highly significant in the authors' regression equations. These results are of questionable value.

By the middle of the 1970s, despite high levels of inflation in most countries, the idea of a link from profits to wages had almost disappeared from the literature. Why this was appears to be a puzzle. The idea was not dropped because repeated empirical experiments rejected it. Most accepted the hypothesis (though Hamermesh (1970) is an exception and may have been influential). The Laidler–Parkin survey of models of inflation in 1975 illustrates how Kaldor's (1959) thesis came to be forgotten: the role of profits is dismissed and product market pressures on wage determination are replaced wholly by labour market pressures. Later work, such as Branson and Rotemberg (1980) and Grubb, Jackman, and Layard (1983), concentrates upon employment and price inflation (and the occasional useful time trend) as influences on the rate of nominal wage growth.

4.3 Recent Research

Over the last ten years there has been a revival of interest in cross-section work on how financial measures such as profitability may influence pay. Slichter (1950), in particular, has been identified as classic research, and British and American economists have re-examined his hypotheses. Two things have given the latest generation of researchers an advantage. The first is the availability of large data sets incomparably better than those used in the 1950s. The second is the technical development of computers capable of handling such data. Some of the new studies, however, continue to use relatively small industry data sets. Little work has been done with panel data, although there are signs that this is changing.

Tylecote (1975) contains relevant empirical work. The author uses data on fifty-eight MLH manufacturing industries to estimate a cross-section wage-change equation for 1954–70, and obtains a corrected R^2 of 0.85. His independent variables are a product market concentration measure, the ratio of sales to total earnings of manual workers, the ratio of total net output minus earnings of manual workers, all divided by earnings of manual workers, average establishment size, the average hourly earnings of male employees (at the start of the sample) and the percentage change in the employment of manual workers. The most general specification produces the equation shown in Table 4.5.

Table 4.5

Independent variables	Coefficient (t−value)	
Constant	3.4	(12.3)
Concentration	0.003	(2.4)
Sales/wages	0.02	(5.9)
(Output-wages)/wages	0.03	(1.1)
Establishment size	0.00	(1.6)
Initial earnings	−0.01	(1.9)
Employment growth	0.00	(0.6)

The author describes the (output-wages)/wages variable as the strike-cost to wage-bill ratio. As can be seen from the equation, various possible proxies for profitability enter positively, and Tylecote argues for a model in which wages are determined in a bargain between two monopolistic opponents.

It is possible to criticize the study. First, as the author himself notes, there is inevitably substantial collinearity between the sales and output variables. Second, although there are intuitive grounds for including each of the explanatory variables, there is no formal model and it is difficult to assess the chosen specification. Third, as ever in this area, simultaneity is ignored. These points notwithstanding, the results contribute a little evidence that wage behaviour may depend upon product market performance.

Pugel (1980) employs US industry data to investigate whether highly profitable industries pay high wages. The author takes as a measure of pay the average hourly earnings of all employees, and calculates an 'excess profit' variable as an adjusted ratio of taxable profits to business receipts. One cross-section regression, for example, gives the result shown in Table 4.6.

Table 4.6 *Log hourly earnings equation*

Variable	Coefficient	t−statistic
Skill index	1.4	(4.7)
Female fraction	−0.3	(6.5)
Non-white fraction	−0.5	(1.5)
Prime age fraction	0.9	(2.6)
South Fraction	−0.2	(3.0)
Unionized fraction	−0.1	(2.0)
Large plant fraction	0.2	(3.4)
Excess profit per hour	0.2	(4.6)
Constant	−11.3	(4.3)
Log likelihood	−61.05	
Number of observations	73	

On the face of it this is significant evidence of a profit effect upon pay. However, this view must be qualified somewhat, because the introduction of 'median years of schooling', instead of the author's calculated 'skill index', halves the coefficient on profits and reduces the t-statistic to 1.8. The log likelihood then improves to -59.6. Surprisingly, the author does not enter together both the labour quality proxies, so it is unclear what happens to the profit variable in the full specification.

Further evidence comes from Geroski, Hamlin, and Knight (1982), who use 1968 data in seventy-three MLH manufacturing industries for Britain. The authors take as their dependent variable the level of average hourly earnings of male manual workers. The wage equation, which is estimated simultaneously with a strike equation, has as explanatory variables: strikes, enterprise size, industry concentration, advertising expenditure, profitability, proportion of skilled workers, proportion of female workers, a geographical variable, the extent of shiftworking, the proportion of workers on payment by results, and the ratio of inventories to final sales. The wage equations explain just under half the variance of the dependent variable.

Geroski, Hamlin, and Knight find that profitability — measured as net output minus the wage bill all over gross output — enters positively in the wage equation. Without industry concentration entered, its t-statistic is approximately 1.9. If concentration is included, however, that falls to 0.7. These results are not strong enough to provide any conclusive evidence, but they are suggestive. Given the inevitable depressing effect that high wages have on profits, it is of interest that profitability ever enters positively in a wage equation.

Mishel (1986) uses a pooled sample of unionized US establishments from the Expenditure on Employee Compensation Surveys, 1968–72, and estimates cross-section wage equations. The data are for establishments, and the author grafts on various industry statistics at points where establishment figures are not available. A wage equation of the following form is estimated:

$$w_{ij} = BX_{ij} + CBS_j + DM_jBS^*$$

in which X is a vector of demographic, industry, union, and size variables; BS measures bargaining structure; M is a dummy variable for a concentrated industry with entry barriers; and BS^* is BS augmented by single plant bargaining.

The author's results, based on a painstaking analysis of his establishment data set, favour the view that wages depend sensitively upon the interaction between union influence and product market structure. Central findings include the following:

(1) A union production worker in a highly oligopolistic industry with high entry barriers enjoys a 16 per cent wage advantage over a similar worker in a competitive industry.
(2) Union workers earn more in the non-competitive sector regardless of the structure of bargaining.

(3) Union gains are highest where they achieve high coverage, practise centralized bargaining and avoid union fragmentation.
(4) Centralized bargaining provides no wage advantage in competitive industries.
(5) Import penetration is associated with lower pay for union production workers.
(6) In equations that include bargaining structure, and other dimensions of union structure, the price–cost margin (the mark-up) enters positively in the wage estimates.

Mishel concludes in favour of the ability-to-pay effect upon wages: 'Overall, the estimates suggest that union workers are rewarded for working in a profitable industry' (p. 103).

Sparks and Wilton (1971) examine wage determination in Canadian manufacturing industry. Data on individual contracts are used: the authors pool time-series observations for fourteen industries. Their explanatory variables include profits, unemployment, price inflation, employment growth, strikes, a relative wage, and productivity. The dependent variable is the rate of change of basic hourly wages. Profit is effectively a real rather than (as in some studies discussed above) a nominal variable, because it is defined as a proportion of assets. The profit variable is significant in each of the reported equations.

The results of Sparks and Wilton (1971) are open to various interpretations. One is that the rate of wage inflation depends on the *level* of profits (defined over the previous four quarters), among other variables. An alternative view follows from the steady state version of the authors' best fitting wage equation, which is denoted by (1.4) on their p. 743. The long-run equilibrium relationship is

$$0 = \text{constant} + \alpha_0 U^{-1} + \alpha_1 \pi - \alpha_2 r + \text{industry dummy variables}$$

where U is unemployment, π is profit, r is the wage of the industry relative to earnings in manufacturing and α_0, α_1 and α_2 are positive coefficients. This equation can be rewritten as an equation with the relative wage as the dependent variable.

Whilst Sparks and Wilton do not discuss this interpretation, it is one which fits in with some other parts of the cross-section literature on pay determination. An industry's wage depends here upon wage-rates elsewhere, the level of unemployment, and the profitability rate. Interestingly, the authors conclude that earlier research failed to recognize that the labour market is 'characterised predominantly by bilateral monopoly' (p. 748).

Hamermesh (1970) makes a highly original contribution by using a pooled sample of union contract data. His study takes sixteen US companies and examines their wage agreements from 1948 to 1967. The data provide 180 observations with the attribute of both a cross-section and a time-series element. Nominal wage inflation is taken as the dependent variable. The independent variables are price inflation, unemployment (at the aggregate level), and the profit rate relative to total assets. Hamermesh also examines the consequences of changes in profitability, and of various kinds of threshold effects of inflation. Interestingly, the profit variables perform generally poorly.

The work of Hamermesh constitutes the best early evidence against the hypothesis that pay depends upon lagged profitability. Possible objections, however, include the following. First, table IV of the paper shows that profit is highly significant when the sample is restricted to the years 1962–7. Moreover, these are the only equations in which the coefficient on price inflation is approximately unity. The other results estimate coefficients of approximately one half, which is theoretically unsatisfactory, as it implies a high degree of money illusion. As the period of 1962–7 was one of low inflation, it may be that some kind of bias, possibly caused by the definition of profits, is entering during the other (inflationary) period. Second, contract wages at the individual level are likely to be affected by wages elsewhere in the economy, which in turn depend over time on the quality of technology and the capital stock. Hamermesh's equations implicitly ignore these factors and constrain the underlying rate of real-wage growth to be constant over each of the years 1948-67. Nevertheless, the paper can be seen as evidence against this book's principal thesis.

Another study, drawing on data from many countries, is OECD (1965), which is a report by a group of independent experts on the economics of pay and jobs. The contributors use partial correlation analysis, but attempt to control for third factors. Unfortunately it is not easy to know how to interpret the report's vast quantities of data. However, the OECD experts concluded in favour of 'the prosperity or ability-to-pay thesis' (p. 18). The thrust of the study is that it is profits rather than employment which shape wages.

One other especially well-known British study is that of Salter (1966). Although his work was directed principally at the issue of how productivity and technical change are related, another matter of direct interest to labour economists was also addressed. Salter's famous conclusion in chapter 9 was:

> There is no tendency for greater than average increases in earnings to be associated with greater increases in output per operative . . . Cross-section correlation analysis deals entirely with variations in the experiences of different industries around the mean experience, and all our results refer to such variation. For example, it is conceivable that industries which exceeded the average increase in output per operative would also exceed the average increase in earnings, and vice versa. If this were the case, a positive correlation would be recorded. In fact, the recorded correlation coefficient is near zero . . . (pp. 114-15).

His explanation drew upon classical theory.

> The finding that inter-industry movements of earnings and output per operative are uncorrelated is not at all surprising. The market for labour is common to all industries and, over the long run, the movement of wages in each industry is primarily determined by the movements of wages in the economy as a whole (p. 115).

One way to object to Salter's argument is to point out that the removal of one or two outliers from his twenty-eight industries' figures will produce a much stronger correlation. Fig. 1.4 of Salter (1966) makes this clear. The author also records the fact that US investigations had often found a significant relationship. Salter cites a study by John Dunlop in which a rank correlation of 0.72 was found.

There is, however, a more crucial objection. An economist would expect that the level of earnings in a firm or industry would be linked — if to anything other than an aggregate variable — to *the value of a man hour not to the physical product of a man hour*. When viewed in this light, Salter's claim is less surprising and somewhat less interesting.

The author (accidentally) makes it possible for the reader to calculate whether pay in an industry is correlated with value productivity in that industry. Late in the book, Fig. 23 depicts the relationship between output per operative and product earnings per operative. The scatter diagram shows both the excellent fit between the two ($r = 0.94$, one of the highest recorded anywhere in the monograph) and that the gradient is only a little below unity. As (where k is a constant) this means

$$\frac{\text{earnings/worker}}{\text{product price}} = k \text{ (output/worker)},$$

it follows that

earnings/worker $= k$ (value of average product).

Hence, despite the conclusions for which Salter's work is famous, his study provides confirmation that average earnings in an industry are proportional to the (value) productivity of the industry's typical employee. This is consistent with the findings of, for example, Slichter (1950), although is not *per se* a profit effect.

Further work has been done by Ball and Skeoch (1981), who examine British data on plants in fifteen manufacturing industries. One finding of particular relevance is that there is a strong positive relationship between pay and (the value of) labour productivity. The authors consider and reject the possibility that this is because either more able or more skilled individuals work in the high productivity plants. Ball and Skeoch conclude that the competitive labour market model 'is less than totally convincing' (p. 71). Although the authors study profitability and its causes, they do not present direct estimates of the effect of profit upon pay.

Excellent new surveys of the American literature on the economics of inter-industry wage differences are presented in Krueger and Summers (1987) and Dickens and Katz (1987). The latter also estimates a large number of cross-section wage equations using individual and industry data of a kind unavailable in Britain. Both papers — written independently but given at the same conference in 1986 — draw the same broad conclusion. Inter-industry wage differentials, the four authors argue, cannot be described simply in terms of compensating differentials for non-monetary aspects of jobs, nor be explained by an appeal to unmeasured employee characteristics, nor seen as some form of temporary disequilibrium. The authors reject the classical model of the labour market.

Both papers claim that pay moves significantly with profitability and product market power, and cite large numbers of prior US studies (some of which we have already reviewed). Dickens and Katz develop their own evidence and propose the following two-step methodology. First, they estimate separate earnings functions on individual data for union and non-union members, controlling for individual characteristics, location, and industry affiliation. Next, they explain the industry fixed effects (the coefficients on industry dummies from individual equations) in terms of broad industry characteristics such as measures of job quality, industry labour market conditions, and employers' ability-to-pay. The union and non-union sectors are treated separately.

Dickens and Katz (1987) contains persuasive evidence that wages depend on the financial performance of the employer. After checking 432 specifications they conclude (for the non-union sector):

The ratio of net income to sales and the average return on capital were both positively related to wages on all specifications tried and were often significantly related when entered by themselves. Profit per employee was nearly always positively related and often significantly positively related when entered by itself (p. 78).

More broadly, the authors argue that there are only three variables which stand out — from the literature survey and their own analysis — as having a consistent relation with wages. Of the dozens they consider, their chosen threesome consists of

(i) average years of education of workers
(ii) profits
(iii) establishment size/capital intensity.

As the authors point out on number (ii), since 'we would expect a negative relation between profits and wages, all else held equal, this is a remarkable result'.

One weakness of the early cross-section British studies is that they use small and possibly unrepresentative data sets. Recent work by Blanchflower, Oswald, and Garrett (1988) employs the Workplace Industrial Relations Surveys (WIRS) of 1984 to pursue the same questions in a more comprehensive way. The survey, which was sponsored in part by the UK government, covers more than 2,000 British establishments and was designed as a representative sample of the economy (the sampling frame was the Census of Employment). The only significant omissions are that only establishments with at least twenty-five employees are included, and that the coal-mining industry is not covered by the survey.

Blanchflower, Oswald, and Garrett (1988) estimate unskilled, semi-skilled, and skilled weekly wage equations on samples of up to 1,200 British establishments in 1984 (see Table 4.7). They examine the influence of

(1) 'insider variables', including the financial performance and oligopolistic position of the establishment
(2) 'outsider variables', including the levels of wages and unemployment in the establishment's geographical area (across approximately sixty-five counties)
(3) other variables, including conventional statistical controls such as the percentages at the establishment of part-time

Table 4.7 *Dependent variable: skilled workers' weekly wages by eatablishment*

	Parameter (*t*−statistic)	Parameter (*t*−statistic)
Insider variables		
Financial performance	0.019	0.023
	(2.29)	(2.91)
Few competitors	0.035	0.029
	(2.(2.20)	(1.88)
Previous year's	−0.0009	−0.0008
employment change	(2.71)	(2.44)
Union recognition	0.029	0.024
dummy variable	(1.43)	(1.21)
Pre-entry closed shop	0.075	0.071
dummy variable	(2.94)	(2.84)
Post-entry closed shop	0.038	0.03
dummy variable	(2.04)	(1.75)
Outsider variables		
County employment	−0.12	—
rate	(4.63)	
County wage-rate	—	0.58
		(8.21)
Other variables[a]		
Adjusted R^2	0.50	0.52
Degrees of freedom	1019	1019

[a] See Blanchflower, Oswald, and Garrett (1988).

workers, manual workers, male workers, and different kinds of skilled workers, and the size of the establishment, its nature, and industry affiliation.

No precise profit statistics were available for the establishments, partly because plants are often treated by accountants not as profit centres but rather as cost centres. However, managers provided a qualitative measure of financial performance, using a fivefold grouping from 'a lot better than average' down to 'a lot below average'. The exact question in the WIRS survey was: 'How would you assess the financial performance of this establishment compared with other establishment/firms in the same industry?' (question 14a, 1984). The authors used the fivefold ordering to create a single variable 'financial performance' where the numbers $+2$, $+1$, 0, -1, -2 were assigned to the ordering 'a lot better than average' down to 'a lot below average'. This is a cardinality restriction and was suggested by unrestricted dummy variable coefficients for the five answers.

The WIRS survey also provides information about the establishment's oligopolistic position. Managers were asked: 'Is this market dominated by your organisation, are there only a few competitors (5 or less) or are there many competitors?' (question 11d, 1984).

Table 4.7 Dependent variable: skilled workers' weekly wages by establishment

When the establishment was described as either monopolistic or as having 5 or less competitors it was assigned to a dummy variable category 'few competitors'. Other insider variables, related to internal performance, were also used by Blanchflower, Oswald, and Garrett (1988). These included statistics on employment growth and a number of unionized variables.

Two examples of the authors' results are given in Table 4.7. There is evidence that the prosperity of the employer influences the level of pay. Other things constant, a plant here rated in the top financial performance groups pays a little under 10 per cent more than a plant in the lowest financial performance group. Further estimates, varying from 0 to 20 per cent according to subsample, are discussed by the authors.

A recent British study has been done by Gregory, Lobban, and Thomson (1987). The paper estimates wage equations using data from the CBI's Databank Survey of Pay Settlements. As its dependent variable the study takes settlement figures for individual manufacturing settlement groups. The explanatory variables are the pressures seen by managers as having influenced the individual agreements. These are captured by qualitative data in the form of ratings, for each of various forces, of 'very important', 'fairly important', or 'not important'. The forces include the level of profits, price competitiveness, the need to recruit or retain labour, the risk of redundancy, and outside and internal wage comparability. Respondents to the CBI Survey choose for themselves how many factors to cite and what weight to attach to them. Gregory, Lobban, and Thomson report that two-thirds cited between two and four influences as 'very important'.

The authors estimate the equation

$$\dot{w}di_t = \beta_0 + \beta_i \dot{p}_t + \sum_{k=1}^{K} \beta_k F_{kit} + \sum_{j=1}^{K} C_{jit} +$$
$$\theta \ln(\frac{w}{p}_{it-1} + e_{it}$$

where $\dot{w}$ is the percentage change in earnings (forecast by managers), $\dot{p}$ is the rate of price inflation, F_k is the binary rating given to the kth factor, C_j is the binary presence or absence of the jth further element in the settlement, and $\ln w/p$ is the log of the level of the real wage. Subscript i refers to the ith settlement group; subscript t denotes time. The equation combines a short-run error correction process with a long-run equilibrium wage relationship.

The data extend from 1978/9 to 1983/4 and cover 212 settlement groups. Neither $\dot{p}$ nor w/p is available from within the CBI Databank, so the authors measure the former by changes in the RPI, and set each w/p to correspond to that from the common starting point of 100 in 1978/9.

Estimation was by Joint Generalized Least Squares, which assumes, among other things, that the error terms (e) have zero covariance both within each year and across groups across years. The $\bar{R}^2$ figures were close to 0.3. There was some evidence of serial correlation and heteroscedasticity, but little of parameter instability across years.

Gregory, Lobban, and Thomson's principal conclusion is of direct interest to our study:

the most important influence on pay settlements over the period, both upwards and downwards, has been profits, their importance as a downward pressure diminishing and as an upward pressure rising as corporate profits first weathered the crisis of 1980-81, then showed a recovery (p. 144).

The authors report that, when profits as an upward pressure are cited as 'very important', the settlement is on average 0.75 percentage points higher than when unimportant. Moreover, profits had the largest coefficient of the variables. There was a similar finding for profits as a downward pressure, which reduced wage increases by 0.8 per cent when assessed as 'very important'. Certain other variables were found to be significant — particularly the need to recruit and retain labour, the cost of living and (in 1980/1) the risk of redundancy. However, the estimated coefficient on price inflation was only 0.2, which appears unacceptably low as it is widely believed that wages move roughly one-for-one with consumer prices. This may be, in part, because the lagged real wage has no cross-section element and hence is dominated by aggregate movements.

Another extensive data set has been used by Nickell and Wadhwani (1987). The authors estimate an average remuneration equation on a panel data set covering 219 UK firms and nine years. Their equation includes as independent variables the following: lagged remuneration, the aggregate UK wage, the industry wage, the output price, the output per man, aggregate unemployment, industry unemployment, the firms' debt–equity ratio, the UK minimum lending rate, a stock market value variable for the firm, the firm's cash balances, the UK union/non-union markup, and an incomes policy dummy variable. Nickell and Wadhwani estimate a fixed effects model in which there is a firm-specific constant and separate dummies for each of the nine years. The authors also test for the effects of capacity utilization and accounting profits (the results are not given) but neither is significant.

Although the study does not find effects of exactly the same kind as other work (and rejects the influence of accounting profits), it is in the same spirit. First, product price and productivity terms are highly significant. Second, the firm's financial position has a powerful influence on pay. Third, the interest rate has a significant depressing effect upon remuneration — conceivably because higher interest rates raise borrowing costs and the costs of holding inventories.

The Nickell and Wadhwani work has advantages over almost all of the earlier research, because it employs longitudinal data on a large number of firms, and it does not use subjective data. Its central conclusion is that both outside unemployment and the employer's degree of financial prosperity shape the level of workers' remuneration. This is the same conclusion as emerges from Blanchflower, Oswald, and Garrett (1988). However, Nickell and Wadhwani (1987) suggest that the accountant's definition of profits is not the appropriate measure of firm performance.

A new paper by Beckerman and Jenkinson (1988) provides further disaggregated evidence on the link from profits to pay. The authors point out the apparent sensitivity of British wages to unemployment over the early 1980s, and explore the hypothesis that profit-push is the explanation for the strong earnings growth over the period. They use data on British manufacturing industries from 1973 to 1986. The mixture of cross-section and time-series elements provides approximately 200 observations.

Both unrestricted and parsimonious models are estimated.

Table 4.8 *Dependent variable: nominal wage change in industry* i.

Independent variables	Parameter	*t*-statistic
Error correction term	0.19	4.2
Aggregate wage change	1.06	25.6
Industry wage $(t-1)$	0.02	2.6
Industry profit per employee $(t-1)$	3.09	2.7
Industry unemployment $(t-1)$	0.06	2.0
Aggregate unemployment	−0.25	2.9
Change in industry productivity	0.02	1.4
Change in aggregate productivity	0.14	2.4
Aggregate productivity $(t-1)$	−0.11	4.8
DW = 2.03		
% standard error = 1.29		

Beckerman and Jenkinson's preferred equation is as shown in Table 4.8. All but the profit variables are included in logarithmic form.

The regressions reveal the importance of inter-industry wage 'following': the rate of change of pay in any one sector depends strongly upon the going rate of wage inflation. Aggregate unemployment has a statistically significant negative effect upon wages, but (surprisingly) industry unemployment has a positive impact. Industry productivity has short-run effects on pay. Aggregate productivity has long-run effects.

There is strong evidence in these results of a relationship between industrial earnings and industrial profit per worker. The lag on profits is found to be one year. The authors do not say whether they tested for (say) a two-year lag but explicitly reject the hypothesis that profitability enters contemporaneously. The Beckerman–Jenkinson study appears to be interesting British evidence of a kind similar to the Canadian findings of Sparks and Wilton (1971).

Finally, Christofides and Oswald (1988), Card (1988), and Dowrick (1987) also examine the way in which product and labour market pressures combine to shape wage-rates. Dowrick estimates cross-section equations for 1975, 1979, and 1983 using British data on approximately 100 industries. The author weights the explanatory variables by profits per worker, so it is difficult to calculate the effect of that variable on its own. However, Dowrick concludes in favour of a model in which profitability affects the equilibrium level of remuneration. Christofides and Oswald (1988) and Card (1988), using Canadian contract data, do not have data on firms' profits, but find a strong positive effect upon pay from industry product price.

4.4 Conclusions

Early econometric evidence on the link from profits to wages is of mixed quality. Cross-section studies provide interesting affirmative evidence: they appear to tackle the issue in a systematic way and to deserve to be taken seriously. Slichter (1950) helped to create this area of research by uncovering the strong rank correlation between pay and employers' prosperity. Much persuasive American evidence now exists, as the surveys by Krueger and Summers (1987) and Dickens and Katz (1987) reveal, and those authors' own results are among the most convincing. The only roughly comparable British work — in terms of sample size — is that of Gregory, Lobban, and Thomson (1987), Nickell and Wadhwani (1987), and Blanchflower, Oswald, and Garrett (1988).

Despite their differences all find strong signs that the wage-rate depends upon the employer's performance. Their conclusions are similar to those from industry studies such as Beckerman and Jenkinson (1988). In the face of this evidence, drawn both from the United States and Great Britain, it is difficult to believe that pay is fixed independently of financial factors such as profitability.

Interpretation of the aggregate time-series work is more problematic. Although many apparently strong results exist (Perry (1962), and Eckstein and Wilson (1962), for example), these are mostly obtained by estimating a nominal wage equation in which nominal profitability is an independent variable, and where often it is the only nominal independent variable. Not only is the rate of price inflation often omitted from these studies' wage equations, but so too is any real productivity trend variable. Not surprisingly, therefore, these equations routinely break down and exhibit serious autocorrelation. Aggregate time-series work does not seem to offer robust evidence, either one way or the other, on the question of whether wages are affected by past or expected profits. Kaldor's (1959) gauntlet has not been seized.

APPENDIX

There is one caveat to this chapter's claim that Kaldor's idea has not been pursued adequately using time-series data. Just as our book was being completed, an important study by Rowlatt (1987) was published (some months after its November data indicates). The author's work is akin to our own: it looks for and finds a profit effect.

Rowlatt assumes that wages are determined by a bargaining process. A trade union which cares only about high real pay is assumed to negotiate with a firm which cares only about profits. A form of Nash bargaining solution is used. Unemployment is taken to depress workers' power relative to that of the firm; profitability influences the equilibrium outcome by affecting the employer's ability to pay.

Estimation is on British manufacturing quarterly data from the mid 1960s to the mid 1980s. A representative estimated equation is:

change in earnings =
    0.8 (0.25 4-year change in the acceptable nominal wage$_{-1}$)
    (9.1)
+ 0.2 (0.25 4-year change in the affordable nominal wage$_{-1}$)
    (−)
+ 0.2 real-wage disequilibrium$_{-3}$
    (4.4)
+ 0.02 real profit per unit of output$_{-3}$
    (2.2)
− 0.01 short-term unemployment$_{-2}$%
    (2.0)
− 0.06 change in short-term unemployment%
    (3.2)
+ dummies
Adjusted R^2 = 0.89
DW = 2.0

where t-statistics are in brackets, all but 'real-wage disequilibrium' and the profit variable are in logarithms, subscripts denote the lag length, and superscripts denote the period over which the change is taken.

The author assumes that

(i) the acceptable wage depends upon inflation, trend productivity and the income tax retention ratio
(ii) the affordable wage depends upon export competitors' prices, input costs, trend productivity and labour taxes
(iii) the real-wage disequilibrium variable is an error-correction term, where the long-run equilibrium wage is defined in a similar way as in(i) but includes a dependence on the terms of trade.
(iv) the lagged profit term is based on the statistics for industrial and commercial companies' real disposable income (net of stock appreciation, and excluding North Sea profits).

Rowlatt examines both constrained and unconstrained equations, and checks for stability and correctness of specification.

For our purposes the author's finding of a significant role for lagged profitability is a notable one. Chapter 7 will suggest a somewhat longer lag than the three quarters used in Rowlatt (1987), and will not use exactly the same definitions. Broadly speaking, however, Rowlatt (1987) and our inquiry are compatible. Hence her corroborative findings are of importance to this study.

5

The Psychology of Equity

5.1 Introduction

If a firm's profits rise, the employees in that company may feel it natural that their pay should increase. This attitude can be seen, for example, in the engineering pay-claim documents studied in Chapter 3. One might even believe it to be widespread in society, because it seems to conform to intuitive notions of fairness.

Is this just muddled thinking? Much research by social psychologists suggests that it is not. Before constructing an economic theory, therefore, it is fruitful to examine what psychologists call *equity theory*. A later section considers recent laboratory experiments and survey data.

The major pioneer of equity theory appears to have been J. S. Adams, a psychologist then working for the General Electric Company in New York City. His work is cited in all standard social psychology textbooks, such as Warr (1985) or Weyant (1986), and stems from the beginning of the 1960s. Homans (1961) is credited with an equivalent idea. Similar views are proposed in Jacques (1961).

Equity theory rests upon one special formula, that is, the target relationship (related to efficiency wage theory):

$$\frac{\text{One's own reward}}{\text{One's own investment (or input)}} = \frac{\text{Other's reward}}{\text{Other's investment (or input)}}$$

This defines 'equity' or 'distributive justice'. It is what agents are assumed to strive towards. In the words of Adams and Rosenbaum (1962): 'we may state that cognitive dissonance exists for Person whenever his cognitions of his job inputs and/or outcomes stand psychologically in obverse relation to his cognitions of the inputs and/or outcomes of other' (p. 161).

In short, an individual is unhappy if he is paid either more or less than he sees as fair. Fairness, or equity, means the equality of reward/input ratios. Individuals assess themselves against 'comparison' others.

The formula given above is rather general. In its typical application, however, 'reward' is financial payment and 'investment' is a mixture of effort and training qualification. Lawler's (1968) survey article contains a discussion of the relationship between equity theory and other psychological models of human motivation.

The main implication and prediction of equity theory is that an individual who believes that his or her own inputs are too high, relative to those of 'comparison' others, will reduce them. Inequity is 'aversive' and human beings will attempt to minimize it. Whether this model provides a useful way to predict behaviour is an empirical question. An obvious theoretical difficulty, however, is that of how people choose those against whom they compare themselves. The theory gives no guidance on this point, which reduces its value. Nevertheless, many social and economic exchanges take place between two agents, and in such circumstances the 'other' of equity theory appears to be obvious. One such exchange is that between a firm and its employees. Another is the relation between different groups of workers (see Wood (1978), and Willman (1982), among others, on the importance of notions of fair differentials).

From an economist's point of view the assumption of inequity minimization looks — except perhaps to the Rawlsian — unconventional. Although it is reminiscent of efficiency wage notions, the lack of normal elements, such as utility functions and constraints on optimization, means that many economists are likely to dismiss it without further thought. Yet that would be unscientific, because it would be the result of prejudice and habits of analysis. The only satisfactory approach is to test, and so try empirically to reject, the theory.

5.2 Adams's Early Experiments

One of the first attempts to test equity theory was undertaken by Adams and Rosenbaum (1962). They conducted two experiments, using university students who did not know they were part of a laboratory test, to see if productivity varied with feelings of overpay and underpay.

The first of these was done in the winter of 1960 in New York. A small sample of twenty-two students at NYU were hired as part-time interviewers. The rate of pay advertised was $3.50 an hour, and subjects were told that the work would last several months. They were assigned randomly into two groups of eleven each. One group was placed in an 'experimental dissonance condition' by being given the impression that they were all being overpaid, whilst the other was a control group. This was done in a preliminary session in the following way.

Experimental subjects were told:

You don't have any (nearly enough) experience in interviewing or survey work of the kind we're engaged in here. I specifically asked the Placement Service to refer only people with that kind of experience. This was *the* major qualification we set. I can't understand how such a slip-up could have occurred. It's really very important for research of this kind to have people experienced in interviewing and survey techniques. [Agonizing pause]

We're dealing with a limited alternative open end kind of questionnaire. There's no 'correct' answer to an item. Research in this area has shown that the nature of the response elicited by a skilled and experienced interviewer is more accurate and representative of the respondent's sentiments and differs substantially from the responses elicited by inexperienced people.

Who interviewed you at Placement? [Experimenter scans the New York University phone directory, picks up the telephone receiver and dials a number. Gets busy signal and slams receiver down. Pause, while Experimenter thumbs paper and meditates.]

I guess I'll have to hire you anyway, but *please* pay close attention to the instructions I will give you. If anything I say seems complicated, don't hesitate to ask for clarification. If it seems simple, pay closer attention. Some of this stuff, on the surface, may appear to be deceptively easy.

Since I'm going to hire you, I'll just have to pay you at the rate we advertised, that is $3.50 per hour.

Control group subjects, however, had a less gruelling time.

Well, this is very good. We can use you for this work. You meet all the qualifications required for the job, which is good, because we often have to turn people down because they're poorly qualified. Poorly qualified people can really make a mess of a study of this kind. Why even the Census, where they were dealing with simple demographic material, got fouled up. They hired inadequately qualified people, some of them housewives for example, and the result was gross deficiencies in their data that were so widely criticized in the press, if you recall. Well, anyway I'm pleased that you have the background we're looking for.

So far as pay is concerned, the people at the Placement Service have probably advised you that we pay $3.50 per hour. This rate of pay is standard for work of this kind performed by people with your qualification (p. 162).

Although the sample of individuals used in this case was small, the idea behind the experiment is a simple and natural one. In the experimental induction period one half of the subjects were made to perceive their own qualifications (or 'inputs' into the job) as out of line with the rewards. They were made to feel unreasonably lucky in their pay.

The experimenters then explained to the subjects that they were to interview adult members of the general public for approximately two and a half hours. Subjects chose their own locations. The interviews required people to assign likely personalities to drivers of different kinds of car. The subjects were each given fifty blank questionnaires, which was known to be a greater supply than could be completed. After the subject returned, with the task completed, he or she was told the real purpose of the interview and the experiment.

One measure of the result is given in Table 5.1. The dependent variable of interest is productivity, namely the number of interviews per minute.

As predicted by equity theory, experimental subjects produced

Table 5.1 *Mean productivity and median distribution of experimental and control subjects*

	Experimental	Control
Cases above median	8	3
Cases below median	3	8
Mean productivity	0.27	0.19

significantly more than control subjects. Adams and Rosenbaum used a non-parametric Chi-square test which showed the findings to be statistically significant at the 5 per cent level on a two-tailed test.

The authors did a second and slightly different experiment in the late spring of 1961. This not only replicated the previous experiment but also studied the effects of inequity where subjects were paid piece-rates. The basic procedures were as before, except that some subjects were allocated

(1) to an overpaid piece-rate group;
(2) to a control piece-rate group.

The prediction from the theory was again that subjects would act so as to regain equity by working differently if overpaid. Those on piece-rates were expected to respond to overly generous rates of pay by doing slower work and thus earning lower total income.

Table 5.2 gives the results. Columns H_e and H_c record the findings from the repeat of the 1967 experiment, whilst columns P_e and P_c document the productivities of the piece-workers. The productivity means have the expected differences but are not significantly different in the statistical sense (as all four groups now had only nine members each, it may not be surprising that it was

Table 5.2 *Median productivity and distribution of hourly and piece-work experimental and control subjects*

	H_e $3.50	H_c $3.50	P_e 30 cents/ interview	P_c 30 cents/ interview
Cases above median	8	4	1	5
Cases below median	1	5	8	4
Mean of productivity	0.27	0.23	0.15	0.20

H_e : experimental hours group. H_c : control hours group.
P_e : experimental piece rate-group. P_c : control piece-rate.
Source: Adams and Rosenbaum (1962, p. 163).

hard to reject the null). However, an interaction test between pay and 'dissonance' was significant.

Adams and Rosenbaum conclude in favour of equity theory. However, they recognize one possible difficulty with the experimentation, that is, that the 'overpaid' subjects worked harder for fear of being sacked in the future:

This explanation is not satisfactory, however. In the first place, if it were valid, the same effects would be predicted for pieceworkers. But, as we have seen, pieceworkers reduce rather than increase their productivity when overpaid. Secondly, in a related study, Arrowood has argued that if the alternative explanation was valid, the results would obtain only when the experimenter was aware of the subject's productivity. He conducted an experiment . . . [which] . . . invalidates the alternative explanation of our results' (p. 164).

Although this counter-objection has much to recommend it, the possibility that workers are merely investing in future job security must be considered a difficulty for the test procedure.

5.3 Later Research

By 1967 other psychologists had begun to try to replicate Adams and Rosenbaum's work. Andrews (1967), for example, begins by pointing out some of the limitations of the early experiments.

(1) Work periods were extremely short.
(2) Individuals were isolated from other employees.
(3) Tasks were unusually simple.
(4) Inequity had been induced only by changing perceptions, not by altering payments.
(5) Overpaid workers may have been striving to protect their jobs.
(6) No underpayment was studied.
(7) Only college students were used.

Although the author does not correct all of these, he does drop 4, 5 and 6, and allows for other changes.

Andrews's study uses a piece-work pay system. Hypothesis 1*a*, in the author's notation, was that when compared with workers assigned to an equitable piece-rate, workers assigned to a lower piece-rate will tend to produce more pieces of work but of a lower quality (and conversely for those on a higher rate). Hypothesis 1*b* predicted differences within experimental groups as a function of previous pay: high earners were hypothesized to produce greater quantity and lower quality.

Andrews hired ninety-six university students and assigned them randomly to interviewing and data-checking. Each of the two groups had three sub-groups (for overpay, equitable pay, and underpay). High pay was fixed at 30 cents per piece; low pay at 15 cents; equitable pay at 20 cents. The asymmetry up and down was chosen deliberately.

Measures of (i) interviewing and (ii) checking quality and quantity were devised. Table 5.3 reports the results for quantity. Both of Hypotheses 1a and 1b are apparently confirmed. Quantity was negatively correlated with the assigned piece-rate and positively correlated with the previous high wage per hour. Mean differences were easily statistically significant. Similar results were found for quality although the significance levels were slightly lower (close to the 5 per cent level).

Table 5.3 *Quantity of work as a function of assigned piece-rate and previous wage experience*

Previous high wage/ hour	15 cents per piece	20 cents per piece	30 cents per piece	Row average
$2.25/hour or more	23.7	18.2	19.6	21.0
$1.60–$2.20	22.2	20.3	17.0	20.0
$1.55 or less	16.7	15.9	15.1	16.0
Column average	21.1	18.9	17.7	19.2

Source: Andrews (1967, p. 41).

Another study is reported in Adams and Jacobsen (1964). They were concerned with the question of whether job insecurity had produced the early findings of Adams's research. Thus they examined whether the manipulation of perceived equity would lead to the same results even when subjects knew there to be little chance of extra work. Their research confirmed that it did. Lawler (1968) has criticized the Adams and Jacobsen work, however, on the grounds that subjects might not have attached zero probability to future employment.

These and similar pieces of research were drawn together in the survey article by Lawler (1968). He was criticial of various aspects of the experiments (doubting, for example, whether it was possible to reject the view that workers aimed for job security when they overproduced). Lawler's main conclusion was that it was only the piece-work laboratory studies which provided evidence in favour of equity theory, and that more research was required.

In 1972 Pritchard, Dunnette, and Jorgensen published a more extensive study of the links from equity to worker productivity. They attempted to design an experiment in which workers were not threatened or made to feel inadequate. A real job setting was created, and a simple task devised (using catalogues). Unlike other studies, this employed workers for a number of consecutive days, and used a larger sample (253) than had been done before.

The authors examined hourly pay and piece-rate pay. Hourly pay was fixed at $2. Under piece-rates, workers were paid according to the following sliding scale:

Productivity	*Remuneration*
16–22 units	$1.60
23–29 units	$2.00
30–above units	$2.40

This gave the investigators an opportunity to see if people willingly chose to produce more units than the minimum required to reach the relevant payment band.

Feelings of overpay and underpay were induced in a simple and ingenious manner. After one day of training, different groups of workers were formed by the experimenters. One group (fifty-eight individuals) was used as a form of control and was told that $2/hour was 'the rate we have been paying college students for this work'. Another (forty-eight individuals) was put onto a piece-rate with equivalent information. However, those in the overpayment-hourly group (twenty-five individuals) were told:

There was a mistake in the flyer you saw. The pay rate for the catalogue job is supposed to be $1.65 an hour. This is the rate we have been paying college students like you in the past few weeks who have worked on this contract. The $2 rate is much too high for this job. I checked with the main office, and since it was our mistake, we decided we would have to pay you at the higher rate of $2/hour, even though we normally pay college students $1.65 (p. 82).

Another 22 individuals were told the reverse:

We have been paying college students like you $2.50 per hour for this job. I checked with the main office, and it was felt that since you tacitly agreed to work for the low rate by coming here to work, we would pay you at the lower $2 rate. This may seem a little unfair, but you did sort of agree to it by coming (p. 82).

Equivalent methods were used to construct groups for underpayment and overpayment within the sliding scale bands.

In testing initially for hourly overpay and underpay the authors found only the weakest support for equity theory's predictions. Mean hourly performance did rise from the underpaid to equitably paid, and from there to overpaid, but these results were not statistically significant. However, in the case of 'naturally occurring inequity', predictions were validated. When individuals were switched, those experiencing overpayment decreased their performance less than equitably paid subjects, who in turn decreased their performance less than underpaid subjects.

Table 5.4 gives some indication of the temporal changes. Although suggestive, the differences there are statistically insignificant.

Table 5.4 *Mean hourly performance for days 1, 2, 3 for hourly pay to interval pay groups*

	Time		
Treatment Group	Day 1	Day 2	Day 3
Underpaid	14.95	18.11	18.37
Equitably paid	16.40	19.40	20.82
Overpaid	16.94	20.18	21.44

Source: Pritchard, Dunnette, and Jorgensen (1972, p. 86).

One of the other recent examinations of equity theory is that by Austin and Walster (1974). Their aim was to test whether persons who are given an equitable reward are happier than persons who receive an inequitable reward, whether persons who are overrewarded are less distressed than those underrewarded, and whether inequitably treated individuals experience less distress if they expected to be so rewarded.

The experimenters used a group of seventy-eight female and thirty-nine male undergraduates at the University of Wisconsin. Rather than studying these students' productivities, as most previous research had done, Austin and Walster were concerned to measure individuals' contentment or discontentment. Subjects were given a proof-reading task and asked to circle errors. They were told that two of them would independently check the same piece of writing, and that an arbitrator would allocate $4 between them according to their relative performance at proof-reading. In practice there was no other reader.

As the going rate of pay in Wisconsin experiments was widely known to be $2, the authors treated that as the likely perceived equitable reward. In some cases expectation were manipulated. Subjects were also required to fill in a *mood adjective form*, to assess their level of contentment. Answers were coded as an index: the larger the number the greater the individual's satisfaction. Electrodes were also attached to the subjects' skin to measure galvanic response, although Austin and Walster note their scepticism of such methods.

As usual in equity experiments, some subjects were overrewarded whilst others were not. The central question of interest was whether excess payments would lower satisfaction (though less than underpayments).

Remarkably, both overpayment and underpayment reduced subjects' levels of contentment. Table 5.5 gives some results. That shows, too, that an underreward is much worse than an excessive one. Statistical significance was checked successfully. A 3 x 3 analysis of variance also supported the hypothesis, and regression analysis produced the same conclusions.

Austin and Walster conclude: 'subjects who were treated equitably were more content and satisfied than were subjects who were either over- or under-rewarded. This finding adds significantly to equity theory, particularly since many critics have been sceptical that inequity would be disturbing to over-rewarded as well as under-rewarded persons' (p. 215).

It is not possible here to provide further information on equity research. A bibliography and discussion is available in Adams and Freedman (1976). The most recent comprehensive source is the monograph by Walster, Walster, and Berschied (1978).

Table 5.5 *Mean change in effect as measured by the mood adjective check list*

Reward Condition	Expectancy			M
	$1	$2	$3	
$1	−1.23	−18.31	−25.08	−14.87
$2	2.46	7.31	2.69	4.15
$3	1.92	− 4.60	3.54	0.28

Source: Austin and Walster (1974, p. 211).

5.4 Laboratory Experiments in the Economics Literature

The institution of wage-bargaining is difficult to capture adequately in a laboratory experiment, because individual subjects know that the conditions are artificial, and because only in the ideal experiment could they be real-life union and management negotiators. However, wage-bargaining also has one unusual and useful characteristic. There is a group of men and women who spend their lives settling actual bargaining disputes — professional labour arbitrators. An experiment performed with such a group of subjects has an opportunity to use the distilled knowledge of many bargaining encounters.

Bazerman (1985) sets up such an experiment. His results provide, in an unconventional way, further support for the thesis that wages are linked to profitability.

Twenty-five hypothetical cases of wage disagreement were constructed. Seven main elements were included in the information on each case. Those elements were:

(1) the inflation rate,
(2) the financial health of the firm (specified as terrible, poor, fair, good, or excellent),
(3) the average wage in the local area,
(4) management's final offer before bargaining impasse,
(5) workers' final offer before bargaining impasse,

(6) the present (i.e. inherited) wage in the company,
(7) the average pay increase elsewhere in the industry.

For each of these there were five different values and, to aid later interpretations, Bazerman imposed the requirement that his twenty-five cases have variables which were orthogonal (that they had zero correlation). By way of example, one of the hypothetical cases was as follows:

In a town with 102,000 people, workers with similar skills and backgrounds to the employees of this radio and broadcasting company were paid $8.31 per hour, while the national wage for this industry was $8.23 per hour. The financial outlook for this company is fair in light of the 11 per cent inflation. The present average wage for this company's union is $8.44 per hour. Contract negotiations have reached an impasse. Both sides, however, have agreed to submit final offers to you, the arbitrator, and to be bound by your decision for a period of 1 year. Comparable pay increases from collective bargaining agreements in the industry are running about 8 per cent this year, management's final offer is $8.56 (a 1.4 per cent increase) while the union's final offer is $9.55 (a 13.2 per cent increase). (Bazerman, (1985, p. 564).)

Each participating arbitrator was sent twenty-five such simulated examples and had to indicate his or her recommended wage settlement. All had also to assign a subjective weight to each of the seven categories.

These hypothetical case details were mailed to each of the members of the US National Academy of Arbitrators plus participants at a regional meeting of the American Arbitrators Association. This yielded sixty-nine usable responses. Arbitrators' judgements about the twenty-five appropriate wage-rates were then used as data in multiple regression equations — one for each arbitrator. The R^2 in such a regression measures the 'consistency' of the arbitrator across the twenty-five cases. The coefficients on the variables correspond to their (estimated) implied importance in shaping arbitrators' decisions.

Of particular importance for our study is the fact that the financial health of the firm was accorded an important role by Bazerman's sample of professional arbitrators. It was ranked first out of seven in the subjective ranking, and third out of seven in the objective one. The average weights (drawn from Bazerman (1985, table 2)) were as shown in Table 5.6.

Table 5.6

	Objective weight (%)	Subjective weight (%)
Inflation rate	4	15
Financial health	20	22
Local wages	7	10
Managers' offer	13	9
Workers' offer	5	11
Wage increases elsewhere	21	16
Present wage	30	17
TOTAL (approx.)	100	100

Bazerman notes the importance of the present wage. This is a kind of fixed effect, however, and presumably embodies past values of the other six variables. Hence it seems appropriate to see the firm's financial performance as one of the two most important factors moulding wage outcomes.

Bazerman's methodology is different from that used in most of the research literature. Moreover, arbitrators' views and actions may not satisfactorily represent the workings of normal wage negotiations, in which no arbitrator is used. Our judgement, even so, is that Bazerman (1985) contributes further confirmation that pay is likely to move with company prosperity. Arbitrators may well behave like real world bargainers.

Another source of information on the economic consequences of fairness is Kahneman, Knetsch, and Thaler (1986). The authors gathered data, using telephone surveys of randomly selected residents of Toronto and Vancouver, about people's reactions to the behaviour of companies in hypothetical circumstances. Not all of the constructed examples concerned wage-rates, but all followed a similar pattern.

Kahneman *et al.* report a number of questions. Two (drawn from p. 733 and using their numbering) are as follows: '*Question 9a*: A small company employs several workers and has been paying them average wages. There is severe unemployment in the area and the company could easily replace its current employees with good workers at a lower wage. The company has been making money. The owners reduce the current workers' wage by 5 per cent.'

Respondents' reactions (N = 195)
    Acceptable   23 per cent
    Unfair   77 per cent

'*Question 9b*: As for question 9a, except: The company has been losing money. The owners reduce the current workers' wages by 5 per cent.'

Respondents' reactions
    Acceptable   68 per cent
    Unfair   32 per cent

It is possible to be sceptical of telephone surveys using questions such as these. Nevertheless, the method may give broadly correct information, and it constitutes one form of evidence. Kahneman *et al.* draw the conclusion that 'when the profit of the employer in the labour transaction falls below the reference level, reduction of even nominal wages becomes acceptable' (p. 733). The different perceptions engendered by the phrase 'The company has been losing money' in question 9 is certainly striking.

Another example created by the authors was the case of Mr Green, a gardener employing two workers at $7 per hour, who discovers that other equally competent workers are willing to work for him at $6 per hour.

Respondents were divided into 2 groups:

(i) those told Mr Green's business was doing well, and
(ii) those told his business was doing poorly.

When asked what would be fair behaviour on Mr Green's part, two-thirds of group (ii) considered it fair for pay to fall (or for workers to be replaced), whilst among group (i) only one-quarter took that view.

Kahneman, Knetsch, and Thaler (1987) document similar examples in fields outside the labour market. They conclude that equivalent rules of fairness apply in industrial pricing and in the fixing of housing rents.

5.5 Britons' Attitudes

One last form of evidence exists. It comes from the British Social Attitude Survey of 1986, which enquired into, among other things, Britons' views about company profits. The Survey, described in Jowell, Witherspoon, and Brook (1987), was designed to cover a representative sample of adults aged 18 and over, living in private households in Great Britain. For practical reasons it was confined to those living in households included in the electoral register. Fieldwork was done after the February 1986 register came into effect.

In 1986 the Survey interviewed approximately 3,100 people. Of these, a subsample of 1,548 individuals was asked the following question:

Suppose a big British firm made a large profit in a particular year. Which one of these things . . . should be its . . . priority?

1. Increase dividends to shareholders
2. Give the employees a pay rise
3. Cut the price of its products
4. Invest in new machinery
5. Improve employees' working conditions
6. Research into new products
7. Invest in employee training
8. Give management a bonus
9. None of these.

Only 5 per cent failed to give one of the answers between 1 and 8.

The second most common answer was: 'Give employees a pay rise' (though individuals did not believe that firms would translate 'should' into 'would'). Individuals thought that only 'Invest in new machinery' should get higher priority. Approximately one-third of the 1,548 respondents said that, of the nine available categories, category 2 (a pay rise) should be ranked either top or second to top. It is not possible to calculate how the pay-rise option was viewed by those who saw it as of lower priority.

These British results accord well with the findings for Canada of Kahneman, Knetsch, and Thaler (1986). Both are compatible with the ideas of equity theory, although they do not constitute a test. It seems that — as introspection suggests — individuals think it morally right that workers' pay should move with profits.

5.6 Conclusions

Equity theory, a standard part of social psychology, and the evidence of Bazerman (1985), Kahneman *et al.* (1986), and Jowell *et al.* (1987), suggests reasons why a firm's profitability might feed through into higher wage-rates. Adams's equity theory, for example, predicts that any decision-maker will compare his or her own reward/input ratio with others' ratios. This implies that a manager whose company's profits increase may feel it right, *ceteris paribus*, to raise its workers' rewards. Those employees, too, will see that as just.

Economists are unaccustomed to theoretical ideas which are not rooted in utility maximization. With some exceptions, they have also traditionally been suspicious of links with psychologists' research. However, as this chapter has shown, laboratory experiments do not reject the psychological model proposed by Adams and others, and they suggest that there are profit effects upon pay. Empirical evidence confirms our intuitions about what is equitable and how that shapes behaviour. There is even some evidence that people dislike being rewarded unjustifiably.

It is possible to be critical of this branch of the social-psychology-cum-economics literature. Much of the research has been done with relatively small samples of subjects, testing hypotheses which are not always clearly defined, in conditions which the typical economist might see as artificial. At the very least, however, the work summarized in this chapter is suggestive. Equity is a concept which economists may have neglected unjustly.

6

The Seniority Model of Wage Determination

6.1 Introduction

The purpose of this chapter is to set out a theoretical model of wage determination which can be used empirically. The framework proposed here is chosen principally because it appears to conform to the stylized facts of industrialized labour markets. Although any list of such facts may be criticized, the following one does not seem unreasonable.

(1) There is regular bargaining, between firms and their workers, about pay and conditions of work.
(2) Except in special circumstances, firms set the numbers of jobs (and the level of investment) unilaterally. This is a logical puzzle, because (according to Leontief (1946) and McDonald and Solow (1981)) in general that is inefficient.
(3) Involuntary lay-offs are typically done by inverse seniority within the plant or firm (so-called 'last in, first out').
(4) Under normal conditions wages are slow-moving: the real wage is one of the least volatile economic variables.
(5) Exceptional recessions can, at the plant level, produce extreme cuts in pay ('concession bargaining'). This occurs when a large proportion of employees face the prospect of redundancy.

Most of these stylized facts are documented in industrial-relations and labour economics textbooks, and in Chapter 3 above. Evidence for the United States and Great Britain is contained also in, for example, Daniel and Millward (1983), Hartman (1965), Farber (1986), Freeman and Medoff (1984), Abraham and Medoff (1985), Oswald (1987), and Oswald and Turnbull (1985). Slichter, Healy, and Livernash (1960) is an early classic.

It is worth noting that many of the models described in Chapter

2 do not allow for the existence of wage negotiations, namely of pay-bargaining. The reason is probably that they were largely developed by US theorists who live in an economy in which four out of five workers are not members of a trade union. For Europe, Australia, and, to a degree, Canada and Japan, this is inappropriate. Large sections of these economies have rates of pay which are fixed by bargains between management and employees.

When bargaining is a central feature of an economy, it is natural to see the process of wage determination as one in which there is rent-sharing between two sides. The firm would like to lower wages. The workers, through their union, would like to raise wages. This conflict of objectives has been discussed by political scientists, politicians, and economists for at least two centuries, and it is not possible in this chapter to explore all its ramifications. The object here is to construct a simple and tractable microeconomic model.

If, as some of the evidence in Chapter 3 suggests, non-union workers earn non-competitive rents, it may be appropriate to analyse their pay as the outcome of an *implicit* bargain. As Pencavel (1985) and others have pointed out, union models have wider application than might be first apparent. The framework developed below need not be thought of as suitable only for the study of unionized markets, although that will be its ostensible focus.

6.2 The Seniority Model

The model is based on the following idea. A majority of workers (the seniors) feel themselves almost entirely insulated from the threat of job loss, and so wish simply to push the wage as high as possible. Their employer earns greater profit if the wage is low, so opposes the workers' aims. Relative bargaining strength then determines the outcome. If the firm is highly profitable, it is easier for employees to extract substantial wage-rates. Their bargaining position is weakened, however, by the existence of any unemployment in the external labour market.

Consider a trade union which agrees with the employer that reductions in the labour force will be by inverse seniority within the firm. A key question is what form of contract this will produce.

It is helpful to begin by thinking of behaviour as being determined by a median-voter rule. The median individual is in this case the person with median seniority (setting aside, as a simplification, any differences in tastes), who is, by definition, half-way down the employment roster.

Fig. 6.1 describes the trade union's preferences in a world of this kind. Wages and employment are on the axes, and the diagram assumes that all workers are equally productive and get the same wage-rate (this assumption could be dropped by adapting a framework such as in Oswald (1984)). The employment level n^s is the median voter's seniority position. For employment points above n^s, this median individual always has a job; for all employment points below that the median voter is necessarily unemployed. Hence region A, the unbounded rectangle above the horizontal line segment On^s, is an indifference zone. The trade union (whose interests here are exactly represented by those of this particular member) does not care which wage-rate, w, or amount of employment, n, holds within the A region. To the right of n^s there are horizontal indifference curves, because the median person is always employed and therefore cares only about the rate of pay. Line I_2 denotes a higher utility than line I_1. For employment levels above n^s this kind of union is indifferent about the total number of jobs.

Assume that — to keep the analytical structure simple — there is no uncertainty and only a single period. A conventional assumption about the employer's preferences is that they can be depicted as concave iso-profit contours (McDonald and Solow

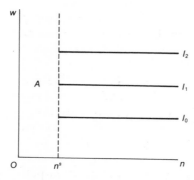

Fig 6.1.   *The union's preference under lay-offs by seniority*

(1981), for example). By definition, then, there is a labour demand curve, dd', given by the locus of the turning-points of these curves. If, in the extreme case, profits are always driven down to some minimum level ($\bar{\pi}$, say), perhaps by costless entry or the threat of entry, the efficient equilibrium is where union utility is maximized subject to that amount of entrepreneurial profit. In the more plausible case, profit depends on bargaining strength. Both cases are considered below.

An efficient outcome can then take two possible forms, and they are described geometrically, as e and e', in Figs. 6.2 and 6.4. The more plausible case, the former, is where the union's indifference curves are tangent to the appropriate iso-profit contour. It is likely to be a Pareto-optimal outcome only in the partial equilibrium sense (one agent's utility is maximized against the other's), but in conventional terminology is an efficient contract. The contract's principal feature is that it is on the labour demand curve. The trade union is locally indifferent to the level of employment; the firm's profits are affected by employment; hence an efficient agreement allows the employer to pick exactly the number of jobs which would have been chosen, given the wage, in an atomistic labour market.

Although this discussion has been in terms of a median voter, that assumption is not necessary to the model. All that is required is that, over a range, some majority know themselves to be insulated from job cuts. Almost any voting system with a known lay-off ordering will produce this.

Fig. 6.2 depicts geometrically a central feature of the analysis. Because (by majority voting and lay-offs by seniority) both the union and the bulk of employees are indifferent to the level of employment, an efficient institutional framework is one in which there is wage-bargaining and the employer fixes the number of jobs unilaterally. This appears to offer a solution to the contradiction — noted years ago — between the presumed efficiency of labour contracts and the empirical lack of employment negotiation. The model also has the property that the trade union will take no direct interest in the elasticity of labour demand, and that a union's preferences can be thought of merely as the desire always for higher wages. Moreover, unlike most other union models, this framework has the apparently realistic property that the union will not shrink over time. The interior solution of Fig. 6.2 is a steady state. It is not the case, in the seniority model developed in this chapter, that the median voter is on the edge of being laid off, nor that the union will shrink each period.

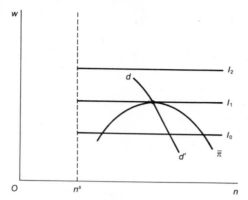

Fig 6.2.   *An interior solution: an efficient contract on the labour demand curve*

A huge decline in demand, which threatens the jobs of large numbers of seniors, will generate so-called concessions bargaining. Fig. 6.3 depicts this extreme form of equilibrium. Employment is then at n^s. It is clear, however, that only a startling market shock could produce a corner allocation like the one in the figure, because the initial employment level was twice as high. Note that n^s could not be a long-run equilibrium in a model with many periods. At the start of the next period there would be a new

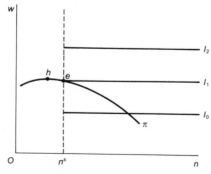

Fig 6.3.   *A corner solution: employment equal to the median voter's seniority*

median voter, at a point equidistant between 0 and n^s, who would wish to impose a much lower number of jobs. With the iso-profit curve $\bar{\pi}$ unchanged, in fact, a point like h would be set, which takes us back to the structural form in Fig. 6.2. Corner equilibria are likely to be exceptional.

The comparative statics of the elementary version — fixed profit — of the model are straightforward. First, a rise in the price of output (an improvement in product demand) leads to an increased equilibrium wage-rate. Second, equilibrium employment is reduced by a rise in the output price, which is a result that is formally identical to the famous 'perverse' employment behaviour documented in the theoretical literature on labour managed firms (Vanek (1970), for example). Fig. 6.4 shows the change in the $\bar{\pi}$ iso-profit contour, from $\bar{\pi}_a$ to $\bar{\pi}_b$, after an increase in the price of output.

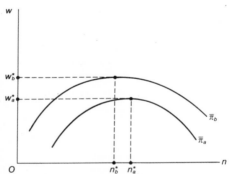

Fig 6.4.   *The effects of an increase in product price (p^a to p^b)*

To check these predictions, it is convenient to write the model in simple form as

$$\text{Maximize } u(w)$$
$$w, n \tag{1}$$
$$\text{s.t. } pf(n) - wn \geq \bar{\pi} \tag{2}$$
$$n - n^s \geq 0, \tag{3}$$

where p is the product price, w is the wage rate, n is employment, $f(n)$ is output and $\bar{\pi}$ is the exogenously fixed market rate of profit. Define a maximum profit function

$$\pi(w, p) = \max_{n} pf(n) - wn, \tag{4}$$

which is homogenous of degree one in (w, p), convex, decreasing in w and increasing in p. Assume it is appropriately differentiable. The problem can be reformulated as that of

$$\text{Maximize } u(w) \tag{5}$$
$$w$$

$$\text{s.t. } \pi(w, p) \geq \bar{\pi} \tag{6}$$

$$n - n^s \geq 0. \tag{7}$$

As long as the first contraint binds, as we should expect, there is only a single wage which will satisfy that constraint. Let it be w^*. Then it follows that, as long as we can ignore corners at $n = n^s$,

$$\frac{dw^*}{dp} = -\frac{\pi_p}{\pi_w} > 0, \tag{8}$$

which establishes the result that wages rise as product prices improve.

The perverse employment prediction can be proved in a number of ways. To use the maximum profit function we need to show that

$$\frac{dn^*}{dp} = \frac{d}{dp}(-\pi_w) \bigg| \pi = \bar{\pi} \tag{9}$$

$$= -\pi_{wp} + \pi_{ww}\frac{\pi_p}{\pi_w} \tag{10}$$

is negative. Because $\pi(w, p)$ is homogenous of degree one,

$$p\pi_p + w\pi_w = \pi \tag{11}$$

$$p\pi_{pw} + w\pi_{ww} = 0, \tag{12}$$

so that, after substitution, and for profit fixed at $\bar{\pi} > 0$, we find that

$$\frac{dn^*}{dp} = \pi_{ww}\left[\frac{w}{p} + \frac{\pi_p}{\pi_w}\right] < 0. \tag{13}$$

Employment falls as the product price increases.

6.2.1. *Bargaining*

A more realistic version of the seniority model, however, is one in which the wage is fixed by the relative bargaining strengths of the two parties. It is convenient to assume that the bargain takes a

Nash solution, which can be justified axiomatically, as in Nash (1953), or strategically, as in Binmore, Rubinstein, and Wolinsky (1986).

Define the status quo or disagreement points of the union and the firm as, respectively, $\hat{u}$ and $\hat{\pi}$. The equilibrium outcome is then given, ignoring corners, by the solution to the symmetric Nash problem (which is easily generalized)

$$\text{Maximize } [u(w) - \hat{u}] [\pi(w, p) - \hat{\pi}], \qquad (14)$$

where, as before, $\pi(w, p)$ is a maximum profit function. It is straightforward to show that the equilibrium wage is an increasing function of the union's status quo utility, a decreasing function of the firm's status quo profit, and an ambiguously signed function of product price.

Again the union and firm have diametrically opposed preferences. One wants a high wage, the other a low wage. The trade union does not weigh up any likely negative consequences for employment (which conforms to Ross's (1948) view that unions take no heed of labour demand curves). The reason is that, around the bargaining equilibrium, the workers do not have the power to raise the wage by very much. Senior workers could not 'price themselves out of jobs' even if they wished to do so, and are unaffected by small declines in employment. These and other aspects of the model are discussed, from different positions, by Turnbull (1988), Disney and Gospel (1988), and Carruth and Oswald (1988).

This model generates the prediction that pay is a function of the profitability of the firm. It is misleading to think of high profits as in a simple sense contemporaneously causing high wages, because the two are determined simultanenously. But profit and pay can accurately be seen as positively related in equilibrium. In this case the appropriate measure of profitability is the per capita difference between $\pi(w, p)$ and $\hat{\pi}$, namely the difference between maximum profit and status quo or delay profit. The proof is as follows.

The first order condition for the Nash maximization in equation (14) is

$$u'(w)[\pi(w, p) - \hat{\pi}] + [u(w) - \hat{u}] \pi_w = 0 \qquad (15)$$

where the requirement for a maximum rather than a minimum is

$$u''(w)[\pi(w, p) - \hat{\pi}] + 2u'(w) \pi_w + [u(w) - \hat{u}] \pi_{ww} < 0,$$

which will hold except when $\pi_{ww} > 0$, an absolute measure of the slope of the labour demand curve, is unusually large.

Equation (15) may be rewritten as a function linking workers' remuneration to profit. By duality theory, employment is

$$n = -\pi_w,$$

so that, more concisely, equation (15) becomes

$$u'(w)\left[\pi - \hat{\pi}\right] - [u(w) - \hat{u}]n = 0 \qquad (15')$$

where for simplicity terms in the maximum profit function have been suppressed. Dividing (15') throughout by n, rearranging, and using a definition of adjusted (net of status quo) profit per employee given by

$$\pi^a \equiv \frac{\pi - \hat{\pi}}{n},$$

equation (15') becomes an implicit function linking w and π^a, namely

$$u(w) = \hat{u} + u'(w)\pi^a. \qquad (16)$$

This is of some importance. It implies that the bargained wage depends both upon status quo (or disagreement) utility and upon adjusted profit.

Equation (16) defines a function relating pay to a measure of the firm's financial performance. The variable π^a describes the per capita amount of the surplus of actual profit over the status quo or disagreement profit. If $\hat{\pi}$ is the negative of fixed costs, π^a is labour's value-added per person. Crucially, the wage is an increasing function of adjusted profit. Differentiating implicitly throughout equation (16), treating π^a as a parameter, gives the gradient

$$\frac{dw}{d\pi^a} = \frac{u'(w)}{u'(w) - u''(w)\,\pi^a} > 0,$$

which (granted $\pi^a > 0$) is positive and less than unity. In this model, therefore, there is *de facto* profit-sharing.

One special case is illuminating. Assume that the representative senior worker is risk-neutral, so that the Nash maximand is

$$\text{Maximize } (w - \hat{w})\,(\pi(w, p) - \hat{\pi}).$$
$$w$$

It then follows that the equilibrium wage is simply

$$w = \hat{w} + \pi^a, \qquad (16')$$

namely, the sum of an external wage-level and an adjusted level of profit per employee. The equilibrium rate of pay depends upon a mixture of what in Carruth and Oswald (1987a) we refer to as 'external' and 'internal' pressures. The former stem from conditions in the outside labour market. The latter are in the spirit of Slichter (1950) and others (see Chapter 3), and depend on the performance of the individual firm itself.

Useful discussions of related bargaining models are provided by Holden (1987), Moene (1988), and Holmlund and Skedinger (1988). The latter is critical of the seniority model.

It might be thought that the natural way for equations such as (16) and (16') to be implemented is by way of an explicit profit-sharing scheme. Although many schemes exist in British establishments (see Blanchflower and Oswald (1988b)), their quantitative importance is small. The same appears to be true of other countries.

6.3 Implementing the Model

To implement the model empirically it is necessary to reduce it to one or more equations for estimation. Variables such as taxes, and other factors and costs of production, must also be incorporated.

Let the union's utility be defined locally by

$$u = u(w, t_2) \qquad (17)$$

where w is the real wage, t_2 is the rate of income tax, and the function $u(..)$ is increasing in the first argument and decreasing in the second.

The firm's objective function is assumed to be

$$\pi = R(n, k, m, t_1, t_3, \alpha) - wn - rk - p^m m - F \qquad (18)$$

where $R(.)$ measures revenue from sales, n is employment, k is capital, m is imported inputs, t_1 is the rate of tax on employment, t_3 is the indirect tax rate, r is the price of capital, p^m is the price of imported inputs, F is fixed costs, and α is a demand shift variable.

Define a restricted profit function

$$\pi^* \, (k, \, \alpha, \, t_1, \, t_3, \, w, \, r, \, p^m, \, F) = \max_{n, \, m} \pi \qquad (19)$$

which maximizes out the employment and imported input levels. Then this function represents the employer's preferences. Equation (17) represents the union's, or senior workers', preferences.

Assume that the wage-bargaining process can be modelled as a Nash bargain of form:

$$\underset{w}{\text{Maximize}} \, (\pi^* - \hat{\pi}) \, (u - \hat{u}) \qquad (20)$$

where $\hat{\pi}$ and $\hat{u}$ are again the profit and utility levels in the event of some delay in negotiating a settlement, or the status quo levels.

The notion of bargaining power enters this framework through these fall-back utilities. An agent which can, by delaying, impose severe costs on the other has negotiating power. Costs can be thought of as the gap between the utility from settlement and that from delay. Thus the greater is $\hat{\pi}$ for the firm ($\hat{u}$ for the union), the stronger is its ability to bargain.

There is no well-developed theory of the determinants of $\hat{\pi}$, $\hat{u}$. The following assumptions are made here. First, it is assumed that

$$\hat{\pi} = \hat{\pi} \, (rk + F), \qquad (21)$$

so that the firm's fall-back utility depends upon the extent of capital plus other fixed costs. Implicit in this is the fact that during a strike the employer has to cover these kinds of costs, but not labour and imported input costs. Output during a strike or other delay is assumed to be zero.

Equivalent forces affect employees. If there is a strike, workers may be able to find some other kind of employment. A union's fall-back or delay utility level is assumed to be determined according to the function

$$\hat{u} = \hat{u} \, (L, \, N, \, \rho, \, w^s), \qquad (22)$$

in which L is the labour force in the economy, N is the number of jobs in the economy, ρ is the 'replacement ratio' of unemployment benefit to the wage, and w^s is the wage available in other sectors. A worker on strike (or his or her spouse) has a greater chance *ceteris paribus* of finding temporary work (i) the lower the labour force, (ii) the greater the total number of jobs, (iii) the higher are unemployment benefits, which reduces the intensity of others' search for work, and (iv) the lower are wages elsewhere, which also reduces other workers' desire for jobs.

Unemployment may be defined as a function of employment and the labour force:

$$U \equiv (L - N)/L. \tag{23}$$

Hence the fall-back utility equation may be written with N substituted out, whereupon

$$\hat{u} = u\,(L, U, \rho, w^s). \tag{24}$$

This will be used at a later point in the empirical work. It is worth noting that our earlier work in Carruth, Oswald, and Findlay (1986) suggests that without such an assumption a seniority model is empirically unsatisfactory.

The solution to the Nash maximization, equation (20), then draws upon equations (17), (19), (21), and (24). That solution defines an equilibrium wage function, at the aggregate level, of form

$$w = w\,(k, \alpha, t_1, t_2, t_3, r, p^m, F, L, U, \rho) \tag{25}$$

where, to recapitulate,

k	= capital stock
α	= demand shock
t_1	= labour tax rate
t_2	= income tax rate
t_3	= indirect tax rate
r	= price of capital
p^m	= price of imported inputs
F	= fixed costs
U	= unemployment rate
ρ	= replacement ratio
L	= labour force

All variables are to be thought of as real. Homogeneity requires that price deflators may be used.

This wage equation is similar to that in Layard and Nickell (1986) and may be estimated on time-series data. One measure of prosperity in the product market which enters directly is the demand shift variable, α. Profitability *per se* is not then an independent variable. If, however, empirical information on α is difficult to collect, and profits data are available, the latter may serve as a proxy for the state of demand, or a proxy for expected demand. This is one way in which profitability in a wage equation may be justified.

An alternative way to justify the inclusion of a profit variable is to appeal to equations such as (16) and (22). The outside wage, w^s, might be modelled as in equation (25).

There are two further ways in which a rationale can be provided. The more unconventional is a psychological or sociological one. It assumes that employees have feelings about the fair level of profit.

Assume, in line with the psychology literature described in Chapter 5, that workers compare their own rewards to those which accrue to the company. Define the union's (or senior worker's) utility as

$$u = u(w, t_2, \pi^\ell) \qquad (26)$$

in which π^ℓ is a measure of the firm's profits in the past (so π^ℓ is lagged profitability). It is plausible, if workers experience feelings of unfairness or relative deprivation as their employer becomes richer, to make the following assumption about the partial derivatives:

$$u_{\pi^\ell} < 0 \qquad (27)$$

$$u_{w\pi^\ell} > 0. \qquad (28)$$

The first assumes that employers feel worse off, at any given wage, the higher are their firm's profits. The second assumes that workers value an extra pound more highly the greater are their firm's profits. By assumption, there is a delay before workers observe profits, which is why π^ℓ rather than π enters, but this is inessential.

Consider the revised version of the Nash maximization where 'jealously' is incorporated. It takes the form (supressing most arguments):

$$\underset{w}{\text{Maximize}} \ (\pi^* - \hat{\pi})(u(w, t_2, \pi^\ell) - \hat{u}). \qquad (29)$$

The first-order condition is then

$$\pi^*_w (u(w, t_2, \pi^\ell) - \hat{u}) + (\pi^* - \hat{\pi}) u_w(w, t_2, \pi^\ell) = 0 \qquad (30)$$

The sign of the comparative static response of wages to lagged profits is given by the formula

$$\text{sgn} \frac{\partial w}{\partial \pi^\ell} = \text{sgn} \{\pi^*_w u_{\pi^\ell} + (\pi^* - \hat{\pi}) u_{w\pi^\ell}\} > 0, \qquad (31)$$

which is positive under the assumptions made.

Although this analysis is consistent with the kind of discussion reported in Chapter 3 on actual negotiations, most economists would consider it unusual. The mechanism at work relies on the idea — related to equity theory — that workers find it unacceptable if their company becomes richer and does not pass on some of the gains. A rise, say, in profits is observed after some time-lag. Employees then feel worse off, because they compare their own efforts and returns with those of the employer. The fair solution is for some of the high profits to be shared out in the form of larger wage payments. According to this model, wage equation (25) must be extended to incorporate a measure of past profitability:

$$w = w (k, \alpha, t_1, t_2, t_3, r, p^m, F, L, U, \rho, \pi^\ell) \qquad (32)$$

This encompasses (25) and makes a convenient form for estimation.

A further reason why pay might depend upon *past* profit levels is because of workers' expectations. Assume that employees must make guesses about their company's future prosperity, and that they look in part at previous financial performance. Then a firm which has done well in the previous period will be predicted, other things constant, to do well in the future. The simplest assumption would be that profits follow a random walk.

The objective of this section has been to suggest a variety of reasons why some measures of profitability might enter an econometric wage equation. It is not possible, using aggregate time-series data, to test among them. Chapter 7 investigates the more fundamental question of whether there is time-series evidence for this class of effects.

6.4 Conclusions

The model developed here is influenced by the stylized facts of wage-bargaining. It assumes that the institution of lay-offs by seniority insulates a core of workers from the possibility of job loss. These senior workers, who make up the majority, dominate their trade union and thus shape its preferences. In consequence, the union acts as if it wishes simply to raise pay, rather than employment, and allows the employer to set the number of jobs unilaterally. Efficient bargains then lie on the labour demand curve, which offers a solution to the inefficiency puzzle noted by Leontief (1946) and McDonald and Solow (1981), among others.

In this framework the firm wishes to keep wage-rates down and the trade union attempts to push them up. The wage which emerges is determined by relative bargaining strength. High external unemployment rates reduce workers' relative negotiating power. High capital and other fixed costs reduce firms' relative negotiating power.

Wage-rates depend in part upon employers' financial prosperity. Equation (16) reveals that the bargained wage is directly shaped by both profit per employee and the status quo or disagreement income level of workers. There are, however, two other ways in which a profitability effect may work. Profits (possibly lagged) could be expected to enter a wage equation because

(1) profitability is a proxy for the state of product demand,
(2) workers' utility depends directly, for reasons of equity or fairness, upon the size of their employers' rewards.

These arguments, when embedded in the framework of the earlier sections, suggest an eclectic reduced-form wage equation of the kind described above. Such an equation is consistent with, but is not a narrowly defined test of, the seniority model of wage determination.

7

Empirical Results for Britain

7.1 Introduction

This chapter applies the theoretical ideas of Chapter 6. Post-war British data are used. Although the majority of the regression equations draw upon annual statistics, quarterly equations are also presented.

Recent work by Layard and Nickell (1986) provides both a foundation and a benchmark for an empirical study of wage determination in Britain. Our tests rely in large part upon their data set and, like a number of other new studies, we attempt to encompass the authors' wage equation. The results given in the chapter also build upon the preliminary investigations reported in Carruth and Oswald (1987a). The central questions will include the following.

(1) Does the wage-rate depend upon the level of profitability? If so, what is the elasticity?

(2) Do real wages fall as unemployment rises, and if so, by how much?

(3) What other factors shape the real wage in Great Britain?

(4) Can we explain the real wage growth of the 1980s?

Number (1) captures the possibility that pay may be affected by 'internal' pressure; number (2) does the equivalent for 'external' pressure.

Our first econometric estimation was done in the summer of 1986. At around the same time, Richard Layard (LSE) and Stephen Nickell (Oxford), and John Muellbauer (Oxford) and co-researchers, began their own inquiries into why British real wages were rising so fast and thus what variable was missing from previous specifications. By the winter of 1986/7 all three groups had become aware of the other two. Our own first attempt (Carruth and Oswald (1987a)), however, was written before that and is encompassed by the equations reported later in this chapter. Halfway through the project, therefore, it was necessary to try to include the variables (long-term unemployment and house prices) which the other teams had begun to advocate. As it turned out, a general specification performed well, and this shaped our later work.

Fig. 1.1 in Chapter 1 shows the close relationship between real earnings and profits, especially when there is a significant downturn in real profits (for instance, the 1975 and 1981 periods). Figs. 7.1 and 7.2 illustrate the movements in real profits, excluding and including North Sea companies respectively (for a full discussion of variable definitions, see Appendix A to this chapter). The most noticeable difference between Figs. 7.1 and 7.2 is the reduced impact of the 1980–1 depression on real profits when North Sea companies are included. It is evident that real-profit levels have grown considerably since 1980. Real profit per employee is the 'missing' variable examined in our empirical investigations.

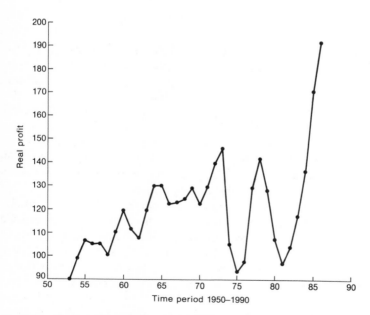

Fig 7.1.   *Real profit excluding North Sea companies 1953–1986*

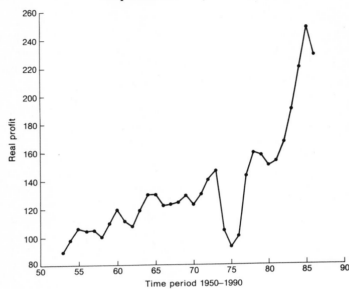

Fig 7.2.   *Total real profit 1953–1986*

Figs. 7.3 and 7.4 present the real product wage-rate and real earnings over the period 1953–86. The series are highly correlated, as we should expect, but the earnings series shows more cyclical sensitivity. While our regression equations concentrate on the explanation of the real product wage, we also include results which explain real earnings.

The missing variable favoured by Layard and Nickell (1986) for the explanation of recent real-wage behaviour is the proportion of long-term unemployed, that is, those unemployed for more than a year as a proportion of total unemployment. Fig. 7.5 shows that this series has increased dramatically since 1980. Bover, Muellbauer, and Murphy (1988) argue that the persistent rises in real wages can be explained by real house prices. Fig. 7.6 demonstrates that house prices have risen fairly consistently since 1977 with one downturn in 1981–2; however, if the influence of house prices works through a geographical mobility (mismatch) problem, then the appropriate variable may be Bover, Muellbauer, and Murphy's measure of regional house price dispersion. We consider both variables in our time-series analysis.

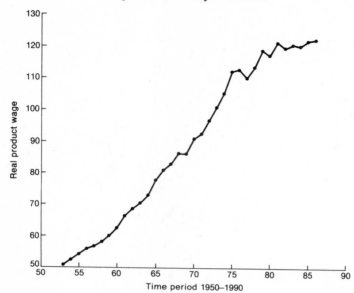

Fig 7.3. *Real product wage 1953–1986*

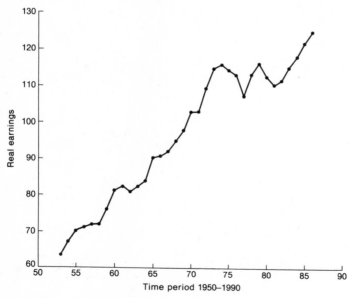

Fig 7.4. *Real earnings 1953–1986*

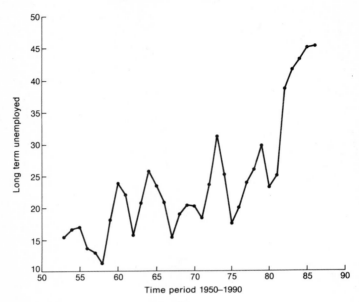

Fig 7.5.   *Stock of long-term unemployed 1953–1986*

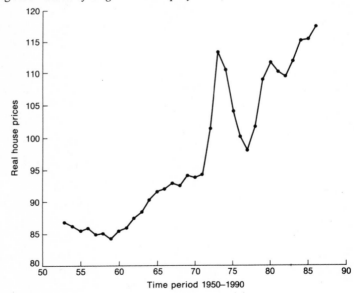

Fig 7.6.   *Real house prices 1953–1986*

The theoretical structure follows from the equations of the previous chapter. They suggest that the real wage will depend upon

(1) the capital stock,
(2) the state of demand,
(3) income, employer, and indirect taxes,
(4) the real interest rate,
(5) import prices,
(6) fixed costs,
(7) the labour force,
(8) the unemployment rate,
(9) the unemployment benefit replacement rate,
(10) profits (lagged).

We also decided to include

(11) the proportion of long-term unemployment,
(12) a house price variable.

Number (11) can be thought of as an adjustment to total unemployment, a composition effect to capture the influence of longer durations of unemployment, which lead to a deterioration of skills, lack of attachment to the labour force, and lower intensity of job search. Number (12) may be considered a labour market 'mismatch' proxy or an adjustment to the price deflator.

The Layard and Nickell (1986) model embodies a natural rate of unemployment or NAIRU. The high unemployment experienced by Britain in the 1980s coexisted with a high level of wage inflation; yet in a natural rate framework, unemployment above the equilibrium level should lead to falling rates of wage inflation. Assuming that the NAIRU has not moved exactly with the actual rise in unemployment, the persistence of British wage inflation in the 1980s raises the possibility that something may have been omitted from the Layard and Nickell (1986) account.

Nickell (1987) provides a detailed analysis of this puzzle. He points out that it is only substantial changes in unemployment (as in 1980–1) which appear to have an obvious effect upon pay-setting. Nickell develops a model in which the duration structure of unemployment helps to shape the real wage. When total unemployment is made up of a disproportionately large number of long-term unemployed individuals (those unemployed for more than one year), downward wage pressure is disproportionately small. This may be because the long-term unemployed have ceased to look actively for work. According to Nickell's model, rises in long term unemployment will, *ceteris paribus*, put upward pressure on wages. The empirical analysis places weight on the rise in 1982 of long-term unemployment of approximately one half.

Bover, Muellbauer, and Murphy (1988) put forward a competing explanation linked to the behaviour of house prices. They argue that there are three ways in which house prices may affect wage settlements. First, house prices, though not included fully in the retail price index, are an important element in the cost of living for many individuals. Second, there is an influence of house prices on labour mobility. Higher house price areas like the South East are not able to attract labour from other regions to fill job vacancies and this adds to labour market mismatch. Finally, house price inflation in excess of retail price inflation may fuel inflationary expectations. Bover, Muellbauer, and Murphy's empirical results find support for a house price variable suitably lagged.

7.2 Empirical Results

The methodological position adopted here is that a successful model of wage determination must encompass earlier empirical work and must have an appropriate dynamic structure. Our estimated model is a generalized version of Layard and Nickell (1986):

$$w_t = a_0 + a_{1i} \sum_{i=1}^{s} w_{t-i} + a_{2i} \sum_{i=0}^{s} k_{t-i} + a_{3i} \sum_{i=0}^{s} \alpha_{t-i} + a_{4i} \sum_{i=0}^{s} t1_{t-i} +$$

$$a_{5i} \sum_{i=0}^{s} t2_{t-i} + a_{6i} \sum_{i=0}^{s} t3_{t-i} + a_{7i} \sum_{i=0}^{s} r_{t-i} + a_{8i} \sum_{i=0}^{s} p^m_{t-i} +$$

$$a_{9i} \sum_{i=0}^{s} U_{t-i} + a_{10i} \sum_{i=0}^{s} L^m_{t-i} + a_{11i} \sum_{i=0}^{s} \pi_{t-i} + a_{12i} \sum_{i=0}^{s} \rho^m_{t-i}$$

+ variables for long-term unemployment and house prices
+ error term,

where w is the real wage, k is the capital stock, α is the demand shock, $t1$ is the labour tax rate, $t2$ is the income tax rate, $t3$ is the indirect tax rate, r is the price of capital, p^m is the price of imported inputs, U is the unemployment rate, ρ is the benefit replacement rate, π is a profitability measure and L is the labour force. This form is close to that in Layard and Nickell (1986).

Our work covered both annual and quarterly data. For the former, it was not possible to consider a truly general dynamic structure. There were not enough degrees of freedom to allow for a complex lag structure. More detailed analysis was feasible for the quarterly data set.

There are a number of ways in which a profit variable could be entered into the regression equation, and various definitions of profits are possible. We adopt what King (1975) calls 'conventional gross profits', namely gross trading profits before depreciation and without an allowance for stock appreciation. Three adjustments are then feasible — allowing respectively for depreciation, stock appreciation, and company taxes. Our experiments suggested that switching from one definition to another made little difference to the time-series results. We deflated gross trading profits by an output price index, and divided by the number of employees in employment, to produce a measure of real profitability per worker. It appears unwise to be overly optimistic about the quality of this variable: figures on declared profits are traditionally unreliable. However, the statistical series may not be devoid of information.

7.2.1. *Annual results*

The annual estimation, following Layard and Nickell (1986), was by instrumental variables. All current dated regressors were thus treated as endogenous (see Appendix A to this chapter for a discussion). As the Statistical Appendix shows, however, a switch to Ordinary Least Squares estimation makes little difference.

Not all of variables (1)–(12) were found to be statistically significant. Equation (1) states our preferred empirical specification. It uses annual data from 1956 to 1983 and has the real product wage as dependent variable. The results are designed to allow comparison with the wage equations presented in work such as Layard and Nickell (1986), Nickell (1987), and Bover, Muellbauer, and Murphy (1988). One slight difference, however, is that the dependent variable in equation (1) includes no 'wedge' term

Equation (1): *Annual*

Real Product Wage Equation	*IV estimation 1956–1983*
ln (unemployment rate$_t$)	−0.07 (9.35)
ln (import/output price index$_t$)	−0.27 (8.14)
ln (capital/labour ratio$_{t-1}$)	1.24 (44.8)
Indirect tax rate$_{t-1}$	0.61 (4.00)
ln (profit per employee$_{t-2}$)	0.05 (3.32)
Proportion of long-term unemployed$_t$	0.10 (1.98)
$\triangle_1$ stock of long-term unemployed$_{t-1}$	−0.17 (2.82)
1n (house price$_{t-2}$)	0.22 (3.61)
Constant	9.56 (97.5)

Model Evaluation Statistics

se = 0.0086	RSS = 0.00144	DW = 2.68
Specification	Chi^2(5)/5	1.74
Forecast	Chi^2(4)/4	0.72
Chow	F(4,15) {OLS}	0.56
Normality	Chi^2(2)	1.03
LM	F(2,17) {OLS}	2.00
Heteroscedasticity		
(square of regressors) F(16,2)		0.08

Notes :

1. t statistics in brackets.

2. All estimation is by David Hendry's program PC-GIVE.

3. An explanation of the model evaluation statistics is given in Appendix B to this Chapter.

calculated from import prices. Those effects are included on the right-hand side instead.

The equation shows the factors which exert a significant statistical impact upon pay in Great Britain. The real wage depends upon the levels of unemployment, import prices, the capital/labour force ratio (which may be thought of as a productivity trend), indirect taxes, profit per employee, the number of long term unemployed as a proportion of total unemployment, and the price of housing. By many standards equation (1) is highly satisfactory. The model evaluation statistics, which provide various diagnostic checks, are well below their critical levels (for a discussion of these statistics see Appendix B to this chapter). The result of the Chow test of parameter stability for the period from 1980 to 1983 — a time of great change in the British economy — is especially strong.

The effect of profitability upon real wages is of particular relevance, and it appears to be pronounced. Profit per worker (where, for this equation, profits include those from North Sea oil) enters in log form with a coefficient of 0.05 and a t statistic above 3. This elasticity appears at first sight to be a small one, but it should be borne in mind that profitability is one of the most volatile of economic variables, whilst the real wage fluctuates relatively little. For example, over the 1980s, real profit per worker has so far doubled, which on these estimates means that as a consequence the real wage, *ceteris paribus,* has risen by 5 per cent over that short period. Later quarterly results, in fact, suggest bigger effects.

A large rise in unemployment from, for example, 7 per cent to 14 per cent will, according to these findings, push down the real wage by 7 per cent. This is close to the effect estimated by Layard and Nickell (1986) and many other recent investigators. This elasticity might again be considered a small one; it gives a precise meaning to, and measure of, so-called wage stickiness. The coefficient's size also suggests a possible reason why some analysts (Beckerman and Jenkinson (1986), for example) have failed to find an effect.

The coefficient on the capital/labour force ration is 1.24 and thus slightly larger than that in, for example, Nickell (1987), which imposes the value of 1.07 for long-run consistency within the Layard-Nickell model of the economy. Indirect taxes work strongly and with a positive sign. In the annual specification it proved impossible to obtain significant effects from other kinds of tax rates.

A question of central importance is whether house prices and long-term unemployment affect the real wage. Nickell (1987) and Layard and Nickell (1986) argue that wage pressure rises as the proportion of long-term unemployment increases. The underlying assumption is that it is only the recently unemployed individuals who look for jobs intensively enough to force down the going level of pay. Bover, Muellbauer, and Murphy (1988) argue that the price of housing should figure in a real-wage equation. One possible reason is that house prices may not be accurately reflected in the retail price index, so that they must be entered independently in the econometric specification. Another possibility, and one favoured by the authors themselves, is that the regional dispersion of house prices may act as a proxy for regional mismatch in the labour market.

As equation (1) makes clear, both of these forces appear to operate. Long-term unemployment works statistically as a change and as a level variable. House prices enter as a level. The steady state coefficients are, respectively, 0.1 and approximately 0.2. The latter elasticity is particularly large.

The dynamic structure of the model is worthy of comment. First, there is no lagged dependent variable, because it was never found to be significant. Second, the unemployment variables work with little or no time-lag. Third, profit per employee and house prices each affect real wages with a lag of two years. It is customary, in modern time-series analysis, to allow the data to determine the lag structure, subject to sensible interpretation. For the profit variable, however, it is possible to suggest an explanation of the two-year delay. Wage determination in Britain is done in advance and by annual negotiation. Moreover, profit statistics for companies appear up to a year after the period to which they apply. This reporting lag, plus the lag caused by yearly wage-bargaining, might be seen as the reason for the lag on profits in the real-wage equation. It may also be that it is expectations of profits which matter and that they are determined by profitability some time ago.

Equation (1) suggests that there are three missing variables from the form of real-wage equation in, for example, Layard and Nickell (1986). They are long-term unemployment, profits, and house prices. To check the robustness of the specification, we experimented by dropping one variable at a time. These experiments are reported in equations (2), (3), and (4).

Equation (2): *Annual*

Real Product Wage Equation	IV estimation 1956–1983
ln (unemployment rate$_t$)	−0.08 (7.23)
ln (import/output price index$_t$)	−0.27 (5.99)
ln (capital/labour ratio$_{t-1}$)	1.24 (34.1)
Indirect tax rate$_{t-1}$	0.75 (3.84)
ln (profit per employee$_{t-2}$)	— —
Proportion of long-term unemployed$_t$	0.13 (2.01)

$\triangle_1$ stock of long-term unemployed$_{t-1}$	−0.18 (2.27)
ln (house price$_{t-2}$)	0.25 (3.42)
Constant	9.52 (77.8)

Model Evaluation Statistics

se = 0.0106	RSS = 0.0022	DW =	1.83
Specification	Chi^2(5)/5		3.08
Forecast	Chi^2(4)/4		13.57
Chow	F(4,16) {OLS}		1.42
Normality	Chi^2(2)		0.36
LM	F(2,18) {OLS}		1.11
Heteroscedasticity			
(square of regressors) F(14,5)			0.38

Equation (2) shows what happens when profit per employee is omitted. The general structure of the model holds up reasonably well: each variable continues to be significant and the coefficients change only marginally. However, the explanatory power of the whole equation is noticeably inferior (the standard error rises from 0.0086 to 0.0106, an increase of approximately 25 per cent). Equation (2) also fails the test denoted Specification, which is Sargan's instrument validity test, and it forecasts the later part of the sample extremely poorly. The evidence suggests that profits per employee, suitably lagged, should enter the real-wage equation, and is consistent with a wealth of other evidence surveyed in earlier chapters.

House prices are dropped in equation (3). Again the result compares unfavourably with equation (1): it fails the Specification test, forecasts badly, and has a standard error of 0.0116. Equation (4) omits both long-term unemployment variables. In this case, interestingly, it is not possible to reject the model. None of the diagnostics quite reach failure levels. However, the standard error of the equation is 0.0100, so explanatory power has been lost by eschewing the equation 1 formulation.

Equation (3): *Annual*

Real Product Wage Equation	*IV estimation 1956–1983*
ln (unemployment rate$_t$)	−0.07 (6.82)
ln (import/output price index$_t$)	−0.20 (5.45)
ln (capital/labour ratio$_{t-1}$)	1.30 (45.6)
Indirect tax rate$_{t-1}$	0.63 (3.07)

ln (profit per employee$_{t-2}$)	0.06 (3.09)
Proportion of long-term unemployed$_t$	0.12 (1.72)
$\triangle_1$ stock of long-term unemployed$_{t-1}$	−0.24 (3.31)
ln (house price$_{t-2}$)	— —
Constant	9.83 (111.5)

Model Evaluation Statistics

se = 0.0116 .	RSS = 0.0027	DW = 2.09
Specification	Chi^2(5)/5	2.30
Forecast	Chi^2(4)/4	15.94
Chow	F(4,16) {OLS}	1.79
Normality	Chi^2(2)	0.25
LM	F(2,18) {OLS}	0.02
Heteroscedasticity		
(square of regressors) F(14,5)		0.24

Equation (4): *Annual*

Real Product Wage Equation	*IV estimation 1956–1983*
ln (unemployment rate$_t$)	−0.06 (6.73)
ln (import/output price index$_t$)	−0.34 (10.2)
ln (capital/labour ratio$_{t-1}$)	1.18 (41.2)
Indirect tax rate$_{t-1}$	0.35 (2.13)
ln (profit per employee$_{t-2}$)	0.05 (2.76)
Proportion of long-term unemployed$_t$	— —
$\triangle_1$ stock of long-term unemployed$_{t-1}$	— —
ln (house price$_{t-2}$)	0.28 (4.45)
Constant	9.45 (93.6)

Model Evaluation Statistics

se = 0.0100	RSS = 0.0021	DW = 2.38
Specification	Chi^2(5)/5	1.02
Forecast	Chi$_2$(4)/4	2.29
Chow	F(4,17) {OLS}	0.34
Normality	Chi^2(2)	0.44
LM	F(2,19) {OLS}	2.99
Heteroscedasticity		
(square of regressors) F(12,8)		0.28

7.2.2. *Quarterly results*

Similar analysis was done on quarterly data. Equation (5) reports the empirical application of the theory of the previous chapter.

Although close to the annual results, the quarterly ones suggested no reliable effect from indirect taxes, but that employer taxes, the unemployment benefit replacement ratio and 'union power' all should enter. The union power variable is Layard and Nickell's (1986) time-series estimate of the union wage differential in Britain.

Equation (5): *Quarterly*

Real Product Wage Equation	*OLS Estimation 1962(1)–1983(4)*
ln (real product wage$_{t-1}$)	0.44 (6.03)
ln (unemployment rate$_{t-4}$)	−0.024 (2.26)
Δ_1 ln (import/output price index$_{t-2}$)	−0.19 (2.60)
ln (capital/labour ratio$_{t-1}$)	0.54 (7.20)
Price surprise$_t$	0.97 (6.48)
Δ_1 employer tax rate$_t$	0.70 (3.59)
Δ_3 proportion of long-term unemployed$_t$	0.0014 (2.08)
ln (profit per employee$_{t-6}$)	0.070 (4.51)
Δ_1 replacement rate$_{t-1}$	0.0058 (3.09)
Replacement rate$_{t-3}$	0.0021 (2.81)
Δ_1 ln (union power$_{t-1}$)	0.53 (1.92)
Δ_1 ln (house price: Lon & SE$_{t-4}$)	0.11 (1.92)
ln (house price: Lon & SE$_{t-7}$)	−0.15 (2.76)
ln (house price: Lon & SE$_{t-8}$)	−0.20 (3.61)
Constant	3.89 (7.18)
+ Seasonals	

Model Evaluation Statistics

se = 0.0172   RSS = 0.0211

Forecast	Chi^2(20)/20	1.25
Chow	F(20,51)	0.59
Normality	Chi^2(2)	0.35
LM	F(5,66)	0.78
Heteroscedasticity (square of regressors) F(30,40)		1.76
Heteroscedasticity (White's) F(27,53)		1.38

As might be expected, the dynamic structure of the quarterly equation is complicated. Again the lag specification was chosen empirically (see Appendix B for a discussion of time-series methodology). A lagged dependent variable works strongly, with a coefficient of just under one half. Unemployment, profits, and the price of housing all come in with lags of at least four quarters, and help to determine the long-run solution. The variables measuring import prices, employer taxes, union power, and the long-term unemployment proportion have only temporary effects. A quarterly earnings equation presented as equation 10 has the long-term unemployment proportion estimated as a level effect, so it will have steady-state implications in this case. Nevertheless, the absence of a level effect in equation (5) is noteworthy.

Profit per employee enters the quarterly real-wage equations with a coefficient of 0.07 and a *t*-statistic above 4. A lag of six quarters easily dominated others (see the estimated equation (9) at a later point for more details). After adjustment for the lagged dependent variable, the profit elasticity of pay can be calculated at approximately 0.13. This is considerably above the estimate derived from annual data. The unemployment elasticity, moreover, has dropped to approximately −0.04 in equation (5).

We examined the possibility that profit should enter only as a difference rather than as a level. Various experiments were done: terms in lagged profitability were dropped systematically from the full autoregressive structure. The strong effect from *t*–6 continued — regardless of which other lagged profit terms were incorporated — to be evident. All our attempts to obtain a profit change effect were rejected by the data.

The 'price surprise' term in equation (5) enters with the expected coefficient of (approximately) unity. It is calculated in the same way as Layard and Nickell's (1986) variable, that is, in terms of the fitted value from a regression explaining inflation (of output prices) in the current period by inflation in the previous four quarters. The capital/labour force ratio has a long run elasticity fairly close to that in the annual estimation. The house price elasticity, in the steady state, is noticeably below that in equation (1). It is less than 0.1, but statistically highly significant.

We did some experiments with a profit variable excluding North Sea oil profits. The two series only diverge significantly at the end of the sample, so it may not be surprising, and is perhaps reassuring, that it makes little difference empirically which variable is included in the regressions. Equation (6) is the equivalent to equation (1) but with profits excluding those from North Sea oil companies. The conclusions are virtually the same. The profit

Equation (6): *Annual*

Real Product Wage Equation	IV estimation 1956–1983
ln (unemployment rate$_t$)	−0.06 (6.76)
ln (import/output price index$_t$)	−0.24 (7.22)
ln (capital/labour ratio$_{t-1}$)	1.20 (39.2)
Indirect tax rate$_{t-1}$	0.70 (4.67)
ln (profit (exc. N Sea oil) ^{a} per employee$_{t-2}$)	0.07 (3.37)
Proportion of long-term unemployed$_t$	0.16 (3.08)
$\triangle_1$ stock of long-term unemployed$_{t-1}$	−0.16 (2.71)
ln (house price$_{t-2}$)	0.23 (3.98)
Constant	9.43 (94.6)

Model Evaluation Statistics

se = 0.0843	RSS = 0.0014	DW =	2.79
Specification	Chi^2(5)/5		1.80
Forecast	Chi^2(4)/4		3.16 (1.70, OLS)
Chow	F(4,15) {OLS}		0.50
Normality	Chi^2(2)		1.00
LM	F(2,17) {OLS}		3.24^b
Heteroscedasticity			
(square of regressors) F(16,2)			0.08

a Note change of definition
b 5 per cent critical value is 3.59

elasticity is slightly greater (than in equation (1)) at 0.07. One slight change is that the proportion of long-term unemployment becomes a somewhat more important variable.

One issue of interest is that of whether it is *expected* profit, rather than actual profit, which should enter the wage equation. Hence we experimented with a variable constructed (in an unrestricted way) from a weighted average of past profit levels. This expected profitability measure was then used as the base-line for the construction of a profit 'surprise' effect. Although the variable entered with the correct positive sign, it was never statistically significant at the 5 per cent level.

Equation (7) reports another variation. In this case the house price variable is altered to one used by Bover, Muellbauer, and Murphy (1988). It is a measure of regional house price dispersion, rather than the absolute level of the house price index, and is an

Equation (7): *Annual*

Real Product Wage Equation	IV estimation 1956–1983
ln (unemployment rate$_t$)	−0.06 (6.76)
ln (import/output price index$_t$)	−0.20 (6.68)
ln (capital/labour ratio$_{t-1}$)	1.22 (39.2)
Indirect tax rate$_{t-1}$	0.60 (3.79)
ln (profit per employee$_{t-2}$)	0.06 (3.86)
Proportion of long-term unemployed$_t$	0.09 (1.67)
$\triangle_1$ stock of long-term unemployed$_{t-1}$	−0.16 (2.67)
Regional house price differential (average of $t-2$ and $t-3$ lags)	0.29 (3.62)
Constant	9.50 (85.2)

Model Evaluation Statistics

se = 0.0908	RSS = 0.0016	DW =	2.71
Specification	Chi^2(5)/5		2.32
Forecast	Chi^2(4)/4		3.94
Chow	F(4,15) {OLS}		0.54
Normality	Chi^2(2)		0.82
LM	F(16,2) {OLS}		1.09
Heteroscedasticity (square of regressors) F(16,2)			0.18

average of the values in periods t–2 and t–3. Equation (7) is almost exactly the same as equation (1). Because of the marginally inferior forecasting performance and equation standard error, however, we prefer the house price level variable and hence the Equation 1 specification.

As a further check we changed the dependent variable to the simpler form of average real earnings (where the deflator was the real price index). This is the variable typically used in policy discussions and by politicians. The results are interesting, if not completely satisfactory. Equation (8) presents the annual case. Despite the change in the dependent variable, and a significant incomes policy dummy in 1977, lagged profits enter in much the same way as before, and the unemployment rate continues to enter strongly negatively. However, long-term unemployment reverses sign, and we find no role for house prices. The equation just fails the Lagrange multiplier test for autocorrelation and has other weaknesses.

Equation (8): *Annual*

Real Earnings Equation	IV estimation 1954–1983
ln (unemployment rate$_t$)	− 0.08 (8.58)
ln (import/output price index$_{t+t-1}$)	− 0.06 (3.06)
Replacement rate$_t$	0.0036 (2.77)
ln (capital/labour ratio$_{t-1}$)	1.28 (19.8)
Employer tax rate	− 1.56 (6.09)
Indirect tax rate	− 0.96 (4.82)
Incomes policy (1977=1)	− 0.0038 (2.58)
ln (profit per employee$_{t-2}$)	0.06 (2.00)
Proportion of long-term unemployed$_{t-1}$	− 0.19 (2.81)
Constant	16.7 (11.9)

Model Evaluation Statistics

se = 0.0113   RSS = 0.0026   DW = 2.49

Specification	Chi^2(5)/5	1.48
Forecast	Chi^2(4)/4	1.32
Chow	F(4,16) {OLS}	0.73
Normality	Chi^2(2)	0.63
LM	F(2,18) {OLS}	3.65
Heteroscedasticity (square of regressors) F(16,3)		0.17

Equation 9 uses quarterly data and presents a full set of lagged profit terms. It reveals the importance of profit levels six quarters earlier. It also demonstrates that the profit terms do not appear to reflect the backward shrinking coefficients of some expectation formulae.

Equation (9): *Quarterly*

Real Product Wage Equation	OLS Estimation 1962(1)–1983(4)
ln (real product wage$_{t-1}$)	0.50 (6.34)
ln (unemployment rate$_{t-4}$)	−0.022 (1.65)
$\triangle_1$ ln (import/output price index$_{t-2}$)	0.24 (3.02)
ln (capital labour ratio$_{t-1}$)	0.52 (5.89)
Price surprise$_t$	1.03 (5.77)
$\triangle_1$ employer tax rate$_t$	0.65 (2.88)
$\triangle_3$ proportion of long-term unemployed$_t$	0.0016 (2.06)
ln (profit per employee$_t$)	−0.038 (1.27)
ln (profit per employee$_{t-1}$)	0.023 (0.68)

ln (profit per employee$_{t-2}$)	0.025 (0.74)
ln (profit per employee$_{t-3}$)	−0.045 (1.44)
ln (profit per employee$_{t-4}$)	−0.0026 (0.08)
ln (profit per employee$_{t-5}$)	0.016 (0.50)
ln (profit per employee$_{t-6}$)	0.085 (2.54)
ln (profit per employee$_{t-7}$)	−0.014 (0.44)
ln (profit per employee$_{t-8}$)	−0.0097 (0.35)
	($\Sigma =$ 0.038)
$\triangle_1$ replacement rate$_{t-1}$	0.0071 (3.40)
Replacement rate$_{t-3}$	0.0028 (3.33)
$\triangle_1$ ln (union power$_{t-1}$)	0.63 (1.80)
Constant	3.91 (6.17)

Model Evaluation Statistics
se = 0.0192   RSS = 0.0243

Forecast	Chi^2(20)/20	1.05
Chow	F(20,46)	0.53
Normality	Chi^2(2)	2.69
LM	F(5,61)	0.82
Heteroscedasticity		
(square of regressors) F(38,27)		0.72
Heteroscedasticity		
(White's) F(27,53)		1.66

The quarterly real-earnings equation is presented as Equation 10. Here we find that profit, long-term unemployment, and house prices are all significant. The equation performs moderately; the forecast and normality tests just fail. The long-run elasticities for the key variables are similar to the real product wage case.

Equation (10): *Quarterly*

Real Earnings Equation	OLS Estimation 1962(1)–1983(4)
ln (earnings$_{t-1}$)	0.77 (14.8)
Employer tax rate$_t$	−0.33 (3.36)
Consumer price surprise$_t$	0.75 (7.15)
ln (unemployment rate$_{t-1}$)	0.050 (3.24)
ln (unemployment rate$_{t-1}$)^3	−0.016 (3.60)
$\triangle_1$ income tax rate$_{t-1}$	0.76 (3.22)
ln (profit per employer$_{t-6}$)	0.040 (3.98)
Proportion of long-term unemployed$_{t-1}$	0.0011 (2.74)
$\triangle_1$ replacement rate$_{t-3}$	0.0026 (2.47)

ln (capital/labour ratio$_{t-2}$)	0.20 (3.29)
ln (house/price Lon & SE$_{t-1}$)	0.091 (3.62)
ln (house/price Lon & SE$_{t-3}$)	−0.116 (3.89)
ln (house/price Lon & SE$_{t-7}$)	0.049 (2.54)
$\triangle_1$ ln (union power$_t$)	−0.037 (2.13)
ln (union power$_{t-1}$)	−0.025 (2.09)
Constant	2.95 (3.76)

Model Evaluation Statistics

se = 0.00951   RSS = 0.0065

Forecast	Chi^2(20)/20	3.05
Chow	F(20,52)	0.58
Normality	Chi^2(2)	6.24
LM	F(5,67)	1.81
Heteroscedasticity (square of regressors) F(29,42)		0.72
Heteroscedasticity (White's) F(27,53)		0.61

7.3 Conclusions

The real-wage rate in Great Britain appears to depend upon the level of past company profits. Although precise estimates are open to objections, our judgement is that the elasticity lies between 0.05 and 0.13, and that it is probably towards the lower end of that band. The lag appears to be one of slightly less than two years.

Many other forces shape the pay of British workers. As Layard and Nickell (1986) first pointed out, real wages follow a productivity trend which seems to be successfully represented by the ratio of capital to the labour force. Unemployment fluctuations move the wage-rate around that trend. Import prices and taxes also play an important role.

Our investigation was stimulated by the growth of real wages in the middle of the 1980s, which seemed to show that a high level of unemployment puts little downward pressure upon pay. We have attempted to shed some light on this issue. The first point of relevance is that the unemployment elasticity of wages is apparently small: the equations reported earlier suggest a value between −0.05 and −0.10. Thus if unemployment doubles, *ceteris paribus*, real wages fall a little less than 10 per cent. We have tried to show that pay depends upon profits: it is known that the profitability of British companies improved enormously over the 1980s.

There may, however, be other parts to the jigsaw. The previously 'missing' variable has been identified by Richard Layard and Stephen Nickell as the proportion of long-term unemployment, and by John Muellbauer and his associates as a measure of house prices. Halfway through out own research project, which was designed to see if companies' financial prosperity affected the wage rate, we attempted to check the Layard–Nickell and Bover–Muellbauer–Murphy arguments. Both turned out to be correct, though each left the profits effect undimmed. It seems that all three variables — profits, long-term unemployment, and house prices — should be included in a real-wage equation for the British economy. The long-term unemployment (level) variable is the weakest statistically.

It is not easy to weigh up the importance of different factors in the wage 'explosion' of the 1980s. However, Table 7.1 documents the annual changes in the three missing variables over the period 1980–7 (the 1987 house price figure was not available). Our model is only estimated to 1983, but if it is an adequate model, robust enough to confront new data, then simple comparative static exercises based on our estimated elasticities (see Table 7.2) should provide useful information. Real profits rose from the bottom of the recession (1981) to stand approximtely 70 per cent higher in 1987. Employment was lower in 1987 than in 1980–1, and real profit per employee roughly doubled over the period. This means on our estimates that, *ceteris paribus*, real-wage levels were 5–13 per cent higher in the later 1980s due solely to the prosperity of British industry. Given the time-lags involved, the strong profit performance of British industry in 1987/8 has yet to feed through into real-wage levels.

The basic point can be made in another way. Our best estimates suggest that the unemployment elasticity of pay is very roughly equal to (minus) the profit elasticity of pay. Both are of the order of one tenth (treating the results, as is probably appropriate, as reliable only to broad orders of magnitude). Over the 1980s, British unemployment and British profitability have both doubled. Our study suggests that the two effects on wage pressure cancel out. This may be one reason why large-scale unemployment has

Table 7.1 *Variable changes 1980–1987*

	Stock of long-term unemployed %	Annual change %	House price index	Annual change %	Profit £bn.	Annual change %
1980	23.2	−22.1	111.7	2.4	26,090.0	−5.7
1981	25.0	7.8	110.3	−1.3	25,858.3	−0.9
1982	38.7	54.8	109.6	−0.6	28,642.7	10.3
1983	41.8	8.0	111.9	2.1	32,270.2	12.7
1984	43.4	3.8	115.2	2.8	36,516.4	13.2
1985	45.2	4.1	115.4	0.2	41,275.8	13.0
1986	46.1	2.0	118.5	2.7	39,088.6	−5.3
1987	47.0	1.9	125.4	5.8	43,210.6	10.4

Notes:

1. The stock of long-term unemployed is the number of males unemployed longer than 52 weeks as a proportion of total male unemployment (Layard and Nickell (1986) and *Department of Employment Gazette*).

2. The house price index is the series used by John Muellbauer which is a UK house price index relative to the output price index, *PBAR* (see Appendix A for a full definition) and weighted by the proportion of owner occupiers.

3. The profit variable is gross profits of all industrial and commercial companies (including North Sea oil companies) deflated by the implicit *GDP* deflator (1980=100). Figures from CSO *Economic Trends*.

4. The elasticity for the stock of long-term unemployed cannot be read as the coefficient because it is not entered as a natural logarithm. The coefficient has to be multiplied by the mean of the stock of long-term unemployed (semi-log argument) which is equal to 0.225. If the 1986 value of this variable is used, the elasticity doubles.

5. The 1986 fall in real profit was caused by the decline in the profitability of the oil sector.

appeared to have no effect upon pay settlements.

Table 7.1 documents the substantial increase in the proportion of long term unemployed, in particular the dramatic rise of over 50 per cent in 1982. It has recently shown signs of levelling out, as the government has targeted measures, for example RESTART, at

Empirical Results for Britain

Table 7.2 *Estimates of long-run elasticities*

	Profits	Long-term unemployment[a]	House prices
Annual (Equation 1)	0.05	0.04	0.22
Quarterly (Equation 5)	0.13	0	0.09

a With the long-term proportion set to 0.4, to reflect its value in the 1980s.

the long-term unemployed. For the period as a whole the proportion of long-term unemployed doubled, indicating on our estimates, *ceteris paribus*, that real-wage levels are roughly 10 per cent higher than they would otherwise have been. Over the period to 1986, real house prices have risen less dramatically, though there has apparently been a continuing surge in house prices, especially in the South East, since then. Given the lags involved, these effects have still to work through to real wage levels. From our results, *ceteris paribus*, real wages have increased by about 2 per cent due to the rise in real house prices in the period 1980–6.

Our judgement is thus that profits and long-term unemployment each contributed significantly to the growth in real wages over the 1980s. House price rises seem likely to generate further wage pressure by the end of the decade.

APPENDIX A
Data Sources and Definitions

The data set is largely that of Layard and Nickell (1986), except for profit and house price data. We should like to express our thanks to Richard Layard, Stephen Nickell, and (for house price statistics) John Muellbauer for making their data available: thanks are also due to Andy Murfin, Andrea Gavosto, Jonathan Haskel, and Paul Kong for help with the details on actual data transformations, etc. The data set has now been extensively updated by Jonathan Haskel (1987), and is in a form which will make future updating easier. As the present work has had a fairly long gestation, and to maintain comparability with Layard and Nickell (1986), we use data series which run from the early 1950s to 1983. It would be easy just to refer the reader to Layard and Nickell (1986) for data explanations: however it may be useful in this context to spell out some of the details of the data transformations relevant to our work, simply to provide better information. Therefore, in the manner of Layard and Nickell (1986), we use the following abbreviations for sources:

BB   *Blue Book, National Income and Expenditure* (yearly)
BLSHA   *British Labour Statistics, Historical Abstract, 1886–1968*
DEG   *Department of Employment Gazette*
ETAS   *Economic Trends Annual Supplement*
ET   *Economic Trends* (monthly)
YB   *British Labour Statistics, Year Book, 1969–76*

Data relate to UK unless otherwise stated.

The chapter's empirical results require knowledge of the following statistical critical values. They are presented here in the order in which they occur in the equations.

$Chi^2(5)/5$ =	2.21	$Chi^2(2)$	= 5.99
$Chi^2(4)/4$ =	2.37	$Chi^2(20)/20$	= 1.57
$F(4,15)$ =	3.06	$F(2,19)$	= 3.52
$F(2,16)$ =	3.63	$F(12,8)$	= 3.28
$F(16,2)$ =	19.43	$F(20,51)$	= 1.78
$F(4,16)$ =	3.01	$F(5,66)$	= 2.36
$F(2,18)$ =	3.56	$F(30,40)$	= 1.74
$F(14,5)$ =	4.63	$F(27,53)$	= 1.68
$F(4,17)$ =	2.96		

A full account of the variables used in the chapter, relying to a considerable extent on the information published by Layard and Nickell (1986), is as follows:

w is the real product wage, which is a labour cost variable equal to $WBAR(1 + t1)/PBAR$, where $t1$ is the employer's tax rate, and PBAR is an output price index. $WBAR$ is an average weekly earnings series of full-time male manual workers adjusted for hours of work and an overtime premium. The actual formula can be found in Layard and Nickell (1986). It should be pointed out that we use a different deflator from Layard and Nickell, as they use P, a value-added price index. The relationship between the two deflators is $(1 + nu).\log PBAR = \log P + nu.\log P_m$ where P_m is an import price index and nu is the share of imports in value added. The sources are BLSHA, YB, DEB and ETAS.

$PBAR$ is an output price index. It is defined as the Total Final Expenditure (TFE) deflator at market prices divided by $(1 + nt3)$ where $nt3$ is the indirect tax rate relevant to the TFE deflator. This is defined as

$nt3 = FCA/(TFE-FCA)$ where FCA is the factor cost adjustment, namely expenditure minus selective employment tax minus national insurance surcharge minus subsidies.

K is the capital stock. The series used is gross capital stock at 1975 replacement cost in £ thousand million. Data from 1958 on is available in various issues of BB. Before 1958 data were interpolated using real investment; for details see Layard and Nickell (1986).

RHO is the replacement ratio. This variable is measured as a weighted average of different family types using the following proportions: single householder 0.36, married couple with no children 0.12, with one child 0.11, with two children 0.16, and with three children 0.12. The components of this weighted average are calculated from the DHSS publication, 'Abstract of Statistics for index of retail prices, Average earnings, Social Security Benefits and Contributions', 1983. This gives data on supplementary benefits, plus rent addition, for each family type and on net income for a one-earner family on average earnings. Annual income on benefit is computed and related to mid-year earnings. This series has been extensively revised in Jonathan Haskel's update, based on work by Andy Sentance.

P_m is the import price index for the UK. The source is ETAS.

N is employees in employment, males and females, mid-year Great Britain. The source is ETAS

U is the male unemployment rate. The series is males wholly unemployed as a percentage of the number of employees (employed and unemployed) at the appropriate mid-year, for the UK. The numbers unemployed exclude temporarily stopped but include school-leavers. The data refer to the pre–1982 definition of male unemployment. More recent data have been appropriately adjusted.

$U52$ is the stock of long term unemployed measured as the proportion of males registered as unemployed for over 52 weeks to total male unemployment. The source is DEG.

L is the labour force and is defined by $\log L = U + \log N$. Note that $\log L - \log N = -\log N/L = -\log (1-(L-N)/L) = L - N/L = U$.

UP is a measure of union power, and is defined to be the log of the union/non-union mark-up. The procedure for obtaining this variable is discussed in Layard, Metcalf, and Nickell (1978). Cross-section regressions have been estimated for each year, 1953–83.

$t1$ is the employment tax borne by the firm. The series is calculated by taking the ratio of two indices; total labour costs per unit of output for the whole economy, 1975=100, and wages and salaries per unit of output for the whole economy, 1975=100. As the series is an index based on 1975=100, the only way to approximate $t1$ is to take logs; so $\log k(1 + t1) = \log k + t1$ and let $\log k$ be absorbed by the regression constant. The labour cost series is published in BLSHA, YB, and the DEG. The wage data can be obtained from ETAS.

$t2$ is the income tax rate. It is derived using the following formula, $t2 = (DT + SS)/HCR$, where DT is direct taxes on household income, SS is household's contribution to social security schemes, and HCR is households' current receipts minus employer contributions to social security schemes. All three series are from OECD National Accounts.

$t3$ is the indirect tax rate. The log of the ratio of the GDP deflator at market prices (1975=100) to the GDP deflator at factor cost (1975=100) yields $t3$ plus a constant. The source is ETAS.

π is the profit series. It is extracted from the Appropriations Account of Industrial and Commercial Companies. The series used is gross trading profits net of stock appreciation (income arising in UK). We also used the series which excluded North Sea oil companies. The annual data prior to 1960 was provided by the Treasury. We should like to acknowledge the help of Barry Naisbitt.

The house price data were obtained from John Muellbauer. For the annual data we used the average level of house prices and the regional house price differential. For the quarterly data we only report results using the average level of house prices in London and the South East. The series were deflated by the output price index PBAR. For a detailed discussion of these series the reader is referred to Bover, Muellbauer, and Murphy (1988).

The *instrumental variables* used for the annual regressions include:

V is the vacancy rate which is registered vacancies corrected by a procedure suggested by Jackman, Layard, and Pissarides (1984). The source is DEG.

URS is the short-term unemployment rate based on individuals who are unemployed for less than 26 weeks. The data are published in BLSHA, YB and DEG.

WT is the deviation of world trade from trend. The world trade measure is the log of the quantam index of world exports from the UN monthly digest of statistics. The actual variable consists of the residuals from the regression of the log of world exports against the quintic trend.

G is real government expenditure. G is calculated from general government expenditure on goods and services in £ million divided by the GDP at factor cost deflator. The source was ETAS.

P^* is the unit value index of world manufacturing exports from the UN monthly digest of statistics.

APPENDIX B

Time-Series Methodology and Diagnostic Tests

1. Methodology

The econometric wing of the economics profession has recently engaged in a lively debate about appropriate empirical methodologies, with time series research the major focus. A good discussion of the issues can be found in Pagan (1987). There he concentrates on three possible research strategies, which are identified with the names of Hendry, Leamer, and Sims. Suffice it to say that we try to follow the procedure advocated by Hendry (1983), so this will be the main focus of what is to follow here.

It is apparent from our approach to the question of wage determination and profitability that we subscribe to the idea of considering a wide variety of evidence, and where appropriate from different disciplines. From this rather general form of encompassing, it may be possible to build a stronger case in favour of our thesis than could be obtained from a favourite time-series regression. Nevertheless it is often useful to present a time series perspective on the problem, and this we have sought to do; however we have not adopted the error correction (co-integration) framework which is gaining in popularity (see the special issue of the *Oxford Bulletin of Economics and Statistics*, August 1986).

With the quarterly data we have taken a general distributed lag approximation to our equilibrium wage function. This is consistent with (*a*) specifying a general model consistent with our theoretical framework of Chapter 6, (*b*) simplifying our model to provide a parsimonious outcome compatible with the data, and (*c*) evaluating the resulting model through testing of the residuals and predictive performance. A discussion of the diagnostic test statistics is provided in the second part of this appendix. With the annual data we were, in our specification search, constrained by a lack of observations, and by our decision to follow the Instrumental Variable approach of Layard and Nickell (1986). However equations (2), (3), and (4) report sensitivity tests.

A contentious issue in the Hendry methodology approach, applicable to virtually all methods of time-series research, is the specification search procedure (model 'discovery'). Leamer (1978) is particularly concerned by the practitioners who 'sinned in the basement', flogging their macroeconometric models, only to be resurrected on the top floor as the 'high priests' of the pedagogic exposition of theoretical econometrics. As Pagan (1987) suggests, the simplification of any general model requires a criterion function and a decision rule. For Least Squares regression models the residual variance plays an important role as we move from general to simpler models. Having selected the parsimonious regression, there remains the issue of what to present in the research report.

McAleer *et al.* (1985), in a response to Leamer (1983), believe that a precise explanation of the simplification search is imperative in any application of Hendry methodology. It is a common practice to present the simplified model without articulating the decisions taken along the way. This can lead to the charge of 'data-mining', or at the least to confusion as to how the final version of the model was discovered. Hendry (1983) contends that this is part of the art of the experienced applied economist, and that the important issue is whether the model satisfies the design criteria and provides useful new insights into a problem. This methodology provides an evolutionary element in the development of better time-series models, so there is never a simple right or wrong alternative.

Our analysis of wage determination and profitability has been in competition with other explanations of what is important in the operation of the labour market. The book's approach to the wage equation has been to try to include these other ideas in the form of a general model, and then to seek a parsimonious outcome. To a certain extent restrictions within PC-GIVE version 4.1 (Hendry, 1986*b*) can limit the dynamic testing of quarterly models (maximum of 35 variables in any regression). Normally quarterly models have an intuitive interpretation for general distributed lags to five periods: for example, reparametrization to annual change and whether the change is increasing or decreasing. This is the essence of the error correction approach, but we did not use this method. Instead we let the data determine the dynamic structure of the models through a process of restriction tests using the F-distribution. At all stages the diagnostic tests were monitored for stability ('parameter constancy') and non-random errors ('data coherency'). An explanation of each of the diagnostic tests presented with the regression equations is given below.

2. Diagnostic Tests

Chow (r, s) = a Chow test for parameter constancy, where r observations have been retained. It has an *F*-distribution with (r, s) degrees of freedom. This tests whether the coefficients in the model have changed over the last r periods.

Chi²(r)/r = a prediction test, comparing within-sample and post-sample variances. It is based on estimating the model up to r periods from the end of the total sample and then forecasting ahead for these r periods. The test has a Chi-squared distribution and, as a rough guide, values (5 per cent level) greater than 2 imply poor *ex ante* forecasts. It should be noted that this test is not meant to be a model selection device. A poor result indicates that the model does not forecast ahead very well, which in some forms of time-series research may be important.

$LM(r, s)$ = the F form of the Lagrange multiplier test for rth order serial correlation of the residuals with (r, s) degrees of freedom. It tests whether the residuals from our model can be explained by their past values up to r periods, along with the explanatory variables of the model. If the residuals can be explained by their past history, then we do not have a classic random error. A failure of this test is suggestive usually of an inappropriate dynamic structure, or of missing variables.

Normality $Chi^2(2)$ = a test for the normality of the residuals due to Bera and Jarque (1981) with critical value (5 per cent level) equal to 5.89. Failure of this test is often caused by an outlier observation.

$H(r, s)$ = a heteroscedasticity test due to White (1980), but in two forms. The first augments the model with squares of the regressors (Hendry, 1986*b*) and the second includes squares and cross products of the regressors. It has an F distribution with (r, s) degrees of freedom. Failure of the test is suggestive of an inappropriate functional form.

Specification $Chi^2(s)/s$ = Sargan's test of the independence of the instruments from the error term, which may also be interpreted as a test of the overridentifying restrictions. If the excluded instruments are not independent of the error term, then the model is misspecified. Again a rough guide for the critical value of this test (5 per cent level) is 2.

Hendry (1983) provides a discussion of these tests and their role in a model evaluation exercise. Essentially, if the tests are not satisfied, then the model under consideration is inadequate. The solution is to reconsider the functional form and/or the dynamic structure of the model, and not simply reach out for an alternative method of estimation. On this view the use of procedures such as Cochrane–Orcutt transformations is misguided, because they may conceal the inadequacies of an estimated model.

8

Conclusions

This book is about pay, prosperity, and the link between the two. Our aim has been to uncover the factors which shape the real wage in a country such as Britain. A principal conclusion, put informally, is that wage-rates depend in part upon whether employers are prosperous. In an economy with high unemployment, but strong company profits, it is possible for there to be no discernible downward pressure on pay. This may be the key to the behaviour of Britain's labour market — particularly the puzzling growth of real wages — over the 1980s.

The view that profitability influences workers' remuneration is not new, nor is it likely to seem surprising to the layman, but it has recently been neglected (or, more precisely, forgotten) by economists. Much of our study is a recapitulation of ideas which post-war labour economists took for granted. Sumner Slichter, Arthur Ross, Richard Lester, Clark Kerr, John Dunlop — all these scholars emphasized the importance of the employing firm's performance in the product market. There is a sense in which this study simply gathers together evidence which was unavailable to earlier generations of researchers. This is partly because of the advent of new computerized data sets and partly as a result of more powerful statistical techniques. Whilst such developments are invaluable, they have in this field encouraged economists to believe that knowledge can be gained only from the computer terminal. The previous generation placed more weight on, and were better informed about, real examples of wage-fixing. Our inquiry attempts to draw upon both kinds of method.

Chapter 2 summarizes modern accounts of the theory of wages. It reveals that a primary concern of the literature has been to derive wage rigidity theorems. Three are particularly well-known, and are those in

(1) implicit contract theory (see, for example, Azariadis (1975, p.1188));

(2) the theory of trade unions (see, for example, McDonald and Solow (1981, p.903));

(3) efficiency wage theory (see, for example, Solow (1979, p.80)).

All of these prove results about the inflexibility of pay in the face of a product price or demand shift. Hence they divert attention away from conditions in the product market and ignore the concept of the inflexibility of pay in the face of excess labour supply. To our knowledge the wage rigidity propositions of (1) to (3) have not been established empirically. The thrust of this study is that they lead in the wrong direction, because in practice product market variables help to fashion the wage-rate. Hence these conventional theorems on wage inflexibility — taught to graduate students across the world — are misleading.

Chapter 3 begins afresh at what is, in a natural sense, the beginning. It collects factual information on the arguments used by negotiators during collective bargaining, including managers' beliefs about the primary influences on their most recent settlement. There is evidence of an incontrovertible kind that managers and union leaders refer to, and think themselves affected by, the financial prosperity of the employing establishment and firm. This does not prove that they are affected. However, it counts as one form of verification of the idea that pay may hinge upon product market performance. Those who are unconvinced must find some other explanation for the fact that the 1984 Workplace Industrial Relations Survey showed that profitability-cum-productivity was the most commonly cited influence upon British wage determination, and that four other surveys examined in Chapter 3 came to similar conclusions.

Previous econometric studies are examined in Chapter 4. The object is to assess the statistical evidence on the relationship between what workers are paid and their employers' prosperity. Early work followed from two separate sources: they were Slichter's (1950) analysis of the cross-section wage structure of the US and Kaldor's (1959) argument that the Phillips curve should have incorporated a profits variable. Two literatures have sprung up; each has ignored the other.

Slichter appears to have been the first to provide empirical support — using rank correlation coefficients — for the hypothesis that 'where management can easily pay high wages they tend to do so, and that where management are barely breaking even, they tend to keep wages down' (p. 88). The author's data were crude and his statistical methods poor by today's standards. But our judgement is that Slichter obtained the correct answer; his 1950 paper ranks as seminal work in the labour economics literature. The equivalent modern US calculations, by Dickens and Katz (1987) and Krueger and Summers (1987), confirm Slichter's findings. They conclude that profitability is one of the two most consistently significant microeconomic influences upon remuneration (the other being individuals' educational levels).

New British econometric work on wages using cross-section and panel data has also uncovered effects from profits, product prices, financial measures, and similar variables. These studies include Gregory, Lobban, and Thomson (1987) on 212 settlement groups over five recent years, Blanchflower, Oswald, and Garrett (1988) on cross-section samples of up to 800 establishments in 1984, and Nickell and Wadhwani (1987) on 219 UK firms over a nine-year period from the early 1970s. Related work, at a higher level of aggregation, is reported in Tylecote (1975), Geroski, Hamlin, and Knight (1982), and Beckerman and Jenkinson (1988). Although each of these six studies has its strengths and weaknesses, and not all focus upon profitability narrowly defined, when taken together they appear to offer convincing grounds for the belief that, just as in the data for the United States, wages are correlated with the prosperity of employers.

Whilst the time-series research promoted by Kaldor (1959) often supports the hypothesis that profits affect pay, its quality is not high enough to allow any faith in the conclusions. Lipsey and Steuer (1961), Bhatia (1962), Eckstein and Wilson (1962), and, to a degree, Perry (1966) present equations which are in all probability seriously misspecified. The equations exhibit signs of autocorrelation, instability, and collinearity problems. By modern standards — a difficult bench-mark for applied work in economics — the findings are questionable. In a sense this was the stimulus for our own work of Chapter 7.

New work by Rowlatt (1987) has also examined the effects of lagged profitability. She estimates a dynamic real-wage model, using British data, which uncovers a statistically significant effect from lagged (smoothed) profit. Whilst Rowlatt's estimating framework is not the same as that of Chapter 7, her results are consistent with those in our study.

More unconventional matters are tackled in Chapter 5. The chapter describes an experiment by Bazerman (1985) which attempts to discover the attitudes of professional wage arbitrators and how those shape their judgements. Profitability was found to be one of the most powerful variables influencing the chosen wage settlement. The chapter also examines experimental tests of Equity Theory, a branch of the psychology literature. They suggest that working relationships are shaped by intuitive judgements about fairness in rewards relative to effort. When one side's reward increases, both parties see it as equitable that the other side's should increase. The evidence of Kahneman, Knetsch, and Thaler (1986) for Canada, and of Jowell, Witherspoon, and Brook (1987) for Britain, reveals that this is how individuals view profits and pay. Greater profit 'should' lead to higher wages.

The study's preferred model of wage determination is set out in Chapter 6. It assumes that wages are determined by collective bargaining between a profit-maximizing firm and a trade union. The union is assumed to operate by democratic voting and to enforce a 'last in, first out' firing rule. Senior members are then insulated from demand shocks of all but the most exceptional kind. Around equilibrium the trade union, which is assumed to be dominated in its voting over wage demands by its seniors, cares entirely about higher pay and puts no weight on employment expansion. The chapter demonstrates that the wage then depends upon an adjusted level of profit per employee. More generally, it is shown that other theoretical arguments can be used to support an empirical wage specification in which profitability enters. They include the ideas that (i) profit is a proxy for the state of product and labour demand and (ii) for reasons of fairness the workers' utilities depend upon their employers' rewards. Our study does not attempt to test among these possibilities, nor to prove that the most convincing way to construct a model of the trade union is to assume locally horizontal indifference curves. The aim instead is to see if the pay–profit prediction common to this analytical family is borne out by the data of the world.

The results of our empirical work are described in Chapter 7. Those who place most weight upon new findings using time-series statistics are likely to see this as the study's central chapter.

Chapter 7 estimates annual and quarterly real-wage equations for Britain. The annual estimation is done for the mid 1950s to 1983; the quarterly estimation uses figures from 1962 to 1983. Methodologically our work has been influenced by the prevailing British view about how time-series econometrics should be carried out. Thus the equations include a great variety of time-lags on the independent variables, and each estimated equation is presented with a number of diagnostic check statistics. Those statistics assess the model's stability and forecasting ability. They also reveal whether the fitted errors are autoregressive, non-normal, or heteroscedastic. Models which failed to pass the tests were rejected and, except in certain circumstances and for reasons of illustration, they are not reported in this study.

The hypothesis of special interest for our work was that of a possible link from the financial performance of companies to the real-wage rate. An initial empirical foundation was required, however, and the one chosen was the real-wage equation in Layard and Nickell (1986). The results of Chapter 7 attempt to encompass the Layard–Nickell framework. Our key new explanatory variable, real profitability per employee, was derived from figures for gross trading profits net of stock appreciation. Figures both including and excluding North Sea oil profits were used (there was little difference in the econometric results). Profit statistics are notoriously unreliable and it appears unwise to be sanguine about those employed in Chapter 7. Nevertheless, these profit data may not be devoid of information.

The flavour of our findings is given by an equation such as number (1) of Chapter 7, which shows that the real-wage depends upon lagged profitability, and also upon the levels of unemployment, import prices, capital to labour force ratio, indirect taxes, the proportion of long-term unemployment, and house prices. The quarterly results of Chapter 7's later equations lead to similar conclusions. Of various tests for robustness — to check whether the apparent significance of profits was spurious — one reported as equation (2) of Chapter 7 was to eliminate the profit variable. As required for the thesis of this study, the model was greatly weakened by such a step. Our judgement from the econometric work is that real wages move with past levels of profits per employee. The elasticity appears to lie between 0.05 and 0.13, so that a doubling of profits (as occurred through the 1980s in Great Britain) would tend to raise pay by between 5 and 13 per cent.

However, such numbers are, at best, only a rough guide to the likely structure of the economy. Truly reliable estimates can come only from better data.

The puzzle of rising British wages in the face of large excess supply of labour has stimulated more work than our own. Around the same time as this study began to take shape, Layard and Nickell (1988) and Bover, Muellbauer, and Murphy (1988) were also being written. The first proposes the proportion of long term unemployment as an explanatory variable (see Nickell (1987) for further estimates). The second argues that the level or dispersion of house prices should be included in the wage equation. Our study attempted to incorporate these variables, and both worked in a satisfactory way. Hence Chapter 7 extends the basic Layard and Nickell (1986) wage equation by including, in all, three extra variables. Calculations of which of the three mattered most in the 1980s are fraught with difficulties. Our own estimate is that house price movements were the least important, and that the other two were of comparable consequence.

This inquiry's conclusion can be put concisely. Changes in profitability lead to changes in pay, and this force, according to our calculations, may be one of the reasons why British wage-rates through the 1980s appeared to be insensitive to unemployment. One downward pressure was counterbalanced by another upward force.

The idea that company prosperity helps to determine employees' pay is supported by different kinds of evidence. Some is informal; some draws upon statistical models. Some comes out of surveys, bargaining documents, and experiments; some springs from cross-section and time-series econometric tests. All of the evidence, however, appears to point in the same direction. It is this agreement out of diversity which best establishes the case.

Statistical Appendix

A1. Introduction

The definitions and sources of the data used in our empirical work were reported in Appendix A of Chapter 7. This appendix provides additional evidence, and more information. First, it reports the results of re-estimating a selection of equations from Chapter 7 using a different, but familiar software package, namely TSP. To make readers feel at home we report the equation output from TSP with a short preamble around each equation to aid comprehension. Second, the appendix includes the raw data used in our empirical work. The information is set out as two TSP data files, one for the quarterly, the other for the annual data. These data files were used to generate the results reported in the first part of this appendix. We hope that this exercise helps to corroborate the results of Chapter 7, in the sense that they are reproduced using different software, and provides enthusiasts with a set of data to consider alternative scenarios.[1]

A2. Corroboration of Chapter 7 Results Using TSP

The estimates presented below are labelled with the corresponding equation numbers of Chapter 7. For the empirical model estimated with annual data, we reproduce three equations from Chapter 7, namely (1), (6), and (7). They are incorporated from a TSP output file, though additional editing has been included to aid understanding of the 'computer notation' variable names. The variables, except for the constant, are in identical order to the presentation of equations (1), (6), and (7) in Chapter 7. A minor deviation is that we have used the OLS estimator for the annual results, rather than the Instrumental Variable estimator used in Chapter 7. The similarity of the results suggests that the simultaneity bias arising from the use of OLS is trivial for these empirical models.

The quarterly result reproduces equation (5) from Chapter 7. Here the estimators are identical (OLS), and the results too. This is reassuring, given that our software package PC-GIVE (Hendry (1986b)) is relatively new,[2] and has still to acquire the extensive 'brand loyalty' that TSP seems to enjoy.

Equation (1) from chapter 7 was our preferred explanation of the real product wage for the period 1956–83. It included the rival explanations for buoyant real wages in the 1980s of real profit, the duration structure of unemployment and real house prices. The TSP result follows.

1. Note that if you extract this data to only one or two decimal places you should not expect to obtain exactly the results reported here.

2. It does depend on estimation algorithms that have been developed over a number of years by David Hendry, Frank Srba, and other colleagues at the London School of Economics and University of Oxford, so it is a well-developed product. The point is that TSP has been around a long time, and has built up a 'brand loyalty' that will take software like PC-GIVE some time to acquire; hence our desire to demonstrate that our results in Ch. 7 can be reproduced by TSP. This is a useful check on estimated equations no matter what software product generates the results.

Current sample: 1956 TO 1983

Equation (1)

Method of estimation = ordinary least squares
Dependent variable: *lwp*

Sum of squared residuals	=	0.136782E–02
Standard error of the regression	=	0.848473E–02
Mean of dependent variable	=	4.73163
Standard deviation	=	0.268079
R–squared	=	0.999295
Adjusted R–squared	=	0.998998
Durbin–Watson statistic	=	2.6991
F–statistic (8, 19)	=	3366.79
Log of likelihood function	=	99.2441
Number of observations	=	28

Variable[3]	Estimated coefficient	Standard error	t–statistic
Constant	9.539296	0.9386387E–01	101.6290
lnur ln (unemployment rate)	−0.7084816E–01	0.7169846E–02	−9.881406
pmp ln (import/output price)	−0.2760456	0.2410796E–01	−11.45039
lkl(−1) ln (capital/labour −1)	1.224981	0.2509461E–01	48.81452
*t*3(−1) indirect tax rate −1	0.5614209	0.1372642	4.090075
lpipbln(−2) ln (profit per employee −2)	0.4938174E–01	0.1470066E–01	3.359151
*pu*52 long-term unemployed	0.8501693E–01	0.4763809E–01	1.784642
*D*1*pu*52 1st difference long-term	−0.1463758	0.5328642E–01	−2.746963

unemployed			
wofnew(−2)	0.2188734	0.5542183E–01	3.949228
ln (house price −2)			

3. An explanation of the variable is given below each TSP variable name. For example, PU52 is the long-term unemployed proportion.

Equation (6) corrected the profit data to remove the influence of North Sea oil companies. The TSP result follows.

Equation (6)

Method of estimation = ordinary least squares
Dependent variable: *lwp*

Sum of squared residuals =	0.130384E–02
Standard error of the regression =	0.828392E–02
Mean of dependent variable =	4.73163
Standard deviation =	0.268079
R–squared =	0.999328
Adjusted R–squared =	0.999045
Durbin–Watson statistic =	2.8113
F–statistic (8, 19) =	3532.12
Log of likelihood function =	99.9147
Number of observations =	28

Variable	Estimated coefficient	Standard error	*t*–statistic
Constant	9.403771	0.9456684E–01	99.44047
lnur	−0.5909427E–01	0.7832314E–02	−7.544932
ln (unemployment rate)			
pmp	−0.2603265	0.2433479E–01	−10.69771
ln (import/output price)			

$lkl(-1)$ ln (capital/labour -1)	1.184616	0.2721899E–01	43.52165
$t3(-1)$ indirect tax rate -1	0.6354504	0.1296994	4.899407
$lpixpbln(-2)$[a] ln (profit per employee -2)	0.6671038E–01	0.1866807E–01	3.573501
$pu52$ long-term unemployed	0.1409795	0.4685622E–01	3.008768
$D1pu52$ 1st difference long-term unemployed	−0.1372137	0.5214224E–01	−2.631526
$wofnew(-2)$ ln (house price -2)	0.2404374	0.5325933E–01	4.514466

[a]The profit variable excludes N. Sea oil companies.

Equation (7) replaced the real house price variable with the house price dispersion variable favoured by Bover, Muellbauer, and Murphy (1988).

Equation (7)

Method of estimation = ordinary least squares
Dependent variable: *lwp*

Sum of squared residuals	=	0.145758E–02
Standard error of the regression	=	0.875869E–02
Mean of dependent variable	=	4.73163
Standard deviation	=	0.268079
R–squared	=	0.999249
Adjusted R–squared	=	0.998933
Durbin–Watson statistic	=	2.7407
F–statistic (8, 19)	=	3159.32
Log of likelihood function	=	98.3543
Number of observations	=	28

Variable	Estimated coefficient	Standard error	*t*–statistic
Constant	9.516764	0.1038988	91.59651
lnur	−0.5658595E–01	0.7683550E–02	−7.364558
ln (unemployment rate)			
pmp	−0.2239871	0.2271422E–01	−9.861093
ln (import/output price)			
lkl(−1)	1.214692	0.2823128E–01	43.02646
ln (capital/labour −1)			
*t*3(−1)	0.5093649	0.1408908	3.615317
indirect tax rate −1			
lpipbln(−2)	0.5928485E–01	0.1489991E–01	3.978872
ln (profit per employee −2)			
*pu*52	0.7126146E–01	0.4931491E–01	1.445029
long-term unemployed			
*D*1*pu*52	−0.1399661	0.5572125E–01	−2.511898
1st difference long-term unemployed			
*av*23*rd*	0.2838288	0.7734596E–01	3.669601
regional house price differential average of *t*−2 and *t*−3 lags)			

Equation (5) contains our preferred quarterly explanation of the real product wage. It too includes the rival explanations for the persistence of real-wage growth in the 1980s.

Current sample: 1962:1 TO 1983:4

Equation (5)

Method of estimation = ordinary least squares
Note: Lagged dependent variable(s) present
Dependent variable: *lrwp*

Sum of squared residuals	=	0.211182E–01
Standard error of the regression	=	0.172464E–01
Mean of dependent variable	=	4.54117
Standard deviation	=	0.220727
R–squared	=	0.995018
Adjusted R–squared	=	0.993895
Durbin–Watson statistic	=	2.0932
F–statistic (16, 71)	=	886.226
Log of likelihood function	=	241.872
Number of observations	=	88

Variable	Estimated coefficient	Standard error	t–statistic
Constant	3.892461	0.5422674	7.178120
lrpw(−1) ln (real product wage −1)	−0.4404972	0.7308246E–01	6.027399
lrue(−4) ln (unemployment rate −4)	−0.239385E–01	0.1059492E–01	−2.259436
dlrpmg2 1st difference ln (import/output price −2)	0.1863961	0.7179642E–01	2.596175
klf(−1) ln (capital/labour −1)	0.5431012	0.7547806E–01	7.195484
rple price surprise	0.9749192	0.1505053	6.477641
dllc	0.7019951	0.1953214	3.594052

1st different employer tax rate			
$d3pu52$	−0.1400785E−02	0.6725479E−03	2.082803
long term unemployed long-term unemployed −3			
$lpipbln(-6)$	0.7009452E−01	0.1553492E−01	4.512061
ln (profit per employee − 6)			
$drer1$	0.5762684E−02	0.1861941E−02	3.094987
Ist difference replacement rate −1			
$rer(-3)$	0.2135261E−02	0.7593976E−03	2.811783
replacement rate −3			
$dlmup1$	0.5273030E−01	0.3012908E−01	1.750146
1st difference ln (union power −1)			
$dlhplsp4$	0.1132917	0.5898173E−01	1.920793
1st difference ln (house price London and SE −4)			
$lhplspb(-7)$	0.1554776	0.5633432E−01	−2.759910
ln (house price London and SE −7)			
$lhplspb(-8)$	0.2041159	0.5648073E−01	3.613903
ln (house price London and SE −8)			
Q1	0.1822095E−01	0.5378370E−02	3.387819
1st quarter seasonal			
Q3	0.1085667E−01	0.4779085E−02	2.271705
3rd quarter seasonal			

Durbin (1970) t–stat. for AR (1)=−0.792680

A3. The Raw Data used in the Study

The data listings produced in this section contain the annual and quarterly data sets used in our empirical work, and are set out in a data file format suitable for TSP to read. TSP comments (annotated with a ?) are used to give a brief explanation of the definition of each data series. A fuller explanation of the data series is given in Appendix A of Chapter 7. For good measure we have included data series that do not appear in our preferred specifications. Full definitions of these series can be found in Layard and Nickell (1986). Note that we reproduce many data series after considerable transformation, for example, the real product wage definition; so it may be a little difficult to work back to the original raw data that were used to compile the variables for the empirical models.

The listings start with the quarterly data, and the annual data follow. The first series for both the quarterly and annual data is a time period identifier (id), which is included to aid interpretation. For example, the 1956 first-quarter observation (1956:1) on the series logarithm of the male unemployment rate (lrue) is 0.1823, the 1967 second quarter (1967:2) is 1.0647, and the 1979 fourth-quarter observation is 1.8245. Every series has exactly the same format as the time period identifier, so it is straightforward to work out the date of any observation for any series. A similar exercise can be carried out for the annual data set.

A3.1. *The Quarterly Data Set*

smpl 1956:1 1983:4:
? note that some of
? the variables do not start until
? after 1956; for instance, the profit data does not
? begin until 1960. Estimation is normally from 1962:1
? once lags have been taken into account.

load id; ? data identifier for quarterly series

1956:1	1956:2	1956:3	1956:4	1957:1	1957:2	1957:3
1957:4	1958:1	1958:2	1958:3	1958:4	1959:1	1959:2
1959:3	1959:4	1960:1	1960:2	1960:3	1960:4	1961:1
1961:2	1961:3	1961:4	1962:1	1962:2	1962:3	1962:4
1963:1	1963:2	1963:3	1963:4	1964:1	1964:2	1964:3
1964:4	1965:1	1965:2	1965:3	1965:4	1966:1	1966:2
1966:3	1966:4	1967:1	1967:2	1967:3	1967:4	1968:1
1968:2	1968:3	1968:4	1969:1	1969:2	1969:3	1969:4
1970:1	1970:2	1970:3	1970:4	1971:1	1971:2	1971:3
1971:4	1972:1	1972:2	1972:3	1972:4	1973:1	1973:2
1973:3	1973:4	1974:1	1974:2	1974:3	1974:4	1975:1
1975:2	1975:3	1975:4	1976:1	1976:2	1976:3	1976:4
1977:1	1977:2	1977:3	1977:4	1978:1	1978:2	1978:3
1978:4	1979:1	1979:2	1979:3	1979:4	1980:1	1980:2
1980:3	1980:4	1981:1	1981:2	1981:3	1981:4	1982:1
1982:2	1982:3	1982:4	1983:1	1983:2	1983:3	1983:4;

Statistical Appendix

load Irue; ? log of the male unemployment rate (U)

0.1823	0.0953	0.1823	0.1823	0.5878	0.4055	0.2624
0.4055	0.7419	0.7885	0.7885	0.9555	1.0986	0.8755
0.7419	0.7885	0.7885	0.5306	0.4055	0.5878	0.6419
0.4055	0.4055	0.6931	0.8329	0.7419	0.7885	0.9933
1.4811	0.0296	0.8755	0.8755	0.8755	0.6419	0.5306
0.5878	0.6419	0.4700	0.4700	0.4700	0.5306	0.4055
0.4700	1.0296	1.1631	1.0647	1.0647	1.1631	1.2528
1.1314	1.1314	1.1631	1.2528	1.1314	1.1631	1.2238
1.2809	1.2238	1.2238	1.2528	1.4110	1.4586	1.5476
1.6292	1.7228	1.5892	1.5686	1.5261	1.4586	1.2809
1.1631	1.0986	1.3082	1.1939	1.3083	1.3083	1.5041
1.5686	1.7750	1.8405	1.9459	1.9169	1.9741	1.9741
1.9741	1.9459	2.0281	1.9741	2.0015	1.9315	1.9879
1.8871	1.9459	1.8405	1.8718	1.8245	1.9459	1.9879
2.1861	2.3125	2.4849	2.5337	2.6101	2.6603	2.7213
2.7014	2.7537	2.7912	2.8154	2.8332	2.8565	2.8273;

load rrt3; ? indirect tax rate ($t3$)

0.1036	0.1041	0.1074	0.1113	0.1037	0.1031	0.1028
0.1084	0.1043	0.1048	0.1023	0.1105	0.1095	0.1055
0.1035	0.1090	0.1037	0.1005	0.1000	0.1026	0.0984
0.1021	0.0962	0.1088	0.1023	0.1047	0.1060	0.1079
0.1012	0.1016	0.1064	0.1042	0.1037	0.1076	0.1075
0.1136	0.1149	0.1128	0.1117	0.1176	0.1112	0.1145
0.1142	0.1236	0.1068	0.1090	0.1085	0.1100	0.1054
0.1101	0.1124	0.1214	0.1169	0.1210	0.1239	0.1256
0.1180	0.1207	0.1226	0.1172	0.1138	0.1212	0.1114
0.1094	0.1045	0.1146	0.1086	0.1100	0.1039	0.1031
0.1029	0.0978	0.0790	0.0948	0.0782	0.0784	0.0669
0.0888	0.0902	0.0893	0.0831	0.0850	0.0868	0.0915
0.0743	0.0937	0.0972	0.1003	0.0794	0.0907	0.0915
0.0982	0.0836	0.0912	0.1074	0.1093	0.1027	0.1050
0.1055	0.1118	0.1087	0.1176	0.1173	0.1242	0.1311
0.1264	0.1278	0.1256	0.1255	0.1289	0.1226	0.1224;

load lrpmg; ? log of the import price index for UK (PM)

0.2476	0.2488	0.2454	0.2419	0.2662	0.2697	0.1978
0.1841	0.1534	0.1190	0.1412	0.1134	0.1238	0.0824
0.1318	0.1233	0.1373	0.0985	0.1208	0.0807	0.0858
0.1049	0.0522	0.0758	0.0545	0.0479	0.0484	0.0346
0.0721	0.0410	0.0850	0.0517	0.0900	0.0451	0.0271

0.0318	0.0471	0.0250	0.0055	0.0050	0.0036	0.0036
0.0072	0.0013	0.0044	0.0270	0.0291	0.0134	0.0480
0.0656	0.0564	0.0550	0.0385	0.0508	0.0465	0.0508
0.0538	0.0480	0.0295	0.0135	0.0046	0.0010	0.0417
0.0684	0.1023	0.1116	0.1022	0.0871	0.0509	0.0126
0.0651	0.0953	0.2283	0.2773	0.2247	0.2043	0.1490
0.1168	0.1041	0.1104	0.1210	0.1756	0.1946	0.2345
0.2749	0.2154	0.1969	0.1739	0.0942	0.1451	0.1153
0.1172	0.0914	0.0896	0.0612	0.0732	0.0414	0.0310
0.0205	0.0438	0.0687	0.0414	0.0141	0.0121	0.0098
0.0192	0.0169	0.0156	0.0086	0.0123	0.0026	0.0162;

load lmup; ? log of the measure of union power (*UP*)

−2.2165	−1.8971	−1.8949	−1.8927	−1.9154	−1.8084	−1.8064
−1.8044	−1.8605	−1.9119	−1.9097	−1.9074	−1.9540	−2.0734
−2.0707	−2.0681	−1.9577	−1.7962	−1.7941	−1.9540	−2.0734
−1.7611	−1.7591	−1.7571	−1.7301	−1.6405	−1.7921	−1.8117
−1.7495	−1.9543	−1.9516	−1.9490	−1.8752	−1.6386	−1.6368
−1.8164	−1.7655	−1.6302	−1.6281	−1.6261	−1.8211	−1.8188
−1.7950	−1.7925	−1.7758	−1.7733	−1.7707	−1.7060	−1.7975
−1.5956	−1.5936	−1.5914	−1.5937	−1.5522	−1.7681	−1.7267
−1.4752	−1.3097	−1.3078	−1.3059	−1.3502	−1.5499	−1.5476
−1.3439	−1.2778	−1.1398	−1.1380	−1.1362	−1.3481	−1.3460
−1.1702	−1.1683	−1.2528	−1.4377	−1.4350	−1.1741	−1.1722
−1.1336	−1.1315	−1.1295	−1.1874	−1.2120	−1.4323	−1.3006
−1.1820	−1.1280	−1.1256	−1.1233	−1.1609	−1.2097	−1.2070
−1.2980	−1.2636	−1.2323	−1.2294	−1.2265	−1.3039	−1.3010
−0.8328	−0.8306	−0.8715	−0.8219	−0.8197	−1.0923	−0.8348
−0.8447	−0.8424	−0.8400	−0.8474	−0.8485	−0.8175	−0.8395
					−0.8460	−0.8435;

load llc; ? employer tax rate (*t*1)

4.4571	4.4560	4.4536	4.4499	4.4583	4.4572	4.4549
4.4536	4.4658	4.4648	4.4623	4.4586	4.4670	4.4660
4.4635	4.4598	4.4658	4.4648	4.4623	4.4586	4.4670
4.4660	4.4635	4.4598	4.4695	4.4684	4.4660	4.4623
4.4719	4.4708	4.4685	4.4648	4.4729	4.4718	4.4695
4.4658	4.4775	4.4764	4.4741	4.4704	4.5009	4.4886
4.4785	4.4931	4.5065	4.4886	4.4875	4.4875	4.4920
4.4920	4.4976	4.5076	4.5087	4.5042	4.4965	4.5031
4.5152	4.5131	4.5076	4.5098	4.5087	4.5240	4.4987
4.5042	4.5174	4.5087	4.5076	4.5120	4.5207	4.5109
4.5250	4.5098	4.5486	4.5358	4.5337	4.5240	4.5283

4.5315	4.5518	4.5591	4.5654	4.5633	4.5612	4.5664
4.5799	4.5961	4.6072	4.5901	4.5981	4.5981	4.5941
4.6052	4.5880	4.6191	4.6230	4.6042	4.6032	4.6102
4.6072	4.6012	4.6032	4.6131	4.6191	4.6082	4.6171
4.6102	4.6082	4.5992	4.5941	4.6022	4.5971	4.5941;

load mmb; ? labour market mismatch variable (Layard-Nickell)

0.0012	0.0217	−0.0015	−0.0028	−0.0032	−0.0026	0.0003
−0.0008	−0.0004	−0.0036	−0.0068	−0.0065	−0.0083	−0.0290
−0.0268	−0.0243	−0.0233	0.0047	0.0049	−0.0006	−0.0004
−0.0012	−0.0041	−0.0003	−0.0035	−0.0062	−0.0061	−0.0058
−0.0070	−0.0061	−0.0048	−0.0035	0.0007	0.0026	0.0032
0.0046	0.0030	0.0002	0.0013	−0.0027	−0.0032	−0.0002
−0.0042	−0.0009	−0.0006	−0.0067	−0.0075	−0.0075	−0.0072
−0.0044	−0.0014	0.0001	−0.0001	0.0009	−0.0006	−0.0015
−0.0037	−0.0046	−0.0051	−0.0079	−0.0029	−0.0097	−0.0092
−0.0136	−0.0218	−0.0138	−0.0147	−0.0097	−0.0064	−0.0058
−0.0040	−0.0017	−0.0011	−0.0032	−0.0049	−0.0098	−0.0101
−0.0151	−0.0169	−0.0152	−0.0123	−0.0078	−0.0041	−0.0024
0.0100	0.0118	0.0107	0.0090	−0.0043	−0.0085	−0.0094
−0.0110	−0.0089	−0.0070	−0.0068	−0.0072	−0.0092	−0.0118
−0.0157	−0.0189	−0.0231	−0.0232	−0.0214	−0.0191	−0.0161
−0.0151	−0.0133	−0.0031	−0.0018	−0.0017	−0.0018	−0.0108;

load klf; ? log of capital–labour force ratio

−3.8428	−3.8404	−3.8379	−3.8289	−3.8258	−3.8228	−3.8136
−3.8047	−3.7968	−3.7952	−3.7871	−3.7851	−3.7849	−3.7785
−3.7765	−3.7725	−3.7713	−3.7636	−3.7579	−3.7539	−3.7507
−3.7392	−3.7359	−3.7287	−3.7283	−3.7220	−3.7125	−3.7083
−3.7086	−3.6963	−3.6870	−3.6860	−3.6744	−3.6680	−3.6632
−3.6536	−3.6419	−3.6354	−3.6253	−3.6210	−3.6091	−3.6031
−3.5962	−3.5914	−3.5725	−3.5639	−3.5571	−3.5412	−3.5258
−3.5158	−3.5084	−3.4948	−3.4828	−3.4736	−3.4663	−3.4529
−3.4419	−3.4299	−3.4177	−3.4064	−3.3870	−3.3833	−3.3721
−3.3629	−3.3625	−3.3510	−3.3443	−3.3398	−3.3316	−3.3156
−3.3030	−3.2887	−3.3014	−3.2757	−3.2784	−3.2668	−3.2558
−3.2547	−3.2582	−3.2512	−3.2391	−3.2356	−3.2354	−3.2300
−3.1892	−3.1863	−3.1889	−3.1794	−3.1663	−3.1664	−3.1690
−3.1621	−3.1509	−3.1475	−3.1456	−3.1349	−3.1226	−3.1206
−3.1198	−3.1099	−3.1098	−3.1080	−3.1101	−3.1037	−3.0982
−3.0938	−3.0925	−3.0863	−3.0745	−3.0821	−3.0863	−3.0769;

load rt2; ? income tax rate (*t*2)

0.0908	0.0933	0.0934	0.0935	0.0943	0.0988	0.0990
0.0991	0.1018	0.1122	0.1123	0.1125	0.1088	0.1076
0.1078	0.1079	0.1086	0.1109	0.1111	0.1113	0.1117
0.1172	0.1174	0.1176	0.1176	0.1238	0.1240	0.1243
0.1226	0.1220	0.1223	0.1225	0.1234	0.1273	0.1276
0.1278	0.1313	0.1441	0.1443	0.1446	0.1445	0.1541
0.1543	0.1546	0.1520	0.1537	0.1540	0.1542	0.1546
0.1663	0.1666	0.1668	0.1693	0.1765	0.1768	0.1770
0.1784	0.1882	0.1885	0.1887	0.1864	0.1886	0.1889
0.1891	0.1842	0.1754	0.1756	0.1758	0.1803	0.1873
0.1876	0.1878	0.1937	0.2141	0.2143	0.2145	0.2186
0.2427	0.2429	0.2431	0.2396	0.2471	0.2473	0.2475
0.2407	0.2298	0.2299	0.2300	0.2289	0.2203	0.2204
0.2205	0.2190	0.2106	0.2107	0.2107	0.2152	0.2216
0.2217	0.2217	0.2264	0.2419	0.2419	0.2419	0.2398
0.2442	0.2442	0.2441	0.2435	0.2440	0.2439	0.2439;

load rer; ? replacement ratio (*RHO*)

37.5362	37.7392	37.7548	37.7698	37.2308	35.8428	35.8565
35.8699	37.3475	41.0056	41.0176	41.0293	40.2334	40.7115
40.7223	40.7325	41.0045	42.3227	42.3319	42.3408	41.9885
41.9962	42.0041	42.0118	42.1091	42.4901	42.4971	42.5037
42.8393	44.2477	44.2536	44.2594	43.6231	42.7872	42.7924
42.7974	44.3382	48.5494	48.5539	48.5584	47.7030	48.3615
48.3657	48.3697	49.5096	53.6263	53.6302	53.6339	52.3255
51.4879	51.4915	51.4951	51.4256	50.5879	50.5915	50.5951
50.9140	51.2916	51.2953	51.2989	51.0147	50.4578	50.4609
50.4658	49.5173	46.1564	46.1609	46.1654	46.8731	46.5039
46.5089	49.5141	46.7709	47.3373	47.3429	47.3489	47.7881
49.6639	49.6705	49.6773	49.4279	50.1830	50.1906	50.1985
50.3756	51.5993	51.6079	51.6171	50.8367	49.4443	49.4543
49.4647	48.6464	45.1054	45.1169	45.1289	45.9205	45.7462
45.7593	45.7729	45.5130	49.7339	49.7488	49.7642	51.2291
54.2366	54.2535	54.2708	53.7409	54.6006	54.6195	54.6389;

load 1k; ? log of the capital stock (*K*)

6.1410	6.1472	6.1536	6.1593	6.1663	6.1732	6.1798
6.1874	6.1940	6.2003	6.2068	6.2110	6.2174	6.2244
6.2315	6.2377	6.2459	6.2538	6.2621	6.2748	6.2830
6.2914	6.3001	6.3070	6.3152	6.3235	6.3352	6.3393
6.3497	6.3575	6.3658	6.3708	6.3803	6.3896	6.3993

6.4110	6.4211	6.4302	6.4430	6.4503	6.4596	6.4682
6.4771	6.4805	6.4990	6.5008	6.5110	6.5224	6.5332
6.5429	6.5528	6.5650	6.5748	6.5840	6.5937	6.6052
6.6146	6.6241	6.6367	6.6456	6.6551	6.6640	6.6730
6.6845	6.6937	6.7022	6.7139	6.7224	6.7364	6.7489
6.7615	6.7747	6.7631	6.7913	6.7991	6.8078	6.8162
6.8237	6.8316	6.8398	6.8482	6.8554	6.8631	6.8707
6.8779	6.8847	6.8916	6.8993	6.9069	6.9137	6.9207
6.9271	6.9343	6.9409	6.9480	6.9546	6.9615	6.9672
6.9732	6.9795	6.9844	6.9885	6.9930	6.9983	7.0032
7.0075	7.0126	7.0183	7.0237	7.0279	7.0327	7.0387;

load lurs; ? log of the short-term unemployment rate (Layard–Nickell)

−4.9254	−4.9751	−4.8536	−4.8353	−4.5467	−4.7089	−4.7751
−4.6290	−4.4011	−4.3477	−4.3110	−4.1944	−4.0342	−4.1886
−4.2986	−4.2038	−4.2337	−4.5954	−4.6794	−4.4060	−4.3402
−4.6523	−4.6032	−4.2145	−4.0613	−4.1945	−4.1791	−3.9488
−3.3967	−3.9612	−4.2256	−4.1651	−4.1080	−4.4269	−4.5954
−4.4512	−4.3257	−4.5737	−4.5893	−4.5150	−4.3975	−4.5913
−4.5431	−3.8646	−3.6740	−3.8648	−3.9291	−3.8073	−3.6907
−3.8683	−3.8954	−3.8365	−3.7206	−3.8923	−3.8697	−3.7759
−3.6738	−3.7819	−3.7939	−3.7634	−3.5367	−3.5061	−3.4345
−3.3484	−3.2695	−3.4812	−3.5557	−3.5899	−3.6458	−3.8776
−4.0218	−4.0617	−3.7813	−3.8298	−3.7510	−3.7215	−3.4912
−3.3947	−3.1826	−3.1488	−3.0763	−3.2091	−3.1075	−3.1570
−3.1672	−3.2427	−3.0795	−3.1741	−3.1729	−3.3066	−3.1586
−3.2997	−3.2409	−3.4380	−3.3168	−3.3694	−3.2057	−3.1971
−2.8972	−2.7739	−2.6294	−2.6951	−2.6743	−2.6957	−2.6802
−2.8151	−2.7358	−2.6911	−2.6478	−2.7369	−2.7032	−2.6768

load rple; ? price surprise variable

0.0000	0.0109	0.0108	−0.0110	0.0138	0.0081	−0.0242
−0.0117	0.0131	0.0034	0.0229	−0.0047	0.0053	−0.0182
0.0229	−0.0085	0.0060	−0.0142	0.0080	−0.0106	−0.0070
0.0234	−0.0270	0.0056	0.0084	−0.0006	0.0060	−0.0056
0.0115	−0.0107	0.0052	−0.0107	0.0171	−0.0153	−0.0085
−0.0016	0.0096	0.0021	−0.0043	−0.0058	0.0034	−0.0003
0.0069	0.0040	0.0007	−0.0054	0.0022	−0.0004	−0.0014
0.0060	−0.0058	−0.0079	0.0035	0.0071	−0.0010	−0.0088
−0.0153	−0.0069	−0.0057	0.0004	−0.0037	0.0029	−0.0156 .
0.0001	0.0051	0.0181	−0.0016	0.0034	0.0027	0.0143
−0.0138	−0.0359	−0.0019	0.0093	−0.0438	−0.0275	−0.0236

0.0181	0.0253	0.0235	0.0152	0.0174	0.0058	−0.0027
0.0386	−0.0467	−0.0249	0.0270	−0.0153	0.0206	0.0118
−0.0007	−0.0148	−0.0058	−0.0063	−0.0082	−0.0233	0.0075
0.0052	0.0117	0.0158	0.0292	0.0031	0.0025	0.0020
−0.0081	0.0006	0.0059	−0.0027	0.0096	0.0000	0.0052;

load pbar; ? output price index (*PBAR*)

14.9868	15.2609	15.2969	15.5132	15.5653	15.7553	15.9508
16.0498	16.1095	16.2565	16.1846	16.2622	16.1792	16.4545
16.2934	16.4838	16.4271	16.6836	16.6633	16.8600	16.9608
16.8672	17.4328	17.2084	17.4178	17.5891	17.5864	17.6905
17.7162	18.0011	17.9043	18.8276	18.2206	18.5362	18.5909
18.7501	18.9529	19.1952	19.3308	19.4431	19.7267	19.9554
20.0856	20.1770	20.4641	20.6037	20.7032	20.8193	21.3412
21.6384	21.8540	21.8752	22.3023	22.4531	22.6185	22.8579
23.5426	23.9755	24.4256	24.9011	25.5526	26.0076	26.8032
27.1320	27.7408	27.8662	28.7668	29.1619	30.0659	30.5036
31.8336	33.4301	35.6548	37.2401	39.7034	41.6460	44.9060
46.6366	48.8172	50.5565	52.7263	54.5607	56.2772	58.1686
61.4887	62.4324	63.6095	64.0812	67.1474	67.8821	69.4895
70.6767	73.5432	75.6750	78.5262	81.4621	85.7057	89.5838
92.4475	93.8637	96.0800	98.0796	100.6755	101.7266	102.4383
105.0532	106.1874	107.6957	109.7330	110.6830	112.5717	113.4615;

load pu52; ? proportion of males who are long-term
        ? unemployed (*U*52)

11.8000	14.1000	13.1000	10.8000	9.4000	13.4000	13.9000
11.6000	10.3000	11.6000	12.2000	12.1000	14.1000	18.9000
20.1000	18.9000	20.2000	24.7000	24.4000	20.9000	20.3000
22.8000	20.9000	16.2000	14.9000	15.6000	16.3000	15.5000
12.6000	16.1000	20.7000	21.1000	19.5000	22.4000	25.7000
23.3000	19.9000	21.8000	22.9000	20.2000	17.3000	18.8000
20.4000	15.4000	11.6000	12.8000	14.9000	15.7000	15.1000
16.7000	18.6000	18.5000	17.2000	18.6000	20.0000	20.1000
17.6000	18.5000	19.8000	20.3000	16.7000	16.5000	17.1000
17.3000	16.6000	18.5000	22.4000	24.7000	24.8000	26.8000
29.5000	30.2000	26.3000	22.5000	23.7000	22.4000	19.6000
16.8000	15.9000	16.9000	16.7000	19.4000	19.5000	23.4000
23.4000	25.1000	23.4000	25.8000	25.5000	27.0000	25.4000
28.2000	27.2000	30.2000	28.8000	30.0000	27.2000	26.5000
22.6000	22.2000	20.8000	22.3000	24.4000	29.2000	32.5000
36.6000	37.8000	39.6000	38.6000	40.4000	40.8000	41.5000;

load ln; ? log of employees in employment

9.9718	9.9766	9.9795	9.9762	9.9740	9.9809	9.9804
9.9771	9.9698	9.9735	9.9719	9.9701	9.9723	9.9788
9.9870	9.9882	9.9952	10.0004	10.0049	10.1063	10.0148
10.0156	10.0210	10.0157	10.0205	10.0245	10.0257	10.0206
10.0143	10.0258	10.0288	10.0327	10.0306	10.0385	10.0454
10.0466	10.0440	10.0496	10.0523	10.0553	10.0516	10.0563
10.0573	10.0439	10.0314	10.0357	10.0391	10.0316	10.0240
10.0277	10.0302	10.0278	10.0227	10.0268	10.0281	10.0243
10.0206	10.0203	10.0207	10.0175	10.0016	10.0043	9.9981
9.9964	10.0002	10.0043	10.0103	10.0163	10.0250	10.0285
10.0324	10.0333	10.0265	10.0340	10.0404	10.0377	10.0271
10.0306	10.0310	10.0281	10.0175	10.0232	10.0258	10.0275
10.0196	10.0266	10.0296	10.0302	10.0244	10.0335	10.0396
10.0466	10.0392	10.0500	10.0539	10.0538	10.0412	10.0420
10.0323	10.0172	9.9968	9.9929	9.9896	9.9805	9.9697
9.9711	9.9676	9.9584	9.9467	9.9546	9.9594	9.9603;

load lrpw; ? log of the real product wage (W)

3.9299	3.9396	3.9658	3.9454	3.9703	3.9600	3.9306
3.9393	3.9543	3.9489	3.9838	3.9711	4.0507	4.0027
4.0355	4.0149	4.0509	4.0547	4.0727	4.0586	4.0739
4.0866	4.0546	4.0791	4.0837	4.0909	4.1152	4.1131
4.1947	4.1854	4.1896	4.1774	4.2292	4.2088	4.2149
4.2188	4.2596	4.2551	4.3483	4.2803	4.3511	4.3248
4.3279	4.3354	4.3458	4.3320	4.4111	4.3535	4.3856
4.3814	4.4805	4.4109	4.4185	4.4303	4.4277	4.4487
4.4748	4.4862	4.4924	4.5090	4.5190	4.5488	4.5092
4.5136	4.5612	4.5382	4.5393	4.5736	4.5684	4.5953
4.6074	4.5745	4.6570	4.6233	4.6235	4.6362	4.6262
4.6530	4.6852	4.6911	4.7024	4.7093	4.7012	4.6900
4.7251	4.6833	4.6901	4.6908	4.6676	4.7242	4.7070
4.7197	4.7130	4.7533	4.7622	4.7572	4.7325	4.7484
4.7807	4.7846	4.8195	4.8302	4.8316	4.8208	4.8463
4.8337	4.8322	4.8248	4.8367	4.8561	4.8417	4.8704;

load rpi80; ? retail price index 1980 base

16.9483	17.3067	17.2043	17.3579	17.5627	17.7163	17.9211
18.1772	18.2284	18.4844	18.2796	18.5356	18.5868	18.4332
18.3820	18.5356	18.5356	18.6380	18.6380	18.8428	18.9452
19.2012	19.4572	19.6621	19.8669	20.2765	20.1741	20.1741
20.4813	20.5837	20.4301	20.5837	20.7885	21.1470	21.3518

21.5054	21.7102	22.2734	22.3758	22.4782	22.6831	23.0927
23.1951	23.3487	23.5023	23.7071	23.5535	23.8607	24.1679
24.7824	24.8848	25.1920	25.7040	26.1137	26.1649	26.4721
26.9841	27.6498	27.9570	28.5202	29.2883	30.3635	30.7732
31.1316	31.6436	32.2069	32.7701	33.5381	34.1526	35.2279
35.7911	37.0200	38.5049	40.8090	41.8331	43.7276	46.3390
50.7424	52.9442	54.7875	56.7844	58.8326	60.2151	62.9800
66.1546	69.0732	70.1485	71.1726	72.4014	74.3984	75.6784
76.9585	79.3651	82.2837	87.7624	90.2202	94.5213	100.0000
102.0993	104.0451	106.5028	111.6743	113.6201	116.4362	118.3308
122.1198	122.6319	123.6047	124.2192	126.7793	128.3666	129.8515;

load lecp; ? log of real average earnings

4.1168	4.1243	4.1579	4.1581	4.1508	4.1466	4.1378
4.1386	4.1445	4.1392	4.1675	4.1620	4.2004	4.2167
4.2432	4.2427	4.2657	4.2677	4.2827	4.2791	4.2737
4.2749	4.2688	4.2655	4.2480	4.2560	4.2818	4.2954
4.3265	4.3470	4.3732	4.3780	4.3921	4.3928	4.4005
4.4104	4.4178	4.4087	4.4203	4.4423	4.4488	4.4463
4.4469	4.4403	4.4388	4.4451	4.4712	4.4775	4.4835
4.4723	4.4910	4.5010	4.4940	4.4997	4.5146	4.5318
4.5447	4.5513	4.5703	4.5832	4.5849	4.5695	4.5831
4.5879	4.6038	4.6173	4.6332	4.6564	4.6606	4.6677
4.6807	4.6776	4.6357	4.6598	4.7045	4.7352	4.7262
4.6857	4.7032	4.7060	4.7027	4.7018	4.7060	4.6819
4.6531	4.6199	4.6270	4.6495	4.6615	4.6890	4.6915
4.6963	4.7096	4.7135	4.6770	4.7161	4.7188	4.7131
4.7499	4.7445	4.7353	4.7163	4.7360	4.7276	4.7347
4.7201	4.7297	4.7439	4.7688	4.7613	4.7656	4.7718;

load pi; ? gross trading profits inc. N. Sea companies (*pi*)

0.00	0.00	0.00	0.00	0.00	0.00	0.00
0.00	0.00	0.00	0.00	0.00	0.00	0.00
0.00	0.00	997.00	944.00	969.00	929.00	942.00
840.00	1009.00	894.00	863.00	902.00	958.00	933.00
844.00	1065.00	1062.00	1147.00	1126.00	1178.00	1184.00
1172.00	1237.00	1200.00	1213.00	1195.00	1161.00	1115.00
1247.00	1214.00	1269.00	1317.00	1153.00	1174.00	1242.00
1256.00	1384.00	1330.00	1412.00	1429.00	1435.00	1362.00
1388.00	1416.00	1446.00	1507.00	1561.00	1577.00	1715.00
1770.00	1830.00	1908.00	1924.00	2066.00	2463.00	2221.00
2054.00	2188.00	1527.00	2107.00	2149.00	2055.00	2038.00

2072.00	2038.00	2416.00	2605.00	2429.00	2662.00	3297.00
3960.00	4372.00	4663.00	4717.00	5281.00	5175.00	5646.00
5197.00	5321.00	6154.00	6386.00	6519.00	6898.00	7130.00
6190.00	6555.00	6584.00	6834.00	7609.00	8347.00	7185.00
8736.00	8725.00	9241.00	9537.00	9764.00	10781.00	10896.00;

load cpsur; ? consumer price surprise variable

0.0000	0.0000	0.0000	0.0000	0.0000	0.0060	−0.0085
−0.0042	0.0098	−0.0068	0.0224	−0.0103	0.0028	0.0171
−0.0045	−0.0047	0.0039	−0.0079	0.0013	−0.0066	−0.0008
−0.0073	−0.0067	0.0016	−0.0016	−0.0087	0.0207	0.0056
−0.0109	0.0096	0.0096	−0.0094	−0.0014	−0.0101	−0.0042
0.0027	−0.0005	−0.0132	0.0114	0.0043	−0.0019	−0.0026
0.0062	0.0000	0.0011	0.0026	0.0130	−0.0114	−0.0055
−0.0145	0.0055	−0.0011	−0.0085	0.0049	0.0094	−0.0029
−0.0052	−0.0082	0.0027	−0.0065	−0.0081	−0.0118	0.0103
0.0082	0.0025	0.0063	−0.0018	−0.0082	0.0011	−0.0124
0.0073	−0.0125	−0.0148	−0.0237	0.0121	−0.0105	−0.0183
−0.0356	0.0144	0.0164	0.0111	0.0236	0.0152	−0.0149
−0.0115	−0.0011	0.0202	0.0183	0.0129	0.0005	0.0034
0.0007	−0.0136	−0.0092	−0.0377	0.0117	−0.0120	−0.0165
0.0368	0.0106	0.0085	−0.0108	0.0146	−0.0020	0.0074
−0.0009	0.0189	0.0092	0.0065	−0.0038	−0.0015	0.0000;

load lf; ? log of labour force (Layard–Nickell)

9.9838	9.9876	9.9915	9.9882	9.9920	9.9959	9.9934
9.9921	9.9908	9.9955	9.9939	9.9961	10.0023	10.0028
10.0080	10.0102	10.0172	10.0174	10.0199	10.0286	10.0338
10.0306	10.0360	10.0357	10.0435	10.0455	10.0477	10.0476
10.0583	10.0538	10.0528	10.0567	10.0546	10.0575	10.0624
10.0646	10.0630	10.0656	10.0683	10.0713	10.0686	10.0713
10.0733	10.0719	10.0634	10.0647	10.0681	10.0636	10.0590
10.0587	10.0612	10.0598	10.0576	10.0575	10.0600	10.0581
10.0565	10.0540	10.0545	10.0520	10.0421	10.0473	10.0451
10.0474	10.0562	10.0532	10.0582	10.0622	10.0680	10.0644
10.0644	10.0633	10.0635	10.0671	10.0774	10.0746	10.0720
10.0784	10.0899	10.0910	10.0874	10.0910	10.0985	10.1007
10.0672	10.0710	10.0805	10.0788	10.0732	10.0801	10.0897
10.0891	10.0852	10.0884	10.0936	10.0895	10.0841	10.0879
10.0930	10.0894	10.0942	10.0965	10.1031	10.1020	10.1015
10.1013	10.1050	10.1046	10.0982	10.1100	10.1191	10.1156;

load lwcp; ? real consumption wage

3.9283	3.9278	3.9665	3.9639	3.9611	3.9466	3.9350
3.9462	3.9519	3.9375	3.9736	3.9680	4.0320	4.0202
4.0360	4.0327	4.0499	4.0680	4.0801	4.0791	4.0891
4.0710	4.0674	4.0745	4.0731	4.0606	4.0915	4.1075
4.1567	4.1644	4.1716	4.1762	4.1946	4.1802	4.1851
4.2001	4.2194	4.1850	4.2872	4.2314	4.2706	4.2405
4.2516	4.2448	4.2435	4.2478	4.3382	4.2769	4.2990
4.2574	4.3605	4.2800	4.2701	4.2671	4.2790	4.2958
4.3124	4.3098	4.3366	4.3519	4.3675	4.3633	4.3764
4.3867	4.4401	4.4301	4.4428	4.4630	4.4452	4.4463
4.4591	4.4530	4.4750	4.4023	4.4550	4.4910	4.4992
4.4476	4.4678	4.4674	4.4745	4.4607	4.4588	4.4259
4.3947	4.3815	4.3884	4.4108	4.4214	4.4627	4.4651
4.4698	4.4879	4.5025	4.4804	4.5077	4.4905	4.4682
4.5305	4.5513	4.5814	4.5207	4.5223	4.5080	4.5269
4.5065	4.5161	4.5244	4.5560	4.5507	4.5462	4.5704;

load pix; ? gross trading profits excl. N. Sea companies (*pi*)

0.00	0.00	0.00	0.00	0.00	0.00	0.00
0.00	0.00	0.00	0.00	0.00	0.00	0.00
0.00	0.00	997.00	944.00	969.00	929.00	942.00
840.00	1009.00	894.00	863.00	902.00	958.00	933.00
884.00	1065.00	1062.00	1147.00	1126.00	1178.00	1184.00
1172.00	1237.00	1200.00	1213.00	1195.00	1161.00	1115.00
1247.00	1214.00	1269.00	1317.00	1153.00	1174.00	1242.00
1256.00	1384.00	1330.00	1412.00	1429.00	1435.00	1362.00
1382.00	1409.00	1439.00	1502.00	1558.00	1575.00	1712.00
1765.00	1821.00	1896.00	1910.00	2051.00	2450.00	2211.00
2048.00	2184.00	1522.00	2106.00	2155.00	2072.00	2065.00
2099.00	2051.00	2399.00	2552.00	2335.00	2545.00	3034.00
3524.00	3864.00	4142.00	4211.00	4723.00	4528.00	5004.00
4430.00	4378.00	4960.00	4859.00	4928.00	4968.00	5173.00
4195.00	4381.00	4144.00	4151.00	4785.00	5430.00	4506.00
5735.00	5269.00	5657.00	5849.00	6116.00	6663.00	6677.00

load lpipbln; ? log of real profits per employee in
? employment incl. N. Sea companies

-9.9718	-9.9766	-9.9795	-9.9762	-9.9740	-9.9809	-9.9804
-9.9771	-9.9698	-9.9735	-9.9719	-9.9701	-9.9723	-9.9788
-9.9870	-9.9882	-1.2842	-1.3595	-1.3367	-1.3963	-1.3925
-1.5024	-1.3575	-1.4602	-1.5124	-1.4820	-1.4228	-1.4501

−1.4992	−1.3403	−1.3408	−1.3179	−1.3016	−1.2815	−1.2862
−1.3062	−1.2603	−1.3090	−1.3080	−1.3317	−1.3714	−1.4280
−1.3236	−1.3416	−1.2989	−1.2729	−1.4141	−1.3941	−1.3550
−1.3613	−1.2767	−1.3151	−1.2695	−1.2683	−1.2728	−1.3317
−1.3387	−1.3366	−1.3346	−1.3094	−1.2841	−1.2943	−1.2343
−1.2132	−1.2059	−1.1727	−1.2022	−1.1506	−1.0141	−1.1355
−1.2603	−1.2469	−1.6641	−1.3932	−1.4439	−1.5337	−1.6068
−1.6315	−1.6942	−1.5562	−1.5123	−1.6221	−1.5640	−1.3849
−1.2493	−1.1725	−1.1298	−1.1263	−1.0543	−1.0945	−1.0369
−1.1437	−1.1525	−1.0465	−1.0503	−1.0663	−1.0480	−1.0600
−1.2231	−1.1659	−1.1645	−1.1438	−1.0593	−0.9680	−1.1141
−0.9452	−0.9537	−0.9011	−0.8766	−0.8696	−0.7923	−0.7905;

load lpixpbln; ? log of real profits per employee in
? employment excl. N. Sea companies

−9.9718	−9.9766	−9.9795	−9.9762	−9.9740	−9.9809	−9.9804
−9.9771	−9.9698	−9.9735	−9.9719	−9.9701	−9.9723	−9.9788
−9.9870	−9.9882	−1.2842	−1.3595	−1.3367	−1.3963	−1.3925
−1.5024	−1.3575	−1.4602	−1.5124	−1.4820	−1.4228	−1.4501
−1.4992	−1.3403	−1.3408	−1.3179	−1.3016	−1.2815	−1.2862
−1.3062	−1.2603	−1.3090	−1.3080	−1.3317	−1.3714	−1.4280
−1.3236	−1.3416	−1.2989	−1.2729	−1.4141	−1.3941	−1.3550
−1.3613	−1.2767	−1.3151	−1.2695	−1.2683	−1.2728	−1.3317
−1.3430	−1.3416	−1.3394	−1.3127	−1.2860	−1.2955	−1.2361
−1.2161	−1.2108	−1.1790	−1.2095	−1.1579	−1.0194	−1.1400
−1.2632	−1.2487	−1.6674	−1.3937	−1.4411	−1.5254	−1.5936
−1.6186	−1.6878	−1.5633	−1.5328	−1.6616	−1.6090	−1.4681
−1.3659	−1.2960	−1.2483	−1.2397	−1.1659	−1.2281	−1.1576
−1.3034	−1.3476	−1.2622	−1.3236	−1.3461	−1.3762	−1.3808
−1.6121	−1.5689	−1.6274	−1.6424	−1.5231	−1.3980	−1.5807
−1.3661	−1.4580	−1.3919	−1.3655	−1.3374	−1.2735	−1.2802;

load hpls; ? house prices in London and South East (John Muellbauer)

2227.71	2303.18	2378.35	2356.02	2320.73	2272.50	2285.31
2347.77	2357.93	2322.90	2359.75	2378.95	2461.78	2435.32
2468.97	2561.52	2585.61	2716.06	2748.62	3070.95	2973.11
3207.72	3308.03	3259.83	3370.92	3324.55	3370.86	3437.70
3472.81	3806.18	3746.19	3808.63	4073.04	4257.98	4213.66
4284.35	4536.02	4493.69	4723.31	4651.60	4665.34	4705.73
4913.25	4481.81	4687.49	4855.38	5033.21	5136.09	5175.13
5150.26	5335.48	5282.91	5383.22	5416.46	5588.99	5606.52
5690.21	5762.43	6121.09	6138.62	6384.27	6687.33	7100.68

7579.30	8211.71	9186.47	10847.43	11913.74	12561.86	12957.69
13209.08	13370.13	13449.90	13386.75	13125.38	13346.56	13202.43
13817.32	14069.93	13898.60	14263.91	14596.28	14876.99	15218.12
15310.58	15377.96	15747.20	16228.83	16880.89	17425.27	19190.88
20772.97	22277.71	24066.17	26002.09	27896.92	28987.70	30096.62
30585.20	30972.88	31020.31	31676.59	31605.59	31589.88	29555.77
31659.97	32690.64	32929.95	34314.41	35089.15	37324.50	37763.84

load lhplspb; ? log of real house prices in London and South East

9.6067	9.6219	9.6517	9.6282	9.6098	9.5766	9.5699
9.5907	9.5913	9.5673	9.5874	9.5907	9.6301	9.6024
9.6260	9.6511	9.6640	9.6977	9.7108	9.8100	9.7716
9.8531	9.8509	9.8492	9.8706	9.8470	9.8610	9.8747
9.8834	9.9591	9.9486	9.9149	10.0148	10.0420	10.0286
10.0367	10.0830	10.0609	10.1037	10.0826	10.0711	10.0682
10.1049	10.0084	10.0392	10.0675	10.0987	10.1133	10.0962
10.0775	10.1029	10.0920	10.0915	10.0909	10.1150	10.1076
10.0929	10.0873	10.1290	10.1126	10.1260	10.1547	10.1846
10.2376	10.2956	10.4032	10.5376	10.6178	10.6402	10.6568
10.6333	10.5965	10.5380	10.4898	10.4060	10.3750	10.2888
10.2965	10.2689	10.2216	10.2055	10.1944	10.1825	10.1721
10.1226	10.1118	10.1168	10.1396	10.1322	10.1531	10.2262
10.2885	10.3186	10.3673	10.4077	10.4413	10.4289	10.4222
10.4068	10.4042	10.3824	10.3827	10.3544	10.3435	10.2699
10.3135	10.3348	10.3280	10.3504	10.3641	10.4090	10.4128;

load ulr; ? long term unemployment rate (Layard–Nickell)

0.0014	0.0016	0.0016	0.0013	0.0017	0.0020	0.0018
0.0017	0.0022	0.0026	0.0027	0.0031	0.0042	0.0045
0.0042	0.0042	0.0044	0.0042	0.0037	0.0038	0.0039
0.0034	0.0031	0.0032	0.0034	0.0033	0.0036	0.0042
0.0055	0.0045	0.0050	0.0051	0.0047	0.0043	0.0044
0.0042	0.0038	0.0035	0.0037	0.0032	0.0029	0.0028
0.0033	0.0043	0.0037	0.0037	0.0043	0.0050	0.0053
0.0052	0.0058	0.0059	0.0060	0.0058	0.0064	0.0068
0.0063	0.0063	0.0067	0.0071	0.0068	0.0071	0.0080
0.0088	0.0093	0.0091	0.0108	0.0114	0.0107	0.0096
0.0094	0.0091	0.0097	0.0074	0.0088	0.0083	0.0088
0.0081	0.0094	0.0106	0.0117	0.0132	0.0140	0.0168
0.0168	0.0176	0.0178	0.0186	0.0189	0.0186	0.0185
0.0186	0.0190	0.0190	0.0187	0.0186	0.0190	0.0193
0.0201	0.0224	0.0250	0.0281	0.0332	0.0418	0.0494
0.0545	0.0593	0.0645	0.0645	0.0687	0.0710	0.0701;

load imps; ? share of imports in value added (*nu*)

0.2056	0.1931	0.1941	0.1803	0.2022	0.1881	0.2026
0.1842	0.1951	0.1942	0.2015	0.1949	0.2020	0.2068
0.2043	0.1983	0.2197	0.2201	0.2211	0.2074	0.2208
0.2094	0.2075	0.1952	0.2186	0.2071	0.2138	0.2014
0.2101	0.2086	0.2218	0.2036	0.2210	0.2211	0.2295
0.2126	0.2124	0.2181	0.2270	0.2109	0.2273	0.2199
0.2310	0.1959	0.2239	0.2288	0.2276	0.2278	0.2458
0.2334	0.2368	0.2193	0.2491	0.2391	0.2376	0.2193
0.2424	0.2521	0.2466	0.2400	0.2650	0.2558	0.2478
0.2403	0.2831	0.2746	0.2647	0.2722	0.2899	0.2826
0.2790	0.2846	0.2993	0.3000	0.2846	0.2754	0.2760
0.2765	0.2770	0.2560	0.2634	0.2874	0.2749	0.2636
0.2801	0.2880	0.2707	0.2496	0.2846	0.2795	0.2735
0.2598	0.2920	0.3111	0.2922	0.2945	0.3174	0.3122
0.2828	0.2660	0.2640	0.2939	0.3116	0.2903	0.2960
0.3139	0.2907	0.2710	0.2878	0.3092	0.2964	0.2842;

A.3.2. *ANNUAL DATA SET*

smpl 1952 1983;
? Layard–Nickell annual data set,
? published in Economica 1986, special
? issue. Note that some of the data
? does not commence till later than 1952,
? and estimation was over the period 1956–83.

load id; ? data identifier for annual data series

1952	1953	1954	1955	1956	1957
1958	1959	1960	1961	1962	1963
1964	1965	1966	1967	1968	1969
1970	1971	1972	1973	1974	1975
1976	1977	1978	1979	1980	1981
1982	1983				

load klf; ? log of capital–labour force ratio

−4.53590	−4.51837	−4.50597	−4.49224	−4.48050	−4.46257
−4.43511	−4.41640	−4.39433	−4.37455	−4.35958	−4.33429
−4.30582	−4.27367	−4.24725	−4.19805	−4.15305	−4.10860

−4.06687	−4.02457	−3.99360	−3.96754	−3.94016	−3.92524
−3.90435	−3.88294	−3.86092	−3.84732	−3.83313	−3.81686
−3.80114	−3.77568;				

load lrpw; ? log of real product wage (W)

4.14167	4.18682	4.23102	4.26421	4.30280	4.30259
4.33069	4.35100	4.40912	4.44478	4.46882	4.48839
4.52228	4.57488	4.64176	4.66008	4.69363	4.73240
4.82545	4.85910	4.91480	4.93936	4.91902	4.97661
4.94910	4.92155	4.97462	5.02247	5.04894	5.05931
5.07679	5.07535;				

load ltl; ? employer tax rate (*t1*)

4.50529	4.50352	4.50585	4.50673	4.50728	4.50492
4.51194	4.51251	4.51015	4.50931	4.51305	4.51647
4.51089	4.51749	4.54455	4.55059	4.55649	4.56271
4.56851	4.56778	4.57086	4.58273	4.57926	4.60517
4.61881	4.63370	4.64140	4.64826	4.64599	4.64835
4.64247	4.63319;				

load lnur; ? log of male unemployment rate (*U*)

−4.13517	−4.07454	−4.26870	−4.50986	−4.42285	−4.13517
−3.81671	−3.72970	−4.01738	−4.07454	−3.77226	−3.57555
−3.91202	−4.07454	−4.01738	−3.50656	−3.41125	−3.41125
−3.32424	−3.05761	−2.97593	−3.32424	−3.32424	−2.90042
−2.64507	−2.60369	−2.63109	−2.70306	−2.44185	−1.98777
−1.83258	−1.78976;				

load lnup; ? log of measure of union power (*UP*)

.00000	−2.40795	−2.65926	−2.40795	−1.96611	−1.83258
−1.89712	−2.04022	−1.83258	−1.77196	−1.66073	−1.89712
−1.83258	−1.66073	−1.77196	−1.77196	−1.60944	−1.56065
−1.34707	−1.34707	−1.17118	−1.17118	−1.38629	−1.17118
−1.20397	−1.13943	−1.27297	−1.23787	−0.89160	−0.83241
−0.84165	−0.84630;				

load pmp; ? log of import price index for UK (*PM*)

0.41142	0.26504	0.23888	0.24070	0.21655	0.18048
0.08163	0.05848	0.04558	−0.00299	−0.03820	−0.02380
−0.02526	−0.05961	−0.07822	−0.10118	−0.03013	−0.03495

−0.06760	−0.11277	−0.15215	−0.00970	0.16699	0.08422
0.13783	0.16174	0.10903	0.09186	0.07849	0.05704
0.08167	0.10510;				

load rho; ? replacement ratio (RHO)

1.00000	40.50000	37.80000	37.50000	37.70000	36.20000
40.09999	40.60000	42.00000	42.00000	42.40001	43.90001
43.00000	47.50000	48.20000	52.60000	51.70001	50.80000
51.20000	50.60000	47.00000	46.59999	47.20000	49.20000
50.00000	51.30000	49.80000	46.00000	45.80000	50.30000
53.50000	54.40000;				

load t2; ? income tax rate ($t2$)

0.08400	0.08600	0.08600	0.09000	0.09300	0.09800
0.11000	0.10800	0.11000	0.11600	0.12300	0.12200
0.12700	0.14100	0.15200	0.15300	0.16700	0.17500
0.18600	0.18800	0.17800	0.18600	0.20900	0.23700
0.24500	0.23300	0.22300	0.21300	0.22000	0.23800
0.24300	0.24400;				

load t3; ? indirect tax rate ($t3$)

1.00000	0.12077	0.11688	0.11799	0.11844	0.11572
0.11058	0.10740	0.10273	0.10307	0.10717	0.10615
0.11235	0.12025	0.12547	0.12787	0.13606	0.15135
0.14659	0.13240	0.11510	0.10586	0.08894	0.08797
0.09214	0.10369	0.09933	0.11247	0.11815	0.12324
0.13273	0.12536;				

load lnurs; ? log of short-term unemployment rate

−6.90776	−4.40714	−4.61220	−4.84597	−4.70278	−4.44305
−4.08876	−4.17274	−4.52175	−4.51168	−4.13018	−4.08578
−4.44646	−4.55068	−4.44475	−3.91603	−3.85423	−3.86038
−3.75844	−3.47668	−3.54461	−3.96174	−3.82173	−3.30716
−3.14725	−3.13201	−3.20030	−3.32174	−2.94390	−2.70905
−2.77115	−2.80429;				

load 1k; ? log of the capital stock (K)

5.40133	5.42583	5.45233	5.47688	5.50167	5.52784
5.55335	5.57973	5.61786	5.65179	5.68256	5.71538
5.74939	5.79027	5.82511	5.86703	5.90808	5.95116
5.98946	6.02635	6.06146	6.09695	6.12992	6.16036

6.18970	6.21720	6.24397	6.26891	6.29490	6.31192
6.32954	6.34616;				

load pbar; ? output price index (PBAR)

26.53300	26.68600	26.98800	28.20100	29.46000	30.78500
31.39100	31.71700	32.13400	33.05301	33.93600	34.77600
35.82800	37.25100	38.71800	39.96800	41.89700	43.68400
46.90300	51.01300	54.90599	60.83900	74.67299	92.27301
107.06500	121.60900	132.80500	149.31600	173.90200	190.64500
203.05100	215.35010;				

load ln; ? log of employees in employment

9.92123	9.92720	9.94429	9.95812	9.97016	9.97441
9.96646	9.97213	9.99420	10.00933	10.01913	10.02167
10.03522	10.04694	10.05436	10.03509	10.02814	10.02677
10.02034	10.00392	10.00406	10.02849	10.03408	10.02677
10.02305	10.02615	10.03289	10.04923	10.04103	9.99177
9.97068	9.95485;				

load ulr; ? long-term unemployment rate

0.00213	0.00264	0.00234	0.00188	0.00164	0.00208
0.00246	0.00437	0.00432	0.00376	0.00363	0.00583
0.00519	0.00399	0.00376	0.00458	0.00629	0.00676
0.00731	0.00867	0.01207	0.01125	0.00908	0.00970
0.01426	0.01755	0.01874	0.01998	0.02015	0.03426
0.06198	0.06983;				

load pu52; ? long-term unemployed proportion (U52)

0.13300	0.15500	0.16700	0.17100	0.13700	0.13000
0.11200	0.18200	0.24000	0.22100	0.15783	0.20805
0.25929	0.23469	0.20907	0.15270	0.19062	0.20497
0.20292	0.18448	0.23674	0.31528	0.25212	0.17628
0.20087	0.23982	0.26032	0.29824	0.23162	0.25007
0.38740	0.41815;				

load lecp; ? log of real average weekly earnings

4.09121	4.11917	4.17939	4.22116	4.23913	4.25354
4.24811	4.29649	4.35822	4.37722	4.36812	4.40412
4.44944	4.48241	4.47899	4.50689	4.53346	4.55682
4.61700	4.62476	4.70305	4.74810	4.77194	4.75812

| 4.72193 | 4.65973 | 4.71080 | 4.73920 | 4.72792 | 4.72086 |
| 4.72576 | 4.76509; | | | | |

load lwcp; ? real consumption wage

4.05803	4.07816	4.11481	4.14196	4.17159	4.17711
4.17317	4.19993	4.26021	4.28579	4.28294	4.30453
4.33619	4.35779	4.38493	4.40371	4.41530	4.42764
4.51172	4.53771	4.60610	4.62435	4.63533	4.62569
4.56997	4.52329	4.58998	4.63513	4.64208	4.60612
4.60354	4.62404;				

load pi; ? gross trading profits incl. N. Sea companies (pi)

2249.00	2394.00	2665.00	3003.00	3092.00	3243.00
3150.00	3498.00	3839.00	3685.00	3656.00	4158.00
4660.00	4845.00	4737.00	4913.00	5212.00	5638.00
5757.00	6623.00	7728.00	8926.00	7838.00	8564.00
10993.00	17712.00	21299.00	24380.00	26773.00	29374.00
33887.00	40978.00;				

load pix; ? gross trading profits excl. N. Sea companies (pi)

2249.00	2394.00	2665.00	3003.00	3092.00	3243.00
3150.00	3498.00	3839.00	3685.00	3656.00	4158.00
4660.00	4845.00	4737.00	4913.00	5212.00	5638.00
5732.00	6610.00	7678.00	8893.00	7855.00	8614.00
10466.00	15741.00	18865.00	19125.00	18717.00	18510.00
21167.00	25305.00;				

load lpipbln; ? log of real profits per employee
              ? in employment incl. N. Sea companies

-0.87621	-0.82545	-0.74655	-0.68494	-0.71145	-0.71201
-0.75265	-0.66387	-0.60598	-0.69025	-0.73431	-0.63264
-0.56201	-0.57375	-0.64234	-0.61836	-0.59947	-0.56130
-0.60508	-0.53253	-0.45191	-0.43483	-0.77529	-0.89486
-0.78630	-0.43979	-0.35019	-0.34861	-0.39920	-0.34915
-0.24818	-0.10115;				

load lpixpbln; ? log of real profits per employee
               ? in employment excl. N. Sea companies

-0.87621	-0.82545	-0.74655	-0.68494	-0.71145	-0.71201
-0.75265	-0.66387	-0.60598	-0.69025	-0.73431	-0.63264
-0.56201	-0.57375	-0.64234	-0.61836	-0.59947	-0.56130

−0.60943	−0.53449	−0.45840	−0.43853	−0.77312	−0.88904
−0.83543	−0.55777	−0.47154	−0.59137	−0.75716	−0.81095
−0.71877	−0.58319;				

load wofnew; ? log of real house price index (John Muellbauer)

0.00000	−0.14157	−0.14831	−0.15779	−0.15176	−0.16408
−0.16187	−0.17144	−0.15833	−0.15207	−0.13348	−0.12241
−0.10053	−0.08793	−0.08385	−0.07410	−0.07751	−0.06050
−0.06412	−0.05895	0.01428	0.12613	0.09942	0.04021
0.00110	−0.01883	0.01731	0.08694	0.11103	0.09793
0.09183	0.11251;				

load av23rd; ? regional house price dispersion variable (John Muellbauer)

0.00000	0.00000	0.00000	0.00000	0.02248	0.02347
0.03105	0.03033	0.02835	0.03510	0.04568	0.07193
0.08190	0.08929	0.09477	0.11136	0.11624	0.10881
0.11224	0.11099	0.10856	0.11872	0.15531	0.19341
0.17428	0.12927	0.10512	0.09974	0.10481	0.13131
0.14898	0.14376;				

load lqpw; ? unit value index of world manufacturing exports (P^*)

0.76821	0.71240	0.72627	0.74855	0.71803	0.70138
0.64175	0.65100	0.65064	0.63890	0.64104	0.63894
0.67650	0.67151	0.65315	0.65977	0.57725	0.57589
0.57270	0.58270	0.58320	0.68099	0.82512	0.79751
0.81963	0.84684	0.79798	0.91109	1.08522	1.12516
1.04187	1.01062;				

load lvr; log of vacancy rate (V)

0.00000	−3.12325	−2.96848	−2.77472	−2.93807	−3.20436
−3.50002	−3.36307	−3.08644	−3.09689	−3.46204	−3.49847
−3.08608	−2.91323	−2.95882	−3.32384	−3.20608	−3.17672
−3.21368	−3.65031	−3.53521	−2.88695	−2.96942	−3.64560
−3.86858	−3.70124	−3.48514	−3.43123	−3.97255	−4.34119
−4.18258	−3.90155;				

load wt; ? deviation of world trade from trend (WT)

0.00000	0.00000	−0.02178	−0.00305	0.05158	0.03412
−0.05077	−0.03690	0.02820	−0.00441	−0.01623	0.01269
0.00546	0.00989	0.00394	−0.04607	0.00125	0.01805
0.01306	0.00456	0.00614	0.04778	0.02828	−0.08123

−0.02031	−0.02888	−0.01328	0.03159	0.03569	0.01614
−0.01404	−0.01149;				

load mm; ? labour market mismatch variable (Layard–Nickell)

0.00000	0.00000	0.16050	0.48662	0.16073	0.27468
0.24430	0.53488	0.35941	0.06475	0.72921	0.66795
0.15944	0.06146	0.18092	0.58648	0.53364	0.03105
0.48665	0.99897	1.26980	0.60319	0.31071	1.54205
0.79335	0.09508	0.43160	0.51789	1.01183	1.80658
1.07650	0.98560;				

load imps; ? share of imports in value added (*nu*)

0.23200	0.23600	0.23200	0.24300	0.22900	0.22700
0.20900	0.21100	0.22600	0.21100	0.20500	0.20500
0.21300	0.20300	0.19700	0.20300	0.22400	0.22000
0.22500	0.22000	0.22300	0.26700	0.33600	0.28200
0.30000	0.29900	0.27800	0.28500	0.25800	0.24700
0.27000	0.24700;				

load lng; ? log of real government expenditure (*G*)

0.00000	9.56100	9.50700	9.49400	9.52300	9.52100
9.49100	9.53400	9.56800	9.61500	9.65800	9.69100
9.75600	9.80300	9.85600	9.94100	9.98100	9.98600
10.02100	10.03400	10.05100	10.14200	10.19500	10.24500
10.25100	10.19200	10.18100	10.20200	10.25200	10.23600
10.24800	10.29400;				

Note: The authors are willing to supply other investigators with a diskette containing these data.

Bibliography

Abraham, K. G. and Medoff, J. L. (1985), 'Length of Service and Layoffs in Union and Non-Union Work Groups', *Industrial and Labour Relations Review*, 38, 87–97.

Adams, J. S. (1963), 'Towards an Understanding of Inequity', *Journal of Abnormal and Social Psychology*, 67, 422–36.

—— (1965), 'Inequity in Social Exchange', in L. Berkowitz (ed.), *Advances in Experimental Social Psychology*, ii, New York: Academic Press.

—— and Freedman, S. (1976), 'Equity Theory Revisited: Comments and Annotated Bibliography', in L. Berkowitz and E Walster (eds.), *Advances in Experimental Social Psychology*, ix, New York: Academic Press.

—— and Jacobsen, P. R. (1964), 'Effects of Wage Inequities on Work Quality', *Journal of Abnormal and Social Psychology*, 69, 19–25.

—— and Rosenbaum, W. B. (1962), 'The Relationship of Worker Productivity to Cognitive Dissonance about Wage Inequities', *Journal of Applied Psychology*, 46, 161–4.

Addison, J. (1986), 'Job Security in the United States: Law, Collective Bargaining, Policy and Practice, *British Journal of Industrial Relations*, 24, 381–418.

Akerlof, G. (1969), 'Relative Wages and the Rate of Inflation', *Quarterly Journal of Economics*, 83, 353–74.

—— (1982), 'Labour Contracts as Partial Gift Exchange, *Quarterly Journal of Economics*, 97, 543–69.

—— and Miyazaki, H. (1980), 'The Implicit Contract Theory of Unemployment Meets the Wage Bill Argument', *Review of Economic Studies*, 47, 321–38.

Andrews, I. R. (1967), 'Wage Inequity and Job Performance: An Experimental Study', *Journal of Applied Psychology*, 51, 39–45.

Ashenfelter, O. C. (1978), 'Union Relative Wage Effects: New Evidence and a Survey of Their Implications for Wage Inflation', in R. Stone and W. Petersen (eds.), *Econometric Contributions to Public Policy*, London: Macmillan.

—— and Layard, P. R. G. (1986), *Handbook of Labor Economics*, Amsterdam: North Holland Publishing.

Atherton, W. (1973), *The Theory of Union Bargaining Goals*, Princeton, NJ: Princeton University Press.

Austin, W., and Walster, E. (1974), 'Reactions to Confirmation and

Disconfirmations of Expectancies of Equity and Inequity', *Journal of Personality and Social Psychology*, 30, 208–16.

Azariadis, C. (1975), 'Implicit Contracts and Under-Employment Equilibria', *Journal of Political Economy*, 83, 1183–202.

Baily, M. N. (1974), 'Wages and Employment under Uncertain Demand', *Review of Economic Studies*, 41, 37–50.

Ball, J. M., and Skeoch, N. K. (1981), 'Inter-Plant Comparisons of Productivity and Earnings', Government Economic Service Paper, No. 38, Department of Employment.

Bazerman, M. H. (1985), 'Norms of Distributive Justice in Interest Arbitration', *Industrial and Labor Relations Review*, 38, 558–70.

Bean, C. R., and Turnbull P. J. (1986), 'Employment in the Coal Industry: A Bargaining Approach', Centre for Labour Economics, Working Paper 830, London School of Economics.

Beckerman, W., and Jenkinson, T. J. (1986), 'What Stopped the Inflation? Unemployment or Commodity Prices?', *Economic Journal*, 96, 39–54.

—— (1988), 'The Wage–Profit Relationship: A Disaggregative Analysis', mimeo, University of Oxford.

Ben–Ner, A., and Estrin, S. (1985), 'What Happens When Unions run Firms?', mimeo, London School of Economics.

Bera, A. K., and Jarque, C. M. (1980), 'Efficient Tests for Normality, Homoscedasticity, and Serial Independence of Regression Residuals', *Economics Letters*, 6, 255–9.

Bhatia, R. I. (1962), 'Profits and the Rate of Change in Money Earnings in the United States 1935–59', *Economica*, 29, 255–62.

Binmore, K., Rubinstein, A., and Wolinsky, A. (1986), 'The Nash Bargaining Solution in Economic Modelling', *Rand Journal of Economics*, 17, 176–88.

Black, J. M., and Bulkley, I. G. (1984), 'Do Trade Unions Reduce the Job Opportunities of Non-Members? An Application of Implicit Contract Theory', mimeo, University of Exeter.

Blair, D., and Crawford, D. (1984), 'Labour Union Objectives and Collective Bargaining', *Quarterly Journal of Economics*, 99, 547–66.

Blanchard, O., and Summers, L. (1987), 'Hysteresis and the European Unemployment Problem', in R. Cross *et al* (eds.), *Unemployment, Hysteresis and the Natural Rate Hypothesis*, Oxford: Basil Blackwell.

Blanchflower, D. (1984), 'Union Relative Wage Effects: A Cross Section Analysis Using Establishment Data', *British Journal of Industrial Relations*, 24, 311–32.

Blanchflower, D. G., and Oswald, A. J. (1988*a*), 'Internal and External Influences upon Pay Settlements', *British Journal of Industrial Relations*, 26, 363–70.

—— —— (1988b), 'Profit-related Pay: Prose Discovered?', *Economic Journal*, 98, 720–30.

—— —— and Garrett, M. (1988), 'Insider Power in Wage Determination', Centre for Labour Economics, Discussion Paper No. 319, London School of Economics.

Booth, A. (1984), 'A Public Choice Model of Trade Union Behaviour and Membership', *Economic Journal*, 94, 883–98.

Borch, K. (1962), 'Equilibrium in a Reinsurance Market', *Econometrica*, 30, 424–44.

Bover, O., Muellbauer, J., and Murphy, A. (1988), 'Housing, Wages and UK Labour Markets', *Oxford Bulletin of Economics and Statistics*, forthcoming.

Branson, W. H. and Rotemberg, J. J. (1980), 'International Adjustment with Wage Rigidities', *European Economic Review*, 13, 309–37.

Brown, D. G. (1962), 'Expected Ability to Pay and Inter-Industry Wage Structure in Manufacturing', *Industrial and Labor Relations Review*, 16, 45–62.

Brown, J. N., and Ashenfelter, O. C. (1986), 'Testing the Efficiency of Employment Contracts', *Journal of Political Economy*, 94, special issue, S40–87.

Brown, W., and Sisson, K. (1975), 'The Use of Comparisons in Workplace Wage Determination', *British Journal of Industrial Relations*, 13, 23–53.

Burda, M. C. (1987), 'Membership, Seniority and Wage Setting in Democratic Labor Unions', mimeo, INSEAD, Paris.

Calmfors, L. (1982), 'Employment Policies, Wage Formation and Trade Union Behaviour in a Small Open Economy', *Scandinavian Journal of Economics*, 84, 345–73.

Calvo, G. (1978), 'Urban Unemployment and Wage Determination in LDCs: Trade Unions in the Harris Todaro Model', *International Economic Review*, 19, 65–81.

—— and Phelps, E. S. (1977), 'Employment Contingent Wage Contracts', *Journal of Monetary Economics*, (supplement), 160–8.

Cappelli, P. (1985), 'Plant-Level Concession Bargaining', *Industrial and Labor Relations Review*, 38, 90–104.

Card, D. (1986), 'Efficient Contracts with Costly Adjustment', *American Economic Review*, 76, 1045–71.

—— (1988), 'Unexpected Inflation, Real Wages, and Employment Determination in Union Contracts', mimeo, Princeton University.

Carruth, A. A., and Disney, R. F. (1988), 'Where Have Two Million Trade Union Members Gone?', *Economica*, 55, 1–20.

—— and Oswald, A. J. (1981), 'The Determination of Union and Non-Union Wage Rates', *European Economic Review*, 16, 285–302.

—— —— (1985), 'Miners' Wages in Post-War Britain: An Application of a Model of Trade Union Behaviour', *Economic Journal*, 95, 1003–20.

—— —— (1987*a*), 'Wage Inflexibility in Britain', *Oxford Bulletin of Economics and Statistics*, 49, 59–78.

—— —— (1987*b*), 'On Union Preferences and Labour Market Models: Insiders and Outsiders', *Economic Journal*, 97, 431–45.

—— —— (1987*c*), 'Testing for Multiple Natural Rates of Unemployment in the British Economy: A Preliminary Investigation', in R. Cross *et al.* (eds.) *Unemployment, Hysteresis and the Natural Rate Hypothesis*, Oxford: Basil Blackwell.

—— —— (1988), 'Industrial Relations and the Seniority Model: A Comment', mimeo, University of Kent.

—— —— and Findlay, L. (1986), 'A Test of a Model of Union Behaviour: The Coal and Steel Industries in Britain', *Oxford Bulletin of Economics and Statistics*, 48, 1–18.

Cartter, A. M. (1959), *Theory of Wages and Employment*, Homewood, Ill.: Richard Unwin.

Christofides, L. N., and Oswald, A. J. (1988), 'Real Wage Determination in Collective Bargaining Agreements', mimeo, University of Guelph, Canada.

Clark, A. (1988), 'Efficient Bargains and the McDonald–Solow Conjecture', mimeo, London School of Economics.

Corden, A. M. (1981) 'Taxation, Real Wage Rigidity and Employment', *Economic Journal*, 91, 309–30.

Daniel, W. W. (1976), *Wage Determination in Industry*, London: Chapel River Press.

—— and Millward, N. (1983), *Workplace Industrial Relations in Britain*, London: Heinemann.

De Bruyne, F., and Van Rompuy, P. (1981), 'Wage Determination in a Unionized Economy', Discussion Paper, University of Louvain, Belgium.

De Menil, G. (1971), *Bargaining: Monopoly Power Versus Union Power*, Cambridge, Mass.: MIT Press.

Dertouzos, J. N., and Pencavel, J. H. (1981), 'Wage and Employment Determination under Trade Unionism: The International Typographical Union', *Journal of Political Economy*, 89, 1162–81.

Dickens, W. T., and Katz, L. F. (1987), 'Interindustry Wage Differences and Industry Characteristics', in K. Lang and J. S. Leonard, (eds.) *Unemployment and the Structure of Labor Markets*, Oxford: Basil Blackwell.

Disney, R. F., and Gospel, H. (1988), 'The Seniority Model of Trade Union Behaviour: A (Partial) Defence', *British Journal of Industrial Relations*, forthcoming.

Dixon, H. (1987), 'A Simple Model of Imperfect Competition with

Walrasian Features', *Oxford Economic Papers*, 39, 136–60.

Dowrick, S. (1987), 'Bargaining and Income Distribution in UK Manufacturing', mimeo, Australian National University.

Dreze, J. H., and Modigliani, F. (1981), 'The Trade-off between Real Wages and Employment in an Open Economy Trade-off (Belgium)', *European Economic Review*, 15, 1–40.

Dunlop, J. T. (1944), *Wage Determination Under Trade Unions*, New York: Macmillan.

Eberts, R. W., and Stone, J. A. (1986), 'On the Contract Curve: A Test of Alternative Models of Collective Bargaining', *Journal of Labor Economics*, 4, 66–81.

Eckstein, O. (1968), 'Money Wage Determination Revisited', *Review of Economic Studies*, 35, 133–43.

—— and Wilson, T. A. (1962), 'The Determinants of Money Wages in American Industry', *Quarterly Journal of Economics*, 70, 379–444.

Eliasson, G. (1975), *Profits and Wage Determination: An Empirical Study of Swedish Manufacturing*, Stockholm: Federation of Swedish Industries.

Farber, H. S. (1978), 'Individual Preferences and Union Wage Determination: The Case of the United Mine Workers', *Journal of Political Economy*, 86, 923–42.

—— (1986), 'The Analysis of Union Behaviour', in O. Ashenfelter and R. Layard, (eds.), *Handbook of Labor Economics*.

Fellner, W. (1949), *Competition Among the Few*, New York: A. A. Knopf.

Flanagan, R. J. (1976), 'Wage Interdependence in Unionized Labor Markets', *Brookings Papers on Economic Activity*, 3, 635–74.

—— (1985), 'Wage Concessions and Long Term Union Wage Flexibility', *Brookings Papers on Economic Activity*, 1, 183–216.

Frank, J. (1985), 'Trade Union Efficiency and Overemployment with Seniority Wage Scales', *Economic Journal*, 95, 1021–34.

Freeman, R. B., and Medoff, J. L. (1984), *What Do Unions Do?*, New York: Basic Books.

Geroski, P. A., Hamlin, A., and Knight, K. G. (1982), 'Wages, Strikes and Market Structure', *Oxford Economic Papers*, 34, 276–91.

Gordon, D. F. (1974), 'A Neoclassical Theory of Keynesian Unemployment', *Economic Inquiry*, 12, 431–59.

Gregory, M., Lobban, P., and Thomson, A. (1985), 'Wage Settlements in Manufacturing, 1979–1984', *British Journal of Industrial Relations*, 23, 339–58.

—— —— —— (1986), 'Bargaining Structure, Pay Settlements and Perceived Pressures in Manufacturing, 1979–84: Further Analysis from the CBI Databank', *British Journal of Industrial Relations*, 24, 215–32.

—— —— —— (1987), 'Pay Settlements in Manufacturing Industry,

1979–84: A Micro-Data Study of the Impact of Product and Labour Market Pressures', *Oxford Bulletin of Economics and Statistics*, 49, (special issue), 129–50.

Grossman, G. (1983), 'Union Wages, Seniority and Unemployment', *American Economic Review*, 73, 277–90.

Grossman, S. and Hart, O. D. (1981), 'Implicit Contracts, Moral Hazard and Unemployment', *American Economic Review*, 71, 301–7.

Grout, P. A. (1984), 'Investment and Wages in the Absence of Legally Binding Labour Contracts: A Nash Bargaining Approach', *Econometrica*, 52, 449–60.

Grubb, D., Jackman, R. A., and Layard, P. R. G. (1983), 'Wage Rigidity and Unemployment in OECD Countries', *European Economic Review*, 21, 11–41.

Hall, R. E., and Lilien, D. M. (1979), 'Efficient Wage Bargains under Uncertain Supply and Demand', *American Economic Review*, 69, 868–79.

Hamermesh, D. S. (1970), 'Wage Bargains, Threshold Effects and the Phillips Curve', *Quarterly Journal of Economics,* 84, 501–17.

Hart, O. D. (1983), 'Optimal Labour Contracts under Asymmetric Information: An Introduction', *Review of Economic Studies*, 50, 3–35.

Hartman, P. T. (1965), *Collective Bargaining and Productivity,* Berkeley: University of California Press.

Haskel, J. (1987), 'The Updated CLE Quarterly GB Data Set', Centre for Labour Economics, Working Paper No. 948, London School of Economics.

Hendry, D. F. (1983), 'Econometric Modelling: The Consumption Function in Retrospect', *Scottish Journal of Political Economy,* 30, 193–220.

—— (1986a), 'Econometric Modelling with Cointegrated Variables: An Overview', *Oxford Bulletin of Economics and Statistics*, 48, 201–12.

—— (1986b), 'User Manual for PC-GIVE Version 4.1'.

Henle, P. (1973), 'Reverse Collective Bargaining? A Look at Some Union Concession Situations', *Industrial and Labor Relations Review*, 26, 956–68.

Hernstadt, I. L. (1954), 'The Reaction of Three Local Unions to Economic Adversity', *Journal of Political Economy*, 62, 425–39.

Hersoug, T. (1983), 'Union Wage Responses to Tax Changes', *Oxford Economic Papers*, 36, 37–51.

Hicks, J. R. (1963), *The Theory of Wages*, (1st edn. 1932), London: Macmillan.

Hieser, R. (1970), 'Wage Determination with Bilateral Monopoly in the Labour Market: A Theoretical Treatment', *Economic Record*, 31, 55–72.

Holden, S. (1987), 'Wage Drift in Norway: A Bargaining Approach', mimeo, University of Oslo, Norway.

Holmlund, B., and Skedinger, P. (1988), 'Wage Bargaining and Wage Drift: Evidence from the Swedish Wood Industry', mimeo, Uppsala University, Sweden.

Holmstrom, B. (1984), 'Equilibrium Long Term Contracts', *Quarterly Journal of Economics*, 98, (supplement), 23–54.

Homans, G. C. (1961), *Social Behavior: Its Elementary Forms*, New York: Harcourt Brace and World.

Howard, W. A. (1969), 'Wage Adjustment and Profit Rates: An Error-Learning Approach to Collective Bargaining', *Industrial and Labor Relations Review*, 22, 416–21.

—— and Tolles, N. A. (1973), 'Wage Determination in Key Manufacturing Industries', *Industrial and Labor Relations Review*, 27, 543–59.

Jackman, R. A., and Layard, P. R. G. (1987), 'Innovative Supply Side Policies to Reduce Unemployment', Discussion Paper No. 281, Centre for Labour Economics, London School of Economics.

—— —— and Pissarides, C. A. (1984), 'On Vacancies', Discussion Paper No. 165, Centre for Labour Economics, London School of Economics.

Jacques, E. (1961), *Equitable Payment*, London: Heinemann.

Johnson, G. E. (1985), 'Work Rules, Featherbedding, and Pareto Optimal Union–Management Bargaining', mimeo, University of Michigan.

Johnston, J. (1972), 'A Model of Wage Determination under Bilateral Monopoly', *Economic Journal*, 82, 837–52.

Jowell, R., Witherspoon, S., and Brook, L. (1987), *British Social Attitudes: The 1987 Report*, Aldershot: Gower.

Juris, H. A. (1969), 'Union Crisis Wage Decisions', *Industrial Relations*, 8, 247–58.

Kahneman, D., Knetsch, J. L., and Thaler, R. (1986), 'Fairness as a Constraint on Profit Seeking', *American Economic Review*, 76, 728–41.

Kaldor, N. (1959), 'Economic Growth and the Problem of Inflation', part ii, *Economica*, 26, 287–98.

Kaufman, R. T. (1984), 'On Wage Stickiness in Britain's Competitive Sector', *British Journal of Industrial Relations*, 22, 101–12.

Kerr, C. (1983), 'The Intellectual Role of the Neorealists in Labor Economics', *Industrial Relations*, 22, 298–318.

Kidd, D. P., and Oswald, A. J. (1987), 'A Dynamic Model of Trade Union Behaviour', *Economica*, 54, 355–66.

King, M. A. (1975), 'The United Kingdom Profits Crisis: Myth or Reality?', *Economic Journal*, 85, 33–54.

Klein, L. R., and Ball, R. J. (1959), 'Some Econometrics of the Determination of the Absolute Level of Wages and Prices', *Economic Journal*, 69, 465–82.

Kotowitz, Y., and Mathewson, F. (1982), 'The Economics of the Union-Controlled Firm', *Economica*, 49, 421–33.

Krueger, A. B., and Summers, L. H. (1987), 'Reflections on the

Inter-Industry Wage Structure', in K. Lang and J. S. Leonard (eds.) *Unemployment and the Structure of Labor Markets*, Oxford: Basil Blackwell.

—— —— (1988), 'Efficiency Wages and the Inter-Industry Wage Structure', *Econometrica*, 56, 259–94.

Kuh, E. (1967), 'A Productivity Theory of Wage levels: An Alternative to the Phillips Curve', *Review of Economic Studies*, 34, 333–60.

Kuhn, P. (1988), 'A Non-Uniform Pricing Model of Union Wages and Employment', *Journal of Political Economy*, 96, 473–508.

Laidler, D. E. W., and Parkin, J. M. (1975), 'Inflation: A Survey', *Economic Journal*, 85, 741–809.

Lawler, E. E. (1968), 'Equity Theory as a Predictor of Productivity and Work Quality', *Psychological Bulletin*, 70, 596–610.

Layard, R., Metcalf, D., and Nickell, S. (1978), 'The Effect of Collective Bargaining on Relative and Absolute Wages', *British Journal of Industrial Relations*, 16, 287–302.

—— and Nickell, S. J. (1986), 'Unemployment in Britain', *Economica*, 53, (supplement), S121–70.

—— —— (1988), 'The Performance of the British Labour Market', in R. Dornbusch and P. R. G. Layard (eds.) *The Performance of the British Economy*, Oxford: Oxford University Press.

Leamer, E. E. (1978), *Specification Searches: Ad Hoc Inference with Non-Experimental Data*, New York: Wiley.

—— (1983), 'Taking the Con out of Econometrics', *American Economic Review*, 73, 30–43.

Leibenstein, H. (1957), 'The Theory of Underemployment in Densely Populated Backward Areas', Ch. 6 of *Economic Backwardness and Economic Growth*, New York: Wiley.

Leontief, W. (1946), 'The Pure Theory of the Guaranteed Annual Wage Contract', *Journal of Political Economy*, 54, 76–9.

Lester, R. (1952), 'A Range Theory of Wage Differentials', *Industrial and Labor Relations Review*, 5, 483–500.

—— and Shishter, J. (1948), *Insights into Labor Issues*, New York: Macmillan.

Lewis, H. G. (1963), *Unionism and Relative Wages in the United States*, Chicago: University of Chicago Press.

Lindbeck, A., and Snower, D. J. (1986), 'Wage Setting, Unemployment, and Insider-Outsider Relations', *American Economic Review*, 76, 235–9.

—— —— (1988), 'Cooperation, Harrassment and Involuntary Unemployment: An Insider-Outsider Approach', *American Economic Review*, 78, 167–88.

Lipsey, R. G., and Steuer, M. D. (1961), 'The Relation between Profits and Wage Rates', *Economica*, 28, 137–55.

McAleer, M., Pagan, A., and Volker, P. A. (1985), 'What will Take the Con out of Econometrics?', *American Economic Review*, 75, 293–307.

McDonald, I. M. (1985), 'The Wage Demands of the Selfish, Plant-Specific Trade Union', mimeo, University of Melbourne.

—— and Solow, R. M. (1981), 'Wage Bargaining and Employment', *American Economic Review*, 71, 896–908.

MacKay, D. I., Boddy, D., Brack, J., Diack, J. A., and Jones, N. (1971), *Labour Markets Under Different Employment Conditions*, London: George Allen and Unwin.

Macurdy, T., and Pencavel, J. H. (1986), 'Testing Between Competing Models of Wage and Employment Determination in Unionized Markets', *Journal of Political Economy*, 94, special issue, S3–39.

Malcomson, J. M. (1981), 'Unemployment and the Efficiency Wage Hypothesis', *Economic Journal*, 91, 848–66.

Manning, A. (1987), 'An Integration of Trade Union Models in a Sequential Bargaining Framework', *Economic Journal*, 97, 121–39.

Marsden, D. (1986), *The End of Economic Man? Custom and Competition in Labour Markets*, Brighton: Wheatsheaf Books.

Martin, D. L. (1980), *An Ownership Theory of the Trade Union*, Berkeley: University of California Press.

Metcalf, D. (1977), 'Unions, Incomes Policy and Relative Wages in Britain', *British Journal of Industrial Relations*, 15, 157–75.

Minford, P. (1983), 'Labour Market Equilibrium in an Open Economy', *Oxford Economic Papers*, 35, (supplement), 207–44.

Mirrlees, J. A. (1976), 'Optimal Tax Theory: A Synthesis', *Journal of Public Economics*, 6, 327–58.

Mishel, L. (1986), 'The Structural Determinants of Union Bargaining Power', *Industrial and Labor Relations Review*, 40, 90–104.

Mitchell, D. J. B. (1982), 'Recent Union Contract Concessions', *Brookings Papers on Economic Activity*, 1, 165–201.

Moene, K. (1988), 'Unions' Threats and Wage Determination', *Economic Journal*, 98, 471–83.

Moore, J. (1981), 'The Rum Tale of a Declining Industry', mimeo, Birkbeck College, London.

—— (1985), 'Optimal Labour Contracts When Workers Have a Variety of Privately Observed Reservation Wages', *Review of Economic Studies*, 52, 37–68.

Mulvey, C. (1978), *The Economic Analysis of Trade Unions*, Oxford: Martin Robertson.

Nash, J. F. (1953), 'Two-Person Cooperative Games', *Econometrica*, 21, 128–40.

Newell, A., and Symons, J. S. (1987), 'Mid 1980s Unemployment', Discussion Paper No. 283, Centre for Labour Economics, London School of Economics.

Nickell, S. J. (1982), 'A Bargaining Model of the Phillips Curve', Discussion Paper No. 130, Centre for Labour Economics, London School of Economics.

—— (1987), 'Why is Wage Inflation in Britain so High?', *Oxford Bulletin of Economics and Statistics*, 49. 103–28.

—— and Andrews, M. (1983), 'Unions, Real Wages and Employment in Britain 1951–79', *Oxford Economic Papers*, 35, supplement, 183–206.

—— and Wadhwani, S. (1987), 'Insider Forces and Wage Determination', mimeo, Oxford University.

Nolan, P., and Brown, W. (1983), 'Competition and Workplace Wage Determination', *Oxford Bulletin of Economics and Statistics*, 45, 269–87.

OECD (1965), *Wages and Labour Mobility*, Paris: Organization for Economic Cooperation and Development.

Oswald, A. J. (1979), 'Wage Determination in an Economy with Many Trade Unions', *Oxford Economic Papers*, 31, 369–85.

—— (1982*a*), 'The Microeconomic Theory of the Trade Union', *Economic Journal*, 92, 576–95.

—— (1982*b*), 'Uncertainty and the Trade Union', *Economics Letters*, 9, 105–11.

—— (1982*c*), 'Wages, Trade Unions and Unemployment: What Can Simple Models Tell Us?', *Oxford Economic Papers*, 34, 526–45.

—— (1984), 'Wage and Employment Structure in an Economy with Internal Labour Markets', *Quarterly Journal of Economics*, 99, 693–716.

—— (1985), 'The Economic Theory of Trade Unions: An Introductory Survey', *Scandinavian Journal of Economics*, 87, 160–93.

—— (1986*a*), 'Unemployment Insurance and Labour Contracts under Asymmetric Information: Theory and Facts', *American Economic Review*, 76, 365–77.

—— (1986*b*), 'Is Wage Rigidity Caused by Lay-offs by Seniority?', in W. Beckerman (ed.), *Wage Rigidity and Unemployment*, London: Duckworth.

—— (1987), 'Efficient Contracts are on the Labour Demand Curve: Theory and Facts', Centre for Labour Economics Discussion Paper No. 284, London School of Economics.

—— and Turnbull, P. J. (1985), 'Pay and Employment Determination in Britain: What are Labour Contracts Really Like?', *Oxford Review of Economic Policy*, 1, 80–97.

Pagan, A. (1987), 'Three Econometric Methodologies: A Critical Appraisal', *Journal of Economic Surveys*, 1, 3–24.

Parsley, C. J. (1980), 'Labour Unions and Wages: A Survey', *Journal of Economic Literature*, 18, 1–31.

Pemberton, J. (1988), 'A Managerial Model of the Trade Union', *Economic Journal*, 98, 755–71.

Pencavel, J. H. (1977), 'The Distributional and Efficiency Effects of Trade Unions in Britain', *British Journal of Industrial Relations*, 15, 137–56.

—— (1984a), 'The Trade-off between Wages and Employment in Trade Union Objectives', *Quarterly Journal of Economics*, 99, 215–32.

—— (1984b), 'The Empirical Performance of a Model of Trade Union Behaviour', in J. Rosa (ed.), *The Economics of Labor Unions: New Directions*, Boston, Mass.: Kluwer-Nijhoff Publishing Co..

—— (1985), 'Wages and Employment under Trade Unionism: Microeconomic Models and Macroeconomic Applications', *Scandinavian Journal of Economics*, 97, 197–225.

Perry, G. L. (1966), *Unemployment, Money Wage Rates and Inflation*, Cambridge, Mass.: MIT Press.

Phelps–Brown, H. (1977), *The Inequality of Pay*, Oxford: Oxford University Press.

Pissarides, C. A. (1981), 'Contract Theory, Temporary Lay-offs and Unemployment: A Critical Assessment', in D. Currie, D. Peel, and W. Peters (eds.), *Microeconomic Analysis,* London: Croom Helm.

—— (1986), 'Trade Unions and the Efficiency of the Natural Rate of Unemployment', *Journal of Labor Economics*, 4, 582–95.

—— (1988), 'Unemployment and Macroeconomics: An Inaugural Lecture', Discussion Paper No. 304, Centre for Labour Economics, London School of Economics.

Prachowny, M. F. (1987), 'Conflict in the Labour Market: Seniority Rules and Unemployment', *Journal of Macroeconomics*, 9, 527–43.

Pritchard, R. D., Dunnette, M. D., and Jorgensen, D. O. (1972), 'Effects of Perceptions of Equity and Inequity on Worker Performance and Satisfaction', *Journal of Applied Psychology*, 56, 75–94.

Pugel, T. A. (1980), 'Profitability, Concentration and the Interindustry Variation in Wages', *Review of Economics and Statistics*, 62, 248–53.

Rees, A. (1977), *The Economics of Trade Unions*, rev. edn., Chicago: University of Chicago Press.

Rosen, S. (1970), 'Unionism and the Occupational Wage Structure in the United States', *International Economic Review*, 11, 269–86.

Ross, A. M. (1948), *Trade Union Wage Policy*, Berkeley: University of California Press.

Rowlatt, P. A. (1987), 'A Model of Wage Bargaining', *Oxford Bulletin of Economics and Statistics*, 49, 347–72.

Salop, S. (1979), 'A Model of the Natural Rate of Unemployment', *American Economic Review*, 69, 117–25.

Salter, W. E. (1966), *Productivity and Technical Change,* Cambridge: Cambridge University Press.

Bibliography

Sampson, A. A. (1983), 'Employment Policy in a Model with a Rational Trade Union', *Economic Journal*, 93, 297–311.

—— and Shephard, D. (1978), 'Rational Expectations, Risk Aversion and the Phillips Curve', University of Sheffield Discussion Paper.

Shapiro, C., and Stiglitz, J. E. (1984), 'Equilibrium Unemployment as a Worker Discipline Device', *American Economic Review*, 74, 433–44.

Shultz, G. P., and Myers, C. A. (1950), 'Union Wage Decisions and Employment', *American Economic Review*, 40, 362–80.

Slichter, S. H. (1947), *Basic Criteria Used in Wage Negotiations*, Chicago: Chicago Association of Commerce and Industry.

—— (1950), 'Notes on the Structure of Wages', *Review of Economics and Statistics*, 32, 80–91.

—— Healy, J. J., and Livernash, R. E. (1960), *The Impact of Collective Bargaining on Management*, Washington, DC: The Brookings Institution.

Smith, A. (1937), *An Inquiry into the Nature and Causes of the Wealth of Nations* (1st edn. 1776), New York: The Modern Library.

Solow, R. M. (1979). 'Another Possible Source of Wage Stickiness', *Journal of Macroeconomics*, 1, 79–82.

—— (1985), 'Insiders and Outsiders in Wage Determination', *Scandinavian Journal of Economics*, 87, 411–28.

Sparks, G. R., and Wilton, D. A. (1971), 'Determinants of Negotiated Increases: An Empirical Wage Analysis', *Econometrica*, 39, 739–50.

Stewart, M. B. (1983), 'Relative Earnings and Individual Union Membership in the United Kingdom', *Economica*, 50, 111–26.

Stiglitz, J. E. (1974), 'Wage Determination and Unemployment in L.D.C's: The Labor Turnover Model', *Quarterly Journal of Economics*, 88, 194–227.

—— (1984), 'Theories of Wage Rigidity', NBER Working Paper N. 1442.

Strand, J. (1983), 'Layoffs, Labor Productivity and Worker Seniority Rules: An Analysis of Some Micro-Macro Institutional and Long Run Equilibrium Aspects of Implicit Contract Theory', mimeo, University of Oslo.

Sutton, J. (1986), 'Non-Cooperative Bargaining: An Introduction', *Review of Economic Studies*, 53, 709–24.

Svejnar, J. (1986), 'Bargaining Power, Fear of Disagreement and Wage Settlements: Theory and Evidence from US Industry', *Econometrica*, 54, 1055–78.

Transport and General Workers' Union, (1971), *The Ford Wage Claim*, London: TGWU.

Turnbull, P. J. (1988), 'Industrial Relations and the Seniority Model of Union Behaviour', *Oxford Bulletin of Economics and Statistics*, 50, 53–70.

Tylecote, A. B. (1975), 'Determinants of Changes in the Wage Hierarchy in UK Manufacturing Industry: A Test of a New Theory of Wage Determination Under Collective Bargaining', *British Journal of Industrial Relations*, 13, 65–77.

Vanek, J. (1970), *The General Theory of Labour Managed Firms*, New York: Cornell University Press.

Wadhwani, S., and Wall, M. (1988), 'A Direct Test of the Efficiency Wage Model Using UK Micro Data', Discussion Paper No. 313, Centre for Labour Economics, London School of Economics.

Walster, E., Walster, G. W., and Berscheid, E. (1978), *Equity Theory and Research*, Boston, Mass.: Allyn and Bacon.

Warr, P. B. (1985), *Psychology at Work*, Harmondsworth: Penguin Books.

Warren-Boulton, F. R. (1977), 'Vertical Control of Labour Unions', *American Economic Review*, 67, 309–22.

Weiss, A. (1980), 'Job Queues and Layoffs in Labor Markets with Flexible Wages', *Journal of Political Economy*, 88, 526–38.

Weyant, J. M. (1986), *Applied Social Psychology*, New York: Oxford University Press.

White, H. (1980), 'A Heteroskedasticity-Consistent Covariance Matrix Estimator and a Direct Test for Heteroskedasticity', *Econometrica*, 48, 817–38.

Willman, P. (1982), *Fairness, Collective Bargaining and Incomes Policy*, Oxford: Clarendon Press.

Wood, A. (1978), *A Theory of Pay*, Cambridge: Cambridge University Press.

Yellen, J. (1984), 'Efficiency Wage Models of Unemployment', *American Economic Review*, Papers and Proceedings, 74, 200–5.

Index

Index

Index